CW01661868

ICSA'S LEGAL LETTERS AND AGREEMENTS

ICSA'S
LEGAL LETTERS AND AGREEMENTS

READY DRAFTED LETTERS AND CONTRACTS FOR COMPANY SECRETARIES AND DIRECTORS

MALCOLM LEATHERDALE LL B, ACIS
Solicitor

ICSA Publishing
CAMBRIDGE

Published by ICSA Publishing Limited,
Fitzwilliam House, 32 Trumpington Street,
Cambridge CB2 1QY, England

First published 1991

© Malcolm Leatherdale, 1991

Conditions of sale
All rights reserved. No part of this publication may be reproduced, stored in a retrieval system or transmitted, in any form or by any means, electronic, mechanical, photocopying, recording or otherwise, without the prior permission of the publisher.

Whilst all reasonable care has been taken in the preparation of this book, the author, publisher and Institute of Chartered Secretaries and Administrators cannot be held liable for any inaccuracies contained within it or for any loss however arising, or for any action taken as a result of following or using the drafts or precedents.

British Library Cataloguing in Publication Data

Leatherdale, Malcolm
ICSA's legal letters and agreements.
1. Business enterprise. Correspondence
I. Title II. Institute of Chartered Secretaries and Administrators.
651.75

ISBN 1–872860–03–6

Designed by Geoff Green
Typeset by Hands Fotoset, Leicester
Printed in Great Britain by BPCC Wheatons Ltd, Exeter

Contents

General introduction

The primary object of this book is to help company secretaries, accountants, administrators and executives who carry out the company secretarial function to perform some aspects of their work more effectively and with greater authority. The description 'company secretary' is used as a convenient generic term and any reference to the masculine also includes the feminine! For most people fulfilling the role, time is at a premium and access to precedents or draft letters should be of help even if only to provide a starting point. Some of the items included relate specifically to private companies but a number have a general application and are relevant to public companies as well.

The range of duties carried out by company secretaries can be quite extensive and will differ in breadth and variety from company to company. In some companies, for example, any matters remotely legal would immediately be referred to solicitors, and in others the secretary would deal with much of the legal work, especially the non-contentious. Where contentious matters and disputes are concerned, and there is a risk of litigation, as a general rule solicitors should become involved fairly early on, the company secretary providing the facts and giving the company's instructions as matters proceed.

There are, however, a number of situations in which it may not be necessary to consult solicitors. In particular, some agreements do not involve a great deal of protracted negotiation between the parties in the way in which, for example, the acquisition or disposal of a business would require. There are a number of what might be called 'domestic agreements' which can be dealt with perfectly well by the company secretary.

Solicitors are able to refer to a wide range of precedents dealing with every kind of agreement, although such precedents include all conceivable aspects of any transaction because they are intended for solicitors who may be acting for either party. In this book, those precedents which are intended to be used by company secretaries dealing with the matter on behalf of their own particular company are drafted on the basis that the company is the 'customer', and where any balance has to be found between the conflicting requirements of the company and the other party, the balance is struck in favour of the company. Naturally, this has not been done to such an extent that the precedent is so one sided as to be unacceptable but occasionally, where there is any room for manoeuvre or latitude, it is in favour of the company. In effect this means that the obligations on the part of the company are slightly less onerous than they could or might otherwise be. This general approach will be looked at again in the individual commentaries and notes to each of the precedents because the weighting varies from one precedent to another and in some cases is not a factor at all.

One of the problems which occurs in practice is that contractual arrangements may be contained in correspondence without a formal agreement ever being concluded as a separate document. This often works well enough but it can be difficult for anyone other than those who originated the correspondence to ascertain easily and exactly what has been agreed because of its disjointed nature. There may also be ambiguity or uncertainty as not every issue has been covered or dealt with systematically.

Then there may be a dispute between the parties as to whose terms and conditions are incorporated in the contract and which, if any, apply. In fact in some cases the question can legitimately be asked 'Is there a contract at all?' In several of the precedents there is provision for a number of the other party's terms and conditions to be incorporated by specific reference. The other party's terms and conditions may be attached to the agreement but only those clauses specifically noted will apply. This is a convenient method because the agreement between the company and the other party is then effectively contained in the one document.

The drafting style of each precedent is intended to be modern, unambiguous and, so far as possible, devoid of legal jargon. Words such as 'hereinbefore' and 'aforementioned' have been outlawed! Solicitors have a reputation for producing documents expressed in language more appropriate to the nineteenth century. Even among some of the leading firms of solicitors this tendency continues, although there has been progress in modernising the style of language in recent years. The overriding intention has been to make the precedents in this book comprehensible and their meaning clear, yet at the same time to ensure that they have full legal effect. To help in achieving this objective all the clauses have separate headings.

Many of the potential users of the precedents will not have had legal training but they will probably have had experience of reviewing legal documents and so long as the precedents are used carefully the final document should be sufficient for the intended purpose. The cardinal rule, however, is that no precedent should be followed slavishly or adhered to as if written in tablets of stone. If a clause is irrelevant discard it; if it needs amending amend it.

All the precedents have been set out in full, which means that in a few cases some of the standard provisions are duplicated. Solicitors are used to dealing with precedents and are happy to extract various clauses from a number of sources in order to produce the required document but this may be a problem for those who are not so experienced. Whatever else the book is intended to be, it is above all designed to be readily usable. Nevertheless, all the precedents will require some adaptation to suit the particular requirements of the transaction and of the individual business but it is hoped that this will be easier to do if the basic precedent is set out as a complete document.

The draft letters which include technical company secretarial letters are those which company secretaries may be required to write from time to time in addition to the general correspondence connected with their company's business. Some of the letters deal with provisions of the Companies Act 1989 which has far reaching implications for companies generally and for the administration of private companies in particular.

The draft letters and precedents are those which are thought to be appropriate to meet the general needs of most company secretaries. Not all of the items will be relevant to every company secretary but a number will be.

In using a precedent there will be the added satisfaction of doing the job oneself without having to rely on outside help which can be (although it hardly needs to be said) time consuming as well as expensive.

Apart from employed company secretaries, firms of practising accountants should find the book of use as accountants are becoming more involved in reviewing and dealing with certain agreements, for example shareholders' agreements and directors' service agreements. Some of the draft letters should also be relevant to those many firms of accountants who carry out the statutory company secretarial work for their client companies. These comments also apply to chartered secretaries in public practice.

PART I

LETTERS

Introduction to the draft letters

Some caution will be required when using any of the following draft letters as a number are intended to be indicative only of the sorts of points which should be raised or dealt with rather than be regarded as the definitive version. Some may be used without much adaptation but others will need to be tailored substantially to suit the circumstances and particularly those which in some way relate to the company's articles of association where strict adherence to the precise wording of the articles must be observed.

The text of each draft letter should therefore be regarded as a framework.

The phrases, sentences or clauses which have square brackets are alternatives or require completion in some way.

CHAPTER 1

SHAREHOLDERS

Commentary on explanatory letter to shareholders of a private company enclosing notice of EGM at which elective resolutions pursuant to section 116 of the Companies Act 1989 to dispense with some of the requirements of the Companies Act 1985 will be proposed

Private companies can now elect to dispense with some of the procedural requirements of the Companies Act 1985 as a result of provisions contained in the Companies Act 1989. This new concept is generally referred to as the 'elective regime'. The Secretary of State may by regulation make further provisions enabling private companies to elect to dispense with other requirements of the Companies Act 1985. As matters stand currently, members of a private company may at a general meeting by unanimous resolution (either in person or by proxy) elect to dispense with the following requirements:

1. Duration of authority to allot shares

Section 80 of the Companies Act 1985 provides that a company can in general meeting authorise the directors to allot shares but the period for which such authority can be given is restricted to a maximum of five years. A private company may now elect to extend the period of five years to a later specified date or to make the period indefinite.

2. The laying of accounts and reports before the company in general meeting

Accounts and reports have to be laid before the company in general meeting in accordance with section 241 of the Companies Act 1985 but a private company may now elect to dispense with this obligation. Even though such an election is made, any member of the company or the auditors may require the accounts to be laid before a general meeting in any one particular financial year. When the accounts are circulated to the members a notice must be included to the effect that any member has the right to require accounts to be laid before the company in general meeting. Any member of the company or the auditors may, if they require the obligation to lay accounts to be restored, deposit a notice in writing to that effect at the company's registered office within twenty-eight days of the accounts and reports being sent out to the members. A meeting of the company must then be convened and the notice of the meeting issued to members within twenty-one days

Explanatory letter to shareholders of a private company enclosing notice of EGM at which elective resolutions pursuant to section 116 of the Companies Act 1989 to dispense with some of the requirements of the Companies Act 1985 will be proposed

Dear Shareholder

Elective resolutions

As a result of some of the provisions introduced by the Companies Act 1989 private companies are now permitted to modify or dispense with a number of the requirements imposed by the Companies Act 1985 provided that the shareholders, by *unanimous* resolution, elect to do so.

Enclosed with this letter is a notice of an extraordinary general meeting to be held on 19 which sets out the elective resolutions which are to be proposed. In order to pass these resolutions it will be necessary for all of the company's shareholders to attend and vote at the meeting, either in person or by proxy. Proxy cards are enclosed together with a stamped addressed envelope* for you to use if you are unable to attend in person. You will see from the notice that the three resolutions which are to be proposed are:

1. that the company dispense with the obligation to hold annual general meetings;
2. that the company dispense with the obligation to lay accounts and reports before the company in general meeting;
3. that the company dispense with the obligation to appoint auditors annually.

I will comment on each proposed resolution as follows:

1. Annual general meeting

As a general rule the business transacted at an annual general meeting is purely formal and in the event that the subsequent two resolutions are passed there would be even less point in continuing to hold annual general meetings in the future. Although the company has [number] shareholders, attendance at AGMs in previous years has tended to be poor and as often as not shareholders have been outnumbered by the directors. There is of course not only a financial cost to

* If the number of shareholders is insufficient to warrant a business reply service.

of the date of the deposit of the member's or auditors' notice. The meeting itself must be held within twenty-eight days of the issue by the company of the notice convening the meeting. If the company has elected to dispense with the holding of annual general meetings, the meeting convened would consequently be an extraordinary general meeting.

3. The holding of annual general meetings

A private company now has the option to dispense with the holding of annual general meetings. This measure will be of particular benefit to companies where the directors are the only shareholders, although it is not restricted to such companies. One incidental aspect which should be borne in mind concerns the rotation of directors. If the company's articles provide for the rotation of directors at an annual general meeting then the articles will require amendment by special resolution to remove this provision.

4. Majority required to authorise short notice of meeting

If a private company wishes to hold a general meeting at short notice sections 369 and 378 of the Companies Act 1985 prescribe a requirement that members holding at least 95 per cent of the shares have to consent. This proportion can now be reduced to 90 per cent.

5. Appointment of auditors annually

It is a requirement (except in the case of a dormant company that has resolved not to appoint) that at each general meeting of the company at which accounts are laid the company shall appoint auditors; but a private company may now dispense with this obligation, in which event the auditors are deemed to be reappointed for each succeeding financial year. However, one of the provisions of section 122 of the Companies Act 1989 is that when an election by a private company to dispense with the annual appointment of its auditors is in force any member of the company may deposit a notice in writing at the company's registered office proposing that the appointment of the company's auditors be terminated. In that event the directors must convene a general meeting of the company for a date not more than twenty-eight days after the date on which the notice was deposited by the member in order to propose a resolution in a form enabling the company to decide whether the appointment of the company's auditors should be brought to an end. The notice convening the meeting must be dispatched to members within fourteen days of the deposit of the notice by the proposing member.

A number of private companies will naturally want to implement some, if not all, of the provisions of the 'elective regime'. It should also be noted that an elective resolution can be passed using the new written resolution procedure. Consequently, if the company but the additional cost in terms of the time which is spent in making the necessary arrangements and which the directors believe could be better employed in running the company's business for the benefit of all. However, any shareholder may in the future by notice given not later than three months before the end of the year require the holding of an AGM in that year.

2. Dispensing with the laying of accounts and reports before the company in general meeting

The annual accounts and reports of the company will continue to be circulated to all shareholders at the appropriate time which in previous years has been during . The effect of the resolution is simply that there will no longer be any formal requirement to lay the accounts and reports before the company in general meeting which will of course be less likely to happen anyway if the decision is taken to dispense with the holding of annual general meetings. It should, however, be understood that any shareholder of the company or the auditors may require the accounts and reports to be laid before the company in general meeting in any particular year and therefore this requirement could always be restored if necessary by the passing of an ordinary resolution. In fact, the Companies Act 1989 specifically stipulates that whenever accounts and reports are sent to shareholders a notice must also be enclosed reminding shareholders that they have the right to reinstate this requirement and setting out the procedure to be followed to bring it about.

If this proposed resolution is passed it will have effect with regard to the accounts and reports for the current financial year which, as you know, ends on 19

3. Appointment of auditors

The company's auditors Messrs have acted for some years and in the opinion of the directors it is likely that they will continue to be reappointed annually for the foreseeable future. As you know at each annual general meeting there is a formal resolution to reappoint the auditors but again if the decision is taken to dispense with the holding of annual general meetings there seems little sense in not dispensing with the obligation to appoint the auditors annually.

The Companies Act 1989, however, provides that any shareholder is entitled on giving notice in writing to the company to propose that the appointment of the auditors be terminated and should such notice be given the directors are obliged to convene a general meeting to decide the matter, such meeting to be held within twenty-eight days of the receipt by the company of the proposing shareholder's notice.

If these resolutions are passed it does not follow that they are irrevocable for all the directors consider that there is no need to hold a formal meeting to pass an elective resolution and all the members confirm their agreement to the resolution in writing this would be perfectly valid. See pages 34 and 36 which set out the procedure governing the passing of written resolutions. However, the letter which follows is drafted on the basis that a formal meeting of the members would be held and, consequently, at least twenty-one days' notice in writing must be given of the meeting.

Elective resolutions can be revoked at any time by the members of the company passing an ordinary resolution to that effect. An elective resolution, or any resolution revoking an elective resolution, must be filed with the Registrar of Companies within fifteen days in accordance with section 380 of the Companies Act 1985.

time. There are not only the safeguards I have already mentioned, but any elective resolution may be revoked in the future by the passing of an ordinary resolution only.

As I have already indicated, if these elective resolutions are to be passed, it is necessary that all shareholders of the company should vote in favour of these elective resolutions and the directors hope that you will agree to do so. If you have any questions or require any further information or assurance, please do not hesitate to contact me either by telephone or by letter. If, however, you would prefer, you are welcome to arrange an appointment to come to my office to discuss any aspect of the proposals with me directly.

Yours

Chairman

Commentary on response by private company to two situations which may arise following the death of a shareholder

Secretaries of companies with a large number of shareholders will be used to dealing with the shareholdings of deceased shareholders. Professional executors will also know what is required but in many situations the executors will not be professional appointees but friends or relatives of the deceased shareholder. They do not always know how to deal with the formalities involved and where the executor is, for example, a widow it goes without saying that a sympathetic and sensitive approach should be adopted.

Two draft letters follow. The first is in response to the widow of a deceased shareholder querying the position with regard to her late husband's shares on the assumption that she is the prospective beneficiary. The second is a response to a personal representative who has obtained a Grant of Probate/Letters of Administration and who wishes to retain the shares for the time being. The position here depends on what provisions are contained in the articles. If regulation 32 of Table A of the Companies Act 1948 applies, until a personal representative becomes the registered holder of the shares he will not be entitled to exercise any rights in relation to meetings of the company and although the shares will continue to qualify for any dividends which may be declared, the regulation contains a proviso to the effect that the directors may at any time give notice requiring a personal representative to elect to be registered himself or to transfer the shares and if such notice is not complied with within ninety days the directors may thereafter withhold payment of all dividends and the like until the requirements of the notice have been complied with and the personal representative has been formally registered. The articles of association of a substantial number of companies will contain this provision and it is open to the directors to give notice accordingly.

The revised equivalent of regulation 32 of Table A of the 1948 Companies Act is regulation 31 of Table A of the Companies (Tables A to F) Regulations 1985 which now only states that if a personal representative does not apply to become the registered shareholder of the shares he will be unable to attend or vote at any meeting of the company. Consequently, the directors do not have the option of withholding the payment of dividends to a personal representative who has not yet elected to have the shareholding registered in his own name if the company's articles are based on the 1985 edition of Table A. Both draft letters incorporate a

Response to letter from widow of deceased shareholder of private company querying position with regard to her late husband's shares

Dear

Your husband's shares in the company

Thank you for your letter of   asking me to let you know what you can do in respect of your late husband's shareholding.

The options open to you are as follows.

Firstly you can keep the shares and in due course request the company to register the shares in your own name. You will be able to apply for this to be done once the Probate Registry has issued the formal grant of probate if your husband left a will, or letters of administration if he did not. Your solicitors will presumably be dealing with the formalities in this regard and I should be grateful if you would ask them to send me a sealed office copy of the formal grant as soon as this has been obtained. Your solicitors should write to the company's auditors, Messrs   , chartered accountants of   , asking for a valuation of the shares for probate purposes.

When I have received the formal grant I will let you have the necessary letter requesting the shares to be registered in your name. This letter of request should be signed by you and returned to me [within ninety days of your receiving it which is the requirement contained in the company's articles of association]. There would be no charge for doing this.

Secondly, you would be in a position to sell the shares without becoming registered yourself as soon as the formal grant has been obtained but only to other shareholders in the company as the company's articles include what are known as pre-emption rights in favour of existing shareholders. This means that where shares are to be sold whether it be by a shareholder who simply wishes to dispose of his shares or the personal representative of a deceased shareholder the other shareholders have the right to apply for those shares in proportion to their existing shareholdings. I enclose an extract from the company's articles which deals with this aspect and I would be happy to discuss the effect and implications with you if you would like to call in to see me. You can do this either before or after your solicitors have obtained the formal grant which I imagine will take two to three months.

Yours

reference to either version of Table A. It is also presumed that any disposal would be subject to pre-emption provisions contained in the company's articles but if there are no such provisions then the relative paragraph in each letter should be adapted accordingly.

Where the total value of the estate of the deceased shareholder is small, which in this context means less than £5,000, it would be open to the company to recognise the widow as the owner of the shares without the need for her to obtain a formal Grant of Probate or Letters of Administration. There are, however, certain risks in agreeing to deal with the matter on such an informal basis. The better course would be to advise the widow to contact the relevant District Probate Registry where she should find that the staff would be able to assist her in obtaining the formal Grant without the need to incur the expense of consulting a solicitor. A specimen form of letter of request can be found in *Company Secretarial Practice*: the manual of the Institute of Chartered Secretaries and Administrators (ICSA Publishing).

Response by private company to receipt of copy of grant of probate/letters of administration from personal representative of deceased shareholder

Dear

Name of deceased shareholder
Number and class of shares

Thank you for your letter dated enclosing the sealed office copy of the [grant of probate] [letters of administration]. I note that you and your fellow [executors] [administrators] do not propose to dispose of the shares for the time being or transfer them to a beneficiary. [The company's articles of association provide that until the personal representatives become the registered holders of the shares they are unable to exercise any right conferred by membership in relation to meetings of the company which in practice would mean that they would be unable to attend company meetings or vote, and that if the directors give notice requiring the personal representatives to elect either to be registered themselves or to transfer the shares and such notice is not complied with within ninety days, the directors may withhold payment of dividends until the notice has been complied with. The directors have decided in accordance with their previous policy that at least one of you should become registered as the holder of the shares and this letter constitutes the requisite notice.] [The company's articles of association provide that until the personal representatives have become the registered holders of the shares they will not be able to attend company meetings or vote.] Apart from what the articles provide, the directors are also of the opinion that it is preferable for personal representatives to apply for one or more of their number to become the registered holders of shares which are to be retained for any length of time.

Accordingly, I enclose a letter of request for you to arrange to have completed. Would you please note that the letter of request needs to be signed by all the [executors] [administrators] named in the [grant of probate] [letters of administration], even if only one or two are to be formally registered. As soon as the letter of request has been signed would you please return it to me together with the share certificate so that the registration formalities can be completed. The certificate will then be returned to you amended.

If in due course you decide with your [co-executors] [co-administrators] that

the shares should be sold it will be necessary to comply with the pre-emption provisions contained in the company's articles. I enclose a copy of the relevant extract from the company's articles which I hope you will find helpful.

Should you require any further information or explanation, please do not hesitate to contact me. If you would find it more convenient, I would be pleased to arrange to meet you and your [co-executors] [co-administrators] to explain matters in more detail and to discuss with you the various options and courses of action open to you.

Yours

Commentary on response by company to female shareholder who has notified her change of name

At first sight this letter may appear to be unduly formal but, regrettably, company secretaries are not alone in having to be on their guard against possible fraud and deception on the part of third parties. The usual situation which requires a letter of this kind is where a female shareholder wishes to adopt an alternative surname without the formality of marriage. A statutory declaration is one stage below the more involved process of changing a surname by deed poll, which can be enrolled in the Enrolment Department of the Central Office of the Supreme Court of Judicature. In this case it is quite sufficient to rely on a statutory declaration but it may not be so in other circumstances. The making of the statutory declaration as to change of name at common law by usage will also show that the adoption of the new surname is expected to be long term and not something which just happens to be convenient for the time being.

Response by company to female shareholder who has notified her change of name

Dear

Your change of surname

Thank you for your letter of the enclosing your share certificate and notifying the company that you now wish to be known by the surname of , although you are not intending to marry at the moment.

Although you will no doubt take legal advice as to whether or not it would be appropriate to change your surname formally by deed, for the purpose of amending your surname in the register of members of this company it will be necessary for you to provide a statutory declaration as to change of name at common law by usage which you should request your solicitor to prepare.

Could you please send me the completed declaration on receipt of which amendments to the register of members and your share certificate will be made. I will then return your share certificate to you.

Yours

Commentary on response to shareholder whose share certificate has been lost

Section 207 of the Companies Act 1989 provides that the Secretary of State may make provision by regulations to permit title to securities to be evidenced and transferred without a written instrument. The intention behind this provision is to allow a company to administer its register of members by computer system under the proposed Taurus scheme. The Secretary of State has yet to make the necessary regulations but it is very unlikely that they will apply to private companies.

Section 207 specifically states that the regulations will be framed so as to secure that the rights and obligations in relation to securities dealt with under the new procedures correspond, so far as practicable, with those that would arise apart from any regulations under the section. The probability, therefore, is that a company's articles would have to be altered if the company wanted to 'dematerialise' its share register and cease issuing certificates. If the regulations do apply to private companies it is extremely doubtful that any would wish to alter their articles as no benefit would result. The likelihood is, therefore, that private companies will continue to issue share certificates and require their production before a transfer of shares can take place.

Unless a shareholder can confirm specifically that the certificate has been destroyed or lost and that there is no room for doubt, the chances are that it has been mislaid and consequently the draft letter responds with the request that the shareholder redoubles his efforts to try and find the certificate.

Although there is only the remote possibility of a fraudulent transfer taking place or being attempted in the case of a private company with few shareholders, as a general rule there is no reason why the company should assume even a minimal risk. Consequently, it would be prudent for the company to obtain an indemnity from the shareholder coupled with the requirement that his bank should be requested to join in the giving of such indemnity, although, here again, it is a question of judgment depending on all the circumstances as to how far this additional requirement should be pursued. A specimen form of indemnity can be found in *Company Secretarial Practice: the manual of the Institute of Chartered Secretaries and Administrators* (ICSA Publishing).

Response to shareholder of private company whose share certificate has been lost

Dear

Lost certificate representing [no.] [class] shares in the company

Thank you for your letter notifying the company that you have lost your share certificate.

Although you say that you have made a search for the certificate at home, it may be possible that it could have been sent to your bank, perhaps with the deeds of your house or some other important documents for safe keeping. Alternatively, you may have sent the certificate to your accountant, solicitor, or other professional adviser. Could you please, therefore, not only make a further search at your home, but also contact any party to whom you may conceivably have sent the certificate at some time in the past.

If, however, you confirm to me that following a further search at home and enquiry of your bank and professional advisers, the certificate has not come to light, the company will consider issuing a duplicate certificate provided you are prepared to give an indemnity and undertaking in respect of your lost certificate. [Your holding is a significant one and consequently] [Although your holding is not a significant one] the company would require your bank to join in with you in giving the indemnity and undertaking which unfortunately may involve you in some expense.

In the event that it proves to be necessary I will let you have the appropriate form of indemnity for your use. If, however, you do locate your certificate could you please nevertheless let me know.

Yours

Commentary on letter to shareholders of a private company enclosing annual report and accounts

An obvious letter perhaps in some ways but it does provide a more personal touch than just putting the accounts, reports and the notice of the annual general meeting into an envelope and sending them 'anonymously' to the shareholders. Its inclusion is a prompt to company secretaries of private companies to consider whether or not such a letter would be worthwhile, although it would be the practice of many company secretaries to write such a letter anyway.

To some extent the content will depend on how far the directors would want to encourage the participation of the shareholders and hence it can be altered or expanded accordingly. Some directors see the shareholders as part of the 'extended family of the company' whose participation is to be welcomed while other directors would take a somewhat less benign view.

An explanatory letter would of course be required if it is intended to deal with any items of business in addition to the formal annual general meeting business. In that case a commentary on each proposed resolution should be included in the letter explaining why the directors are of the opinion that the additional resolutions should be approved; for an example see the letter commencing on page 5.

Although there is reference in the letter to a proxy card, it is of course only in the case of a listed public company that there is an obligation to issue proxy cards or forms to shareholders. Where companies have adopted regulations 70 and 71 of Table A to the Companies Act 1948 or regulations 60 and 61 of the 1985 version of Table A the form which such proxy should take is set out and if the company does not circularise proxy cards itself a shareholder would be required to draft and submit his own form, which he would be unlikely to do. There is no reason why a private company could not itself issue proxy cards in the prescribed form if it wished to do so, although it may leave itself open to the charge that such an exercise is wasteful and unnecessary bearing in mind the attitude of many shareholders to general meetings, and annual general meetings in particular.

Letter to shareholders of a private company enclosing annual report and accounts

Dear Shareholder

Annual report and accounts

Enclosed with this letter are copies of the company's accounts for the year ended , together with the directors' and auditors' reports.

Also enclosed is a notice of the company's AGM to be held on and a proxy card for you to complete in accordance with the instructions. You will also find a stamped addressed envelope* to enable you to return the proxy card as the directors would like to encourage all shareholders, including those unable to attend, to participate in reaching these formal but none the less important decisions.

Although you may complete and return the proxy card this would not preclude you from attending the AGM if you subsequently decided you would like to do so.

Immediately following the AGM an informal reception will be held for shareholders during the course of which the directors will be pleased to talk to as many shareholders as possible. The reception will last for approximately one hour and light refreshments will be served.

Yours

* If the number of shareholders is insufficient to warrant a business reply service arrangement.

Commentary on letters from private company to shareholders where a shareholder has notified intention to dispose of part or all of his shareholding

Many private companies have incorporated in their articles of association pre-emption provisions of varying complexity which operate in the event of a proposed disposal of part or all of a shareholding by an existing shareholder or the personal representatives of a deceased shareholder. Such pre-emption provisions, however, do not usually apply to proposed transfers in favour of a member of the intending transferor's family or the family of a deceased shareholder.

It is not uncommon in the case of private companies formed since 1985 to find that in addition to pre-emption provisions, clause 24 of Table A of the Companies (Tables A to F) Regulations has been expressly varied to the effect that the directors can in their absolute discretion and without assigning any reason decline to register the transfer of any share whether or not it is a fully paid share, with the exception of a transfer to a member of the intending transferor's family or an existing member of the company. The articles of private companies which incorporate Part II of Table A of the Companies Act 1948, which gives the directors absolute discretion to decline to register any share.

The pre-emption provisions usually stipulate that the company's auditors shall be asked to certify a fair value of the shares (although it is not always clear whether it is the company or the intending transferor who should do so or who should bear the cost) at the time the intending transferor serves notice on the company of his intention to dispose of his shares. The first of the three letters which follow is drafted on this basis.

Alternatively the provisions may simply require the intending transferor to state a price when giving notice of his intention to the company and for the company in turn to notify the other shareholders of that price. It is then open to any of the other shareholders who wish to challenge the price to object within a specified period and to request the directors to ask the company's auditors to certify a fair value, although again it is not always clear who should bear the cost of doing so. The second letter has been drafted on this alternative basis.

The position may be less straightforward where there are no pre-emption provisions or any mechanism providing for the valuation of the company's shares but the articles contain the amended version of clause 24 of Table A of the Companies (Tables A to F) Regulations or Part II of Table A of the Companies Act

Letter from private company to shareholders where a shareholder has notified intention to dispose of part or all of his shareholding and where the pre-emption provisions contained in the company's articles require a fair value to be fixed by the company's auditors

Dear Shareholder

Proposed sale of ordinary shares of £ each owned by

Mr has given notice in writing to the company stating that he wishes to transfer [the whole of his shareholding of ordinary shares] [ordinary shares]. The letter from Mr constitutes a transfer notice for the purposes of article of the company's articles of association. In accordance with that article Messrs , the company's auditors have at the request of [the directors] [Mr] certified in writing that a fair value of each share is £ . The auditor's certificate is dated 19 .

Consequently, the company has by virtue of the receipt of the transfer notice been appointed agent for Mr for the sale of his shares. As the holder of shares you are entitled to apply for shares, being the proportion calculated by reference to the number of shares which you already hold in the company. If you wish to take up part or the whole of your entitlement, please complete and return the enclosed application form.

In the event that some of the other shareholders do not take up their full entitlement and you would like to acquire more shares would you please indicate on the application form how many additional shares you would want should any be available.

This offer remains open until 19 and please therefore ensure that your application form is returned by that date. Even if you do not wish to apply for any of the shares, please would you nevertheless write to the company by the closing date stating that you have declined the offer.

Yours

1948 has been incorporated. In either situation, if a shareholder wanted to sell his shares to an outsider he would need to seek the co-operation of the directors and establish what their attitude would be to such a proposed sale. If the response from the directors was to the effect that such a sale would not be permitted but a sale to existing shareholders would be, the intending transferor would have to negotiate with other existing shareholders who may be interested in acquiring his shares. If there are only a few shareholders a personal approach could be made by the intending transferor but if there are a number it would be sensible to persuade the directors to circularise the other shareholders to see if any would want to acquire the shares that were available. There is no reason why in this case the intending transferor should not be asked to meet the cost of doing so. The third draft letter is the one which might be appropriate in this situation.

If the articles of a company formed since 1985 do not contain any pre-emption provisions and clause 24 of Table A of the Companies (Tables A to F) Regulations has been incorporated without amendment so that the directors' discretion to refuse a transfer to anyone is very limited, it may nevertheless be that in the event of a shareholder wishing to transfer his shares, the only likely purchasers would be existing shareholders, in which case the third draft letter can be adapted accordingly. The directors may well be minded to co-operate in finding existing shareholders who might want to acquire the shares rather than see the shares go to an outsider.

Letter from private company to shareholders where a shareholder has notified intention to dispose of part or all of his shareholding and the pre-emption provisions give the other shareholders the option to request the auditors to value the shares

Dear Shareholder

Proposed sale of ordinary shares of £ each owned by

Mr has notified the company that he wishes to transfer [the whole of his shareholding of ordinary shares] [ordinary shares] at a price of £ per share. The letter from Mr constitutes a transfer notice for the purposes of article of the company's articles of association.

Consequently, the company has by virtue of the receipt of the transfer notice been appointed agent for Mr to sell his shares. As the holder of shares you are entitled to apply for shares, being the proportion calculated by reference to the number of shares which you already hold in the company. If you wish to take up part or the whole of your entitlement please complete and return the enclosed application form.

In the event that the other shareholders do not take up their full entitlement and you would like to acquire more shares, would you please indicate on the application form how many additional shares you would want should any be available.

This offer remains open until 19 and please therefore ensure that your application form is returned by that date. Even if you do not wish to apply for any of the shares, please would you nevertheless write to the company by the closing date stating that you have declined the offer.

If, however, you do not consider the price specified in the transfer notice to be a proper or fair one you have the right to request the company's auditors to certify in writing how much, in their opinion, is the fair value of each share. If it is your wish that the company's auditors be asked to give such a certificate, please respond immediately you receive this letter as if you do not do so within twenty-one days of its date (not the date you receive it) you will lose the right of referral to the auditors. The amount then certified by the auditors would be deemed to be the price per share at which Mr 's shares are offered for sale, which of course may be more or less than the present offer price. The directors are not in a position to speculate as to what the outcome of any request to the auditors to

value the shares would be [even though the articles provide that in arriving at a valuation the auditors shall (state any assumptions to be made by the auditors) [because there are a number of different ways in which the shares could be valued depending on what criteria the auditors consider appropriate and the articles do not specify any guide lines which the auditors should observe in arriving at a valuation].

It should be noted, however, that the articles also provide that Mr would not be able to revoke the transfer notice unless the directors were to agree to a request from Mr to that effect. Consequently, should the auditors reduce the value of the shares it does not necessarily follow that the sale of the shares would not proceed at the lesser figure.

Whatever may be your initial response to this offer, you will be notified of the outcome in due course.

Yours

Letter from private company to shareholders where a shareholder has notified intention to dispose of part or all of his shareholding but the articles do not include any pre-emption provisions or any mechanism for an auditors' valuation of the shares

Dear Shareholder

Proposed sale of ordinary shares of £ each owned by

Mr has notified the company that he wishes to transfer [the whole of his shareholding of ordinary shares] [ordinary shares] at a price of £ per share.

The company's articles provide that the directors may in their absolute discretion and without assigning any reason decline to register the transfer of a share whether or not it is a fully paid share. As this right of veto is discretionary the directors could, if they chose, allow a transfer of shares to a person other than an existing shareholder but this has not been the policy adopted in the past and there are no compelling reasons to vary this practice now. Mr has been informed accordingly and his response has been to request the directors to circularise the existing shareholders to inform them that his shares are available for purchase.

Consequently, the directors propose that existing shareholders should be invited to apply for the shares in proportion to their present holdings. On this basis you are entitled to apply for shares, being the proportion calculated by reference to the number of shares which you already hold in the company. If you wish to take up part or the whole of your entitlement please complete and return the enclosed application form.

In the event that the other shareholders do not take up their full entitlement and you would like to acquire more shares, would you please indicate on the application form how many additional shares you would want should any be available.

This offer remains open until 19 and please therefore ensure that your application form is returned by that date. Even if you do not wish to apply for any of the shares, please would you nevertheless write to the company by the closing date stating that you have declined the offer.

At this stage it is not intended to ask the auditors to certify what in their opinion would constitute a fair price for the shares, partly because of the cost which would be involved and partly because there are a number of different ways in which the shares could be valued depending on what criteria the auditors chose to adopt.

The options which are open to Mr , should he not receive applications for all of the shares on offer, are (a) that he could sell those for which there is an acceptance and retain the balance, (b) reduce the price to a point where there is a better chance that all the shares would be taken up, or (c) ask the auditors to value the shares [at his own cost] and on receipt of that valuation to circularise all shareholders again to see if the price fixed by the auditors might result in sufficient acceptances being received from existing shareholders.

Whatever may be your initial response to this offer you will be notified of the outcome and any decision of Mr if the offer is not taken up in full.

Yours

CHAPTER 2

AUDITORS

Commentary on letter to private company's auditors enclosing copy of intended written resolution(s) pursuant to section 113 of the Companies Act 1989

Section 113 of the Companies Act 1989 provides that the members of a private company can do anything which may be done by resolution in general meeting (or by resolution of a meeting of any class of members) by a unanimous written resolution other than to remove a director or an auditor before his period of office expires. To be valid the written resolution must be signed by all of the members of a company or on their behalf. The date of the resolution will be the date on which the last member signed it or it is signed on his behalf. The resolution which is sent to each member for signature must state accurately the terms of the resolution. It is not a requirement that the signatures of the members should appear on a single document and separate letters from each individual member will suffice. The resolution, together with the signatures of the members, must be kept in the company's general meeting minute book.

This procedure dispenses with the need for previous notice to be given or for a formal meeting to be held.

There is one proviso, however, in that a copy of any resolution which it is proposed should be dealt with as a written resolution must be sent to the company's auditors. This requirement in effect preserves the auditors' existing entitlement to receive notices of general meetings and to attend and speak at a general meeting in so far as any item of business concerns them as auditors. The auditors have seven days from receipt of the copy of the proposed written resolution to express their opinion that:

1. it does not concern them as auditors; or
2. it does so concern them but it is not necessary for the resolution to be considered by the company at a formal general meeting; or
3. it does so concern them and it should be considered at a formal general meeting.

If the auditors respond confirming that either of the first two alternatives above apply or the auditors do not respond at all within the seven day period the resolution will, subject to the unanimity of the members, come into effect automatically.

It is a matter of judgment for the company secretary to decide whether or not the

Letter to private company's auditors enclosing copy of intended written resolution(s) pursuant to section 113 of the Companies Act 1989

Dear

Proposed written resolution

We enclose a copy of the written resolution which it is proposed should be passed in accordance with section 113 of the Companies Act 1989. We have not yet circularised the members with the resolution as we would prefer to receive your response beforehand.

As you will see, the proposed resolution is an ordinary resolution to increase the authorised share capital in the company to £1,000,000. We do not have any immediate plans to issue further shares in the company but, as we want to reprint the memorandum and articles of association shortly it would seem sensible for the authorised share capital to be increased before the reprint takes place.

On the face of it this proposed resolution does not concern you as auditors, but if you decide that it does and that it should be considered at a formal general meeting of the members would you please notify us to that effect, stating your reasons, within seven days from the day on which you receive this letter.

If you do not consider that the proposed resolution concerns you as auditors, would you please nevertheless confirm that in writing within the seven day period so that on receipt we will be able to send the proposed resolution to the members of the company for each of them to approve in writing.

Yours

proposed resolution should be referred to the auditors before the members are circularised or contemporaneously. In most cases it is unlikely that the auditors would be concerned or consider that they are concerned to the extent that they would require the resolution to be considered at a formal general meeting of the company. However, there will be few occasions where it would be necessary to pass a resolution so quickly that there would be insufficient time to obtain the clearance of the auditors within the seven day period and therefore it would generally seem to be the better practice to refer proposed written resolutions to the auditors before the resolutions are circulated to the members.

CHAPTER 3

DIRECTORS

Commentary on letter to non-executive director of private company following appointment at board meeting

Directors are usually appointed for the first time at a board meeting and very rarely at an annual general meeting, except perhaps in the case of those companies where day to day control is in the hands of the members as a whole, for example a company formed for the purpose of managing or administering a block of flats.

When a non-executive director is appointed a number of matters have to be dealt with and the way in which this is done deserves proper consideration. The circumstances of the appointment should be taken into account, as well as the character and personality of the appointee.

In a number of cases it may be appropriate to deal with some or most of the points mentioned in the draft letter in person immediately following the board meeting. On the other hand, it would be prudent for the company secretary specifically to write to the appointee, drawing his attention, for example, to his obligations to disclose any interests of his in the shares and debentures (if any) of the company and of any interest he may have or acquire in contracts or other business arrangements with the company. There will then be a clear record of the company secretary having discharged this responsibility. The legal and regulatory regime to which all directors (not only directors of listed companies) are now subject is more stringent than it used to be. It is incumbent on the company secretary, therefore, to underline, where he has the opportunity to do so, the legal duties and responsibilities which arise on the appointment of a director, even if to do so may appear unduly formal.

One point which should be noted is that for the purposes of section 317 of the Companies Act 1985 which imposes a duty on a director to declare the nature of any interest in a contract or proposed contract with the company, a general notice given to the directors of the company is only appropriate where the director is a shareholder of the other company or is a member of a firm with which the company proposes to contract, or where the director is to be regarded as interested in any contract which may be made with a specified person who is connected with him. A general notice for the purposes of section 317 is not effective where the director's interest in the contract or prospective contract arises as a result of his being a director only of the other company involved. Where the company's articles incorporate regulations 85 and 86 of Table A of the Companies (Tables A to F)

Letter to non-executive director of private company following appointment at board meeting

Dear

Your appointment as non-executive director

Following your appointment as a non-executive director of the company today, I thought that it would be useful if I wrote to you setting out a number of matters which I hope you will find helpful. Although I know that you have been a director of XYZ Limited for some years, this is your first appointment as a non-executive director and as it happens you are also the first non-executive director to be appointed by this company. So it would be as well for both of us to be certain that we have the necessary information to deal with the various requirements, legal as well as practical.

Although I know you have looked at the company's memorandum and articles of association, you should have your own copy to retain and this is now enclosed. You will note that there is no requirement that a director should hold any qualification shares in the company. Nor are any directors required to retire by rotation.

I enclose a schedule setting out the dates of the board meetings for the rest of this calendar year together with details of the basis on which you may claim expenses for attendance at board meetings. Normally an agenda with supporting papers is circulated to directors approximately a week before a meeting.

In order that I can notify the Companies Registry of your appointment, can you please let me have all your forenames and, if appropriate, any former forenames or surnames. I have taken it that your nationality is British and that your business occupation is that of an [engineer]. If you have any other directorships, apart from that of XYZ Limited, could you please let me have a list of the names of the companies concerned, distinguishing where appropriate between holding companies and their subsidiaries. Can you please also let me know your date of birth as it is now a requirement that this information be notified to the Companies Registry.

If you would like your director's fees to be sent direct to your bank could you please provide me with the address, sort code and the number of your account.

In addition to the specific duties imposed on directors by the Companies Acts,

Regulations 1985 the situation with regard to the giving of a general notice is expanded and reference in the letter should be made accordingly.

This draft letter is an attempt to strike a balance between the formal and the informal and yet deal with the essential points.

The paragraphs marked with an asterisk are those which should be incorporated into the three other letters which follow.

and related legislation, directors are under a general duty to act in good faith and to exercise their powers for the benefit of the company as a whole. Consequently, directors' personal interests should not be allowed to conflict with their overriding duty to act for the benefit of the company. This is what the law terms to be a fiduciary duty, although in certain circumstances, which I will come to in a moment, the rigid application of this rule can to some extent be relaxed in particular circumstances and provided that certain conditions are met.

* If you have any interest however remote, even as a trustee, or your wife or a son or daughter under the age of eighteen has any interest in the shares of the company (there are no debentures), would you please let me know in writing within five days of today as this is a legal requirement. Details, which must include the price paid or received, of any acquisitions or disposals of shares in the future, however arising, by you or a member of your family must be notified to me in writing within five days of the occurrence of any such transaction. It is your obligation to give such notice in writing to me even though the likelihood is that I will be or will become aware of any such transaction as a matter of course. Failure to comply will render you liable to imprisonment or a fine, or both.

* I now turn to the requirement on the part of directors to disclose any interest in contracts with the company. The Companies Act 1985 states that a director of a company who is in any way, whether directly or indirectly, interested in a contract (which includes any transaction or arrangement whether or not constituting a contract) or proposed contract with a company has a duty to declare the nature of his interest at a meeting of the directors of the company. In the case of a proposed contract the declaration shall be made at the meeting of the directors at which the question of entering into the contract is first taken into consideration or if the director was not at the date of that meeting interested in the proposed contract, at the next meeting of the directors held after he became so interested, and where the director becomes interested in a contract after it is made the declaration shall be made at the first meeting of the directors held after he becomes so interested.

* The relevant section of the 1985 Act also provides that a general notice given to the directors of a company by a director to the effect that he is a member (i.e. shareholder) of a specified company or of a firm and is to be regarded as interested in any contract which may after the date of the notice be made with that company or firm, or he is to be regarded as interested in any contract which may after the date of the notice be made with the specified person who is connected with him (which means a spouse, son or daughter, including stepson or stepdaughter, under the age of eighteen) is regarded as sufficient declaration of interest in relation to any such contract.

* Failure to comply will render you liable to a fine.

* [The company's articles incorporate an amended version of regulation 84 of Table A of the Companies Act 1948 which provides that a director shall not vote in respect of any contract or arrangement in which he is interested and if he shall

do so his vote shall not be counted, nor shall he be counted in the quorum present at the meeting. Provided, therefore, you have disclosed the *nature* of your interest in any contract to the directors, which means the board as a whole and not to some directors only or to a committee of the board, and it is resolved without your vote that the contract be entered into, you would not be accountable to the company for any profit which may accrue to you from such contract.]

* [The company's articles incorporate regulations 85 and 86 of Table A of the Companies (Tables A to F) Regulations 1985. Regulation 85 states that provided a director has disclosed to the directors, which means the board as a whole and not to some directors only or to a committee of the board, the *nature and extent of any material interest* of his, a director notwithstanding his office

(a) may be a party to or otherwise interested in any transaction or arrangement with the company or in which the company is otherwise interested;
(b) may be a director or other officer of, or employed by, or a party to any transaction or arrangement with, or otherwise interested in, any body corporate promoted by the company or in which the company is otherwise interested; and
(c) shall not by reason of his office be accountable to the company for any benefit which he derives from any such office or employment or from any such transaction or arrangement or from any interest in any such body corporate and no such transaction or arrangement shall be liable to be avoided on the ground of any such interest or benefit.

For the purposes of regulation 85, regulation 86 provides that a general notice given to the directors that a director is to be regarded as having an interest of the nature and extent specified in the notice in any transaction or arrangement in which a specified person or class of persons is interested shall be deemed to be a disclosure that the director has an interest in any such transaction of the nature and extent so specified. You will note that the circumstances in which this general form of notice can be given are not so restricted as in the case of the general notice permitted by the Companies Act itself.

The company's articles also incorporate regulations 94 and 95 of Table A of the Companies (Tables A to F) Regulations 1985, the effect of which is that a director is not entitled to vote at a board meeting on any resolution concerning a matter in which he has directly or indirectly an interest or duty which is material and which conflicts or may conflict with the interests of the company (subject to specific exceptions) and that a director would not be counted in the quorum present at a meeting in relation to a resolution on which the director is not entitled to vote.]

I appreciate that the obligations with regard to the declaration of any interests in contracts or transactions with the company is less than straightforward and I would be happy to discuss these requirements with you further if you would like me to do so.

Can you please let me have all the personal information requested as soon as practicable so that I can prepare the Companies Registry notice of appointment form. I will then be able to send you the completed form for you to sign and return to me for forwarding to the Companies Registry.

If there is anything which is not clear, or there is any further information you require, please do not hesitate to let me know. Finally, on a personal note I very much look forward to working with you in the future.

Yours

Commentary on letter to full time employee following appointment as a director of private company at board meeting

The appointee will, as likely as not, already be known to the company secretary, and this will have some bearing on the style in which the letter is written. It is just as important, if not more so, that the appointee in this situation should be clearly informed in writing as to his responsibilities as a director. An employee who becomes a director has probably not been a director of a company before, whereas a non-executive director may well have been. Furthermore, where the company secretary and the newly appointed director have been colleagues for some time it may be that much more difficult for the company secretary to adopt the more formal stance which would be required in 'laying down the law'. A letter may therefore be the best way out of any dilemma.

The same general observations mentioned in the commentary on the letter to the non-executive director also apply in this case.

The draft incorporates a reference to a directors' service agreement and whether this is appropriate will depend on the company's practice. Not all directors have formal service agreements with their company. If it is usual for the company to require its directors to enter into such an agreement it would undoubtedly be the better course to have given the prospective director a copy or draft some weeks before his appointment is scheduled to be made so that he can consider the implications of the agreement and, if necessary, take legal advice. As some of the provisions in the service agreement are for the benefit of the company in that they place restrictions on the director both during and following the termination of his employment, the director may be reluctant to accept the agreement in its entirety. If the agreement is only presented to the director after he has already been appointed, the company's negotiating position will clearly have been undermined. This aspect therefore needs to be carefully considered and any differences resolved before the appointment is made. The agreement can be executed by the company and the newly appointed director at the relative board meeting and be dated accordingly.

Letter to full time employee following appointment as a director of private company at board meeting

Dear

Your appointment as a director

Following your appointment as a director of the company today, I thought that it would be useful if I wrote to you setting out a number of matters which I hope you will find helpful.

A copy of the company's memorandum and articles of association is enclosed for you to retain. I do recommend that you read this document because it sets out the internal rules by which the company is regulated.

Next I enclose a schedule of the board meeting dates for the rest of this calendar year. Normally an agenda with supporting papers is circulated to directors approximately a week before a meeting.

[I enclose a copy of the company's standard form of director's service agreement which is different from your existing contract of employment [as the company's chief engineer] for you to consider. We will need to discuss this agreement as soon as possible and I would hope that we could do this within the next week.]

[I enclose [a photocopy] [the duplicate] of your director's service agreement which you signed at the board meeting today for your retention.]

As I have all your personal details already, I have been able to prepare the form notifying the Companies Registry of your appointment. I enclose a photocopy of this form so that you can check to make sure that the contents of the original are correct. If any amendments to the form are required can you please let me know as soon as possible so these can be made before you sign.

At the same time as you sign the Companies Registry form I will also ask you to let me have a specimen of your signature as you are to become a signatory to the company's bank accounts.

The position of director is one of some responsibility, as I am sure you already appreciate. You do take on a number of legal obligations once you become a director, which means that in certain circumstances you have to act in a particular way. In addition to the specific duties imposed on directors by the Companies Acts, and related legislation, directors are under a general duty to act in good

faith and to exercise their powers for the benefit of the company as a whole. Consequently, directors' personal interests should not be allowed to conflict with their overriding duty to act for the benefit of the company. This is what the law terms to be a fiduciary duty, although in certain circumstances, which I will come to in a moment, the rigid application of this rule can to some extent be relaxed in particular circumstances and provided that certain conditions are met.

* Take in all the clauses (or the alternatives as the case may be) marked with an asterisk in the first precedent, amending as necessary.

I appreciate that it is unlikely you will ever find yourself in a position where disclosure is required, but to avoid any room for misunderstanding I must draw these obligations specifically to your attention at the outset.

On a personal note I would like to say how pleased I am that you have been appointed a director. We have worked as colleagues for some years now and, notwithstanding 'your elevation', I hope that we can continue to work together as well as we have in the past.

If there is anything which is not clear, or if you feel that you require further information, please do not hesitate to let me know.

Yours

Commentary on letter to non-executive director of listed public company following appointment at board meeting

In many respects the format of this letter is similar to the letter to a non-executive director of a private company, but there are a number of material differences.

The likelihood is that the appointee will be a seasoned and experienced director of a number of other companies. It will therefore be a matter of judgment for the company secretary to decide to what extent the appointee should be informed about his obligations, even though he should be well aware of what these comprise.

There have, however, been a number of well-publicised defaults on the part of directors in recent years and the consequences of such breaches have been dealt with severely in the criminal courts. These cases demonstrate that some directors are, to say the least, cavalier in the way in which they regard the law and the manner in which they discharge their role as directors and their responsibilities to shareholders. A company secretary should be resolute in drawing the attention of directors to their duties and obligations and, as important, be able to show that he has done so.

Letter to non-executive director of listed public company following appointment at board meeting

Dear

Your appointment as a non-executive director

Following your appointment as a non-executive director of the company today, I thought that it would be useful if I wrote to you setting out a number of matters which I hope you will find helpful. It would be advisable for both of us to be certain that we have the necessary information to comply with the various legal and Stock Exchange requirements, as well as dealing with a number of practical matters.

Although I know you have seen a copy of the company's memorandum and articles of association, you should have a copy to retain and this is now enclosed. You will note that one-third of the directors retire by rotation each year, but as you have been appointed at a board meeting rather than at an annual general meeting you will also be subject to retirement at the next annual general meeting in . Your re-election as a director at that meeting will be dealt with in the usual way as part of the formal business.

I enclose a schedule setting out the dates of the board meetings for the rest of this calendar year together with details of the basis on which you may claim expenses for attendance at board meetings. Normally an agenda with supporting papers is circulated to directors approximately a week before a meeting.

In order that I can notify the Companies Registry and the Stock Exchange of your appointment, can you please let me have all your forenames and, if appropriate, any former forenames or surnames. I have taken it that your nationality is British and that your business occupation is that of an [engineer]. I am aware that you have a number of other directorships and I should be grateful if you would please let me have a list distinguishing where appropriate between holding companies and their subsidiaries. Can you please also let me know your date of birth.

If you would prefer your director's fees to be sent direct to your bank could you please provide me with the address, sort code and the number of your account.

In addition to the specific duties imposed on directors by the Companies Acts and related legislation directors are under a general duty to act in good faith and

to exercise their powers for the benefit of the company as a whole. Consequently, directors' personal interests should not be allowed to conflict with their overriding duty to act for the benefit of the company. This is what the law terms to be a fiduciary duty, although in certain circumstances, which I will come to in a moment, the rigid application of this rule can to some extent be relaxed in particular circumstances and provided that certain conditions are met.

I also enclose a copy of the share-dealing rules operated by the company which must be observed in order to comply with the requirement of the Company Securities (Insider Dealing) Act 1985 and the Model Code for Securities Transactions by Directors of Listed Companies issued by the International Stock Exchange.

* Take in all the clauses (or the alternatives as the case may be) marked with an asterisk in the first precedent, amending as necessary.

I should also mention that it is a Stock Exchange requirement that in most circumstances information concerning a proposed contract or transaction between a director and the company will have to be circulated to shareholders for them to approve in general meeting.

The Companies Act 1985 also requires that the company's accounts must contain particulars of any other transaction or arrangement with the company or a subsidiary of it in which a person who at any time during the financial year was a director of the company or its holding company had, directly or indirectly, a material interest.

Can you please let me have all the personal information requested as soon as practicable so that I can prepare the Companies Registry notice of appointment form. I will then be able to send you the completed form for signature and return to me for forwarding to the Companies Registry.

If there is anything which is not clear, or there is any further information you require, please do not hesitate to let me know. Finally, on a personal note I very much look forward to working with you in the future.

Yours

Commentary on letter to full time employee following appointment as a director of listed public company at board meeting

Although this letter follows the general format of the three previous letters in this series there are, as with the other letters, sufficient material differences to warrant the letter being dealt with separately. The same general observations mentioned in the commentaries on the three previous letters apply where relevant.

Invariably, a full time employee of a listed company who is appointed a director will be required to enter into a director's service agreement and such agreement should have been agreed fully before the appointment is made.

Letter to full time employee following appointment as a director of listed public company at board meeting

Dear

Your appointment as a director

Following your appointment today as a director of the company, I thought that it would be useful if I wrote to you setting out a number of matters which I hope you will find helpful.

A copy of the company's memorandum and articles of association is enclosed for you to retain. I do recommend that you read this document because it sets out the internal rules by which the company is regulated.

You should be aware that one-third of the directors of the company retire by rotation each year, although as you have been appointed at a board meeting part way through the current financial year rather than at an annual general meeting you will be subject to retirement at the next annual general meeting of the company to be held in . Your re-election as director at that meeting will be dealt with in the usual way as part of the formal business.

I enclose a schedule setting out the dates of the board meetings for the rest of this calendar year. Normally an agenda with supporting papers is circulated to directors approximately a week before a meeting.

I enclose [a photocopy] [the duplicate] of your director's service agreement, which you signed at the board meeting today, for your retention.

As I have all your personal details already, I have been able to prepare the form notifying the Companies Registry of your appointment. I enclose a photocopy of this form so that you can check to make sure that the contents of the original are correct. If any amendments are required can you please let me know as soon as possible so these can be made before you sign the form. I have taken it that you do not have any other directorships, but if that is not the case please let me know.

When you come to see me to sign the Companies Registry form I will also ask you to let me have a specimen of your signature as you are to become a signatory to the company's bank accounts.

The position of director is one of some responsibility, as I am sure you already appreciate. You do take on a number of legal obligations once you become a director, which means that in certain circumstances you have to act in a particular

way. In addition to the specific duties imposed on directors by the Companies Acts, and related legislation, directors are under a general duty to act in good faith and to exercise their powers for the benefit of the company as a whole. Consequently, directors' personal interests should not be allowed to conflict with their overriding duty to act for the benefit of the company. This is what the law terms to be a fiduciary duty, although in certain circumstances, which I will come to in a moment, the rigid application of this rule can to some extent be relaxed in particular circumstances and provided that certain conditions are met.

I also enclose a copy of the share-dealing rules operated by the company which must be observed in order to comply with the requirements of the Company Securities (Insider Dealing) Act 1985 and the Model Code for Securities Transactions by Directors of Listed Companies issued by the International Stock Exchange.

* Take in all the clauses (or the alternatives as the case may be) marked with an asterisk in the first precedent, amending as necessary.

I should also mention that it is a Stock Exchange requirement that in most circumstances information concerning a proposed contract or transaction between a director and the company will have to be circulated to shareholders for them to approve in general meeting.

The Companies Act 1985 also requires that the company's accounts must contain particulars of any other transaction or arrangement with the company or a subsidiary of it in which a person who at any time during the financial year was a director of the company or its holding company had, directly or indirectly, a material interest.

To avoid any room for misunderstanding I must draw these obligations specifically to your attention.

On a personal note I would like to say how pleased I was that you have been appointed a director. We have worked as colleagues for some years now and, notwithstanding 'your elevation', I hope that we can continue to work together as well as we have in the past.

If there is anything which is not clear, or if you feel that you require further information, please do not hesitate to let me know.

Yours

Commentary on annual reminder to a director of obligations to disclose interests in contracts and shares

Section 232 of the Companies Act and schedule 6 require a company's accounts, which for practical purposes means the annual accounts, to contain particulars of 'any other transaction or arrangement with the company or a subsidiary of it in which a person who at any time during the financial year was a director of the company or its holding company had, directly or indirectly, a material interest'.

There is some doubt as to what constitutes a 'material interest' for the purposes of this requirement, and in practice it is up to the board of directors to decide what is or is not a material interest which would require disclosure in the accounts. There is also some debate as to whether the transaction is one which is material in the context of the company's financial position as a whole or is material in the sense that the director concerned has a substantial interest in the particular transaction or arrangement. The prudent approach is to err on the side of caution and to disclose any interest in a transaction concerning the existence of which a shareholder would expect to be notified.

It is the requirement to ensure that disclosure is made for the purposes of section 232 that prompts the need for an annual reminder to be circulated to directors but it also fulfils the purpose of reminding directors to bring up-to-date details of any other disclosures which they are obliged to make and which they may have overlooked.

Section 317 of the Companies Act 1985 imposes on directors an obligation to disclose to the board of directors any interest, whether direct or indirect, in a contract or proposed contract which includes any transaction or arrangement (whether or not constituting a contract). Thus any interest has to be declared whether or not it is material and there is therefore a distinction between the requirements of section 317 and section 232 and schedule 6 referred to above.

For the purposes of section 317 a general notice given to the directors of a company by a director to the effect that:

(a) he is a *member* of a specified company or firm and is to be regarded as interested in any contract which may after the date of a notice be made with that company or firm, or
(b) he is to be regarded as interested in any contract which may after the date of a

Annual reminder to a director of obligations to disclose interests in contracts and shares

Dear

I am writing to you as I usually do at this time of the year to remind you of the obligations imposed by the Companies Acts requiring you to declare any interests you may have or are likely to have in any contracts or arrangements with the company or in the shares or debentures of the company.

As you know, section 317 of the Companies Act 1985 provides that if you are directly, or indirectly, interested in *any* contract or proposed contract or other business arrangement (whether or not a contract and whether material or not) with the company you must declare the nature of that interest at a meeting of the directors of the company.

Although you have provided a general notice of interests in accordance with [section 317[3] of the Companies Act 1985] [regulation 86 of Table A of the Companies (Tables A to F) Regulations 1985], if that notice needs amendment please let me know so that I can let you have a replacement to complete and return to me for submission at the next board meeting. If you are a director of any company with which this company has contracted or is considering contracting, you must make a separate disclosure in respect of any existing or proposed transactions to the directors at the next board meeting, although it would be helpful if you were to notify me of the details as soon as possible.

In addition to the obligation imposed by section 317, section 232 of the Companies Act 1985 and Schedule 6 require a company's accounts to contain particulars of 'any other transaction or arrangement with the company or a subsidiary of it in which a person who at any time during the financial year was a director of the company or its holding company had, directly or indirectly, a material interest'. Please consider particularly whether these requirements relate to you.

You are, as you know, also required to notify the company of any interests, however remote, in its shares [or debentures] and of any changes, however arising, in those interests. You are obliged to notify the company in writing within five days (excluding Saturday, Sunday and Bank Holidays) of any event which affects such interests and you must provide full details of any acquisition or notice be made with a specified person who is connected with him within the meaning of section 346,

is deemed a sufficient declaration of interest in relation to any such contract.

To be effective such notice has to be given at a meeting of the directors, or the director must take reasonable steps to secure that it is brought up and read at the next meeting of the directors after it is given. Failure to comply may result in a fine.

If a company's articles incorporate regulation 84 of Table A of the Companies Act 1948, then, provided a director declares the nature of his interest in a contract or proposed contract with the company at a meeting of the directors and provided he does not vote or be counted in the quorum, he shall not be liable to account to the company for any profit realised by any such contract or arrangement.

If a company's articles incorporate regulation 85 of Table A of the Companies (Tables A to F) Regulations 1985, then, provided a director discloses the nature and extent of any material interest to the directors and provided he does not vote or be counted in the quorum, a director can continue to be a party to and benefit from such transaction or arrangement.

A director must always recognise his fiduciary and statutory obligations as a director however inconvenient this may be.

A director's position with regard to the disclosure of any interest in contracts or other business arrangements is less clear when compared with his obligation to declare or disclose any interest in the company's securities. The rules relating to disclosure of any interest in the company's securities are more straightforward because there is a specific time scale within which the notice has to be given and the interests which are required to be disclosed are defined in schedule 13 of the Companies Act 1985. Section 324 imposes an obligation to notify the company within five days where a director acquires or disposes of an interest in the company's securities. Failure to comply may result in imprisonment or a fine, or both.

In the case of most private companies it is unlikely that problems will arise as the number of shares in issue will not be great and dealings will be comparatively rare and where a private company has pre-emption provisions which operate in the event of a proposed transfer, the company will itself be involved in the transfer arrangements. Nevertheless, the law applies equally to a private company as it does to a public company whose shares may be listed and directors must not only be aware of the disclosure requirements but also observe them.

disposal of shares [or debentures], stating the price paid or received, if any, and also provide full details of any assignment of any rights granted by the company to subscribe for its shares [or debentures].

The same rules relating to disclosure of an interest in shares [or debentures] apply to any interests of your [wife] [husband] [and your children who are under the age of eighteen]. I enclose a photocopy of the register of director's interests showing the entries which relate to you for you to check and return to me with any comments.

As always I am more than ready to discuss with you any situation or circumstances where you are not sure if a declaration or disclosure has to be made.

Yours

CHAPTER 4

CONTRACTS IN THE ORDINARY COURSE OF BUSINESS (INCLUDING RETENTION OF TITLE)

Commentary on letter from seller to buyer offering to sell goods in accordance with seller's own standard terms and conditions

As a general but self-evident statement, both parties to a transaction would prefer their own terms and conditions (if they have them) to be incorporated into the contract. Whose terms and conditions are to apply where there is a conflict or inconsistency in the wording will depend on a number of factors one of which is the relative bargaining position of each party.

If the market conditions are such that the seller is in the stronger position, he can generally impose his conditions with little or no variation or compromise. Another factor is the extent to which either party's contract formation procedures are efficient and the certainty with which the contract comes into being. The process can often be confused with letters and order/acceptance forms flying backwards and forwards in what has been judicially expressed as 'the battle of the forms', so that at the end of the process it is not always clear whose terms and conditions apply. If the buyer submits his own terms and conditions with his order but the seller's acceptance of the order is subject to the seller's own terms and conditions, then if there is no subsequent negotiation or discussion the buyer, by reason of his acquiescence, may be deemed to have accepted the seller's terms and conditions. By the same token a seller may be held to have accepted a buyer's terms and conditions if there is tacit acceptance by the seller or the seller, by his actions, accepts the buyer's terms and conditions. It would, however, be too simplistic to say that the conditions which are the last to be submitted before the contract is performed will be the ones which apply should there be any conflict or inconsistency. The facts and circumstances surrounding the formation of the contract would need to be scrutinised to establish what, if anything, the parties agreed.

The purpose of this series of letters is to suggest a framework within which to conclude a contract in the ordinary course of business in correspondence. Even where there has been a course of dealing between the company and the other party it would be preferable, unless the frequency is such as to make it impracticable, for each and every transaction to be the subject of a separate contract.

The first draft letter that follows is specific and uncompromising in tone and for use where the seller is in a position to impose his standard terms and conditions in the knowledge that the buyer will have to accede.

Letter from seller to buyer offering to sell goods in accordance with seller's own standard terms and conditions

Dear

Type of goods and quantity

[Thank you for your enquiry dated requesting us to supply you with 1,000 widgets.] [We refer to our telephone conversation on the when you requested us to supply you with 1,000 widgets.] We confirm that the price for each widget is £ .

We would be prepared to sell to you 1,000 widgets but only on the basis that you agree to accept our standard terms and conditions of sale which are incorporated in the enclosed order form. If you wish to proceed with the purchase you must please complete our order form, sign it and return it to us for acknowledgment and acceptance.

It is our established practice to contract only on this basis and we are unable to consider any variation. However, if there are any aspects of our terms and conditions which are not clear, or you are uncertain as to their effect, we would naturally be prepared to discuss any such queries with you.

Yours

Commentary on buyer's reply to seller stipulating that buyer's own terms and conditions should be incorporated into the contract

The next two letters are alternative responses to the last letter.

If the prospective buyer is confident that the seller is anxious to contract, he may decide that he can impose some or all of his own terms and conditions.

The problem for a buyer, however, is that it is unlikely that his terms and conditions will be appropriate in all respects for every kind of transaction in which he becomes involved. The seller's terms and conditions will relate specifically to the supply of the goods manufactured by him and be framed accordingly. Care must therefore be taken to ensure that a buyer does not insist on his terms and conditions being incorporated where it is inappropriate to do so. The buyer is more likely to achieve some variation or agreement if he restricts himself to those terms and conditions which he considers to be of particular importance. However, if the buyer is confident that he is in a strong bargaining position and it is relevant to do so, he can respond with the first letter. If, on the other hand, he is prepared to limit his objections to a number of specific points the second letter would be the more appropriate.

Buyer's reply to seller stipulating that buyer's own terms and conditions should be incorporated into the contract

Dear

Type of goods and quantity

We acknowledge your letter of the enclosing the order form incorporating your company's own standard terms and conditions of sale. We note that you are not prepared to agree to any variation.

However, it is not this company's practice to accept the imposition of a seller's terms and conditions as we have our own which we use for contracts of this kind. There are, as you know, many suppliers of widgets and we would be able to place our order elsewhere without difficulty, as we have done on previous occasions. We accordingly return your order form unsigned.

We enclose our own purchase order form which incorporates this company's terms and conditions. If you wish to proceed please return one copy dated and signed by way of confirmation and acceptance within the next seven days, failing which this order will automatically lapse.

Yours

Buyer's alternative reply to seller proposing that some of buyer's own terms and conditions should be incorporated into the contract

Dear

Type of goods and quantity

We acknowledge your letter of the enclosing the order form incorporating your company's own standard terms and conditions of sale. We note that you will not agree to any variation.

Although we are prepared to agree the majority of your terms and conditions nevertheless we consider that some amendments should be accepted by you as follows:

1. *Price*

   Your condition entitles you to increase the price at your sole discretion without prior reference to us. Condition of our terms and conditions states that there can be no increase in the price without our prior written consent. We therefore propose that our condition should prevail in this respect.

2. *Payment*

   Your condition stipulates that payment is to be made within fourteen days of your receipt of the order whereas our condition states that payment shall be made within twenty-eight days of receipt by us of the goods. We consider that our condition should apply as the projected delivery date is two months from the date you acknowledge the order and it is unreasonable that we should be expected to pay the full contract price so far in advance of the delivery date.

3. *Warranty and liability*

   The warranty period specified in your condition is for a period of six months only but we consider this period should be extended to twelve months.

   Subject to your written agreement to these proposed variations we would return your completed order form attaching to it a copy of this letter and your response.

Yours

Commentary on letter from buyer to seller offering to buy goods in accordance with buyer's own standard terms and conditions

In some situations, the buyer may wish to take the initiative. The tone of this letter is terse and uncompromising. Whether or not a letter on this basis would be appropriate is a question of judgment, depending as always on the bargaining position of the parties, any time constraints and to what extent it is necessary for the buyer to impose his own terms and conditions. The other aspect to bear in mind, as already mentioned, is that the seller's terms and conditions will have been drawn up specifically for the purpose of his business and the supply of his products, and a buyer's terms and conditions are unlikely to be appropriate in all respects for every kind of transaction in which he becomes involved.

The letter is not only intended to be perceived by the seller as firm but should also enable the contract to be concluded with the minimum of correspondence which could otherwise become protracted and confused.

The letter contains two alternative suggestions on how to proceed. The first is to enclose a blank purchase order form incorporating the terms and conditions and invite the seller to accept, in which event the completed purchase order form will then be sent to him. The second is to enclose the completed purchase order form at the outset in the hope that the seller will accept it without further ado.

For administrative and processing purposes it may be preferable for the seller's own order form to be used, notwithstanding the fact that the order form incorporates the seller's terms and conditions. If that course is adopted then the order form should be endorsed with a simple statement to the effect that the buyer's terms and conditions in use at the date the contract is entered into are to apply in substitution for the seller's terms and conditions. A copy of the buyer's current terms and conditions should be firmly attached or stapled to the seller's order form and preferably initialled by both parties.

Letter from buyer to seller offering to buy goods in accordance with buyer's own standard terms and conditions

Dear

Type of goods and quantity

Thank you for sending us the sample of the widget manufactured by your company. We would be prepared to purchase 1,000 widgets at a price of £ subject to your agreement that our standard terms and conditions of purchase which are incorporated in the enclosed [blank purchase order form] [signed and completed purchase order form] are accepted. The delivery date which we require is 19 .

It is our established practice to contract only on this basis and we are unable to agree to any variation. As your company is not the only manufacturer of widgets we would be able to obtain what we require from an alternative source without difficulty as we have done on previous occasions.

[As soon as we have your written confirmation that you are prepared to proceed on this basis we will let you have our completed and signed purchase order form.]

Yours

Commentary on seller's reply to buyer whose confirmation of proposed order contained a stipulation that buyer's own terms and conditions should be incorporated into the contract

The next letter is a response to a buyer who has written the previous letter. In the initial discussions the buyer may have neglected to mention that it was his intention to adopt this stance and may well have waited until the discussions had progressed to the point where it was possible to gauge the likely reaction of the seller to such a requirement.

For the reasons already mentioned the seller is usually in a better position to impose his terms and conditions and that is more so where the goods to be supplied are technically complex and have a high monetary value.

Seller's reply to buyer whose confirmation of proposed order contained a stipulation that buyer's own terms and conditions should be incorporated into the contract

Dear

Type of goods and quantity

We acknowledge your letter of the enclosing your standard terms and conditions of purchase which you wish to incorporate into the proposed contract between us.

However, we return the copy of your standard terms and conditions as it is our practice to contract only on the basis that our standard terms and conditions of sale apply. We therefore enclose our own order form which incorporates these terms and conditions for your consideration.

We would point out that at the moment there is a lead time of approximately six weeks due to the unprecedented demand for widgets. It is only when a contract is formally concluded that those widgets which are the subject of the contract are taken into our production schedule. Consequently, the longer it is before the contract is concluded, the later it will be before we can supply the widgets to you.

If you wish to proceed on the basis of our normal practice would you please sign the enclosed order form without amendment and return it to us as soon as practicable. On receipt we will send you a completed copy which will include the delivery date.

Yours

Commentary on letter from selling company to receiver/ liquidator of buyer company requiring return of goods delivered where ownership and title have been retained by the selling company

Companies which sell goods in the course of trade (excluding retail sales) usually do so on the basis of written terms and conditions of sale which include a clause to the effect that title and ownership of the goods remains with the selling company until payment has been made in full. This concept was first judicially approved in the decision in 1976 known as the Romalpa case. However, since 1976 the principle has been refined as a result of a number of other decisions by the Courts.

Not content with keeping the drafting of retention of title clauses simple, draftsmen started to extend the scope of such clauses in an attempt to retain title and ownership even where the goods supplied had been incorporated by the large company into its own products for onward sale. However, such a provision will be ineffective unless registered as a charge under section 395 of the Companies Act 1985, and if a claim is made by the selling company against the receiver/liquidator of the insolvent buyer company, it will be void as against the receiver or liquidator.

Attempts have also been made to project the seller's right of retention to the proceeds of sale received by the buyer company for its products which incorporated the seller's materials and for which payment had not been received by the seller. The effect of such a provision is to create a charge over a book debt and, again, if this charge is not registered against the buyer company in accordance with section 395, the retention of title clause will fail in its purpose.

Unless the goods are of considerable value and the number of transactions carried out by the selling company are relatively few, it is impracticable to register charges against the various buyer companies with which it deals. In practice, therefore, a retention of title clause is more likely to be effective where the goods supplied have been delivered to the buyer company's premises but have not been either resold or used in the manufacture of other goods, or where, for example, the goods have been supplied to a building site but have not yet been incorporated into the structure of the property in the process of being built.

There are, however, additional problems unique to the sale of goods to a building sub-contractor in that if the employer/developer has already paid for the goods, either to the main contractor or to the sub-contractor to whom the goods were supplied, the rights of the employer/developer will override and negate the effect of

Letter from selling company to receiver/liquidator of buyer company requiring return of goods delivered where ownership and title have been retained by the selling company

Dear Sir

Description of goods
Date delivered
Date of invoice

We note that you have been appointed [receiver] [liquidator] of Limited/PLC. On the we delivered 1,000 widgets to [specify address]. Condition of our standard terms and conditions of sale which are printed on the reverse of the purchase order form dated provides that ownership of and title to the widgets is reserved by us and does not pass to the purchaser until payment in full has been made. This clause also provides that on giving reasonable notice we have the right to enter the premises where the goods are located in order to repossess the goods. This letter constitutes such notice.

[May we please hear from you immediately so that the necessary arrangements can be made for the widgets to be collected and returned to us.]

Yours faithfully

the retention of title clause contained in the contract between the selling company and the sub-contractor.

Usually a Romalpa clause will include a provision to enable the selling company to have access to the buyer company's premises in order to reclaim the goods. The letter refers to such a provision.

A retention of title clause will be ineffective where a buyer company is the subject of an administration order made pursuant to the Insolvency Act 1986 because the selling company will be unable to take any action of any kind to reclaim goods in the possession of the buyer company except with the leave of the Court.

CHAPTER 5

BANKING AND FINANCE

Commentary on request to bank to open designated or joint venture account

Although the next letter relates to a joint venture agreement for the construction of a building comprising shop units, the principle is applicable to any other kind of joint venture or similar business arrangement. The parties should agree the banking arrangements at the outset so that the account can be opened as soon as practicable. It would depend on the circumstances as to whether the letter should state the reasons for the account being opened and what payments and receipts are likely to be made, but the bank would expect to have some idea of what the purpose of the account would be and of the time for which the account is likely to remain open.

Request to bank to open designated or joint venture account

Dear

Joint venture account with Limited relating to the construction of [description]

We have recently concluded a joint venture agreement with Limited relating to the construction of shop units at . Limited is providing £ as part of the finance to enable the construction work to proceed and these funds are to be paid directly into a joint venture account to be opened as soon as practicable.

The building programme is expected to commence on and will take approximately twelve months to complete.

Leases will then be granted and each of the incoming tenants will pay a premium to be negotiated at the time. These premiums, together with any rents collected in advance, will be paid by our solicitors into the joint venture account as each lease is completed. In addition, the sale proceeds arising from the sale of the freehold interest will in due course be credited to the account.

Would you please therefore open a joint venture account in the names of both companies and let us have the necessary mandate which we will arrange to complete. There will be four signatories to the account, Messrs and of this company and Messrs and of Limited. All cheques in excess of £ will require two signatures, one on behalf of each company.

The likelihood is that the account will remain open for approximately two years.

Yours

Commentary on letter to bank varying bank mandate

From time to time the arrangements which govern the operation of the company's bank accounts have to be amended. This must be done formally and it is good practice to enclose a certified extract of the relative board resolution with the letter.

Letter to bank varying bank mandate

Dear

The company's mandate dated

The board of directors resolved at its meeting on the that the present cheque signing arrangements should be varied. At the moment any cheques in excess of £ require the signatures of two directors or one director and the secretary. The board has now decided to increase the threshold to £ . We enclose a certified copy of an extract of the minutes of the board meeting resolving that this variation should be made.

We should be grateful if you would acknowledge receipt of this letter and confirm that the bank will operate the account in accordance with the new arrangements with immediate effect.

Yours faithfully, for and on behalf of Ltd/PLC

....

Director

....

Secretary

Commentary on initial enquiry to factoring company

The provision of factoring services has become more widespread in recent years and the demand for such services appears set to increase for a number of reasons, not least as the result of fluctuating economic and trading conditions. A factoring arrangement, depending on its nature (and there are various forms) can be a profound one so far as a company is concerned because a number of fundamental implications arise. In effect a company is surrendering part of its independence in exchange for a price.

One of the primary reasons for entering into a factoring arrangement is to accelerate the payment of cash either to ease cash flow problems or to make available cash for other purposes connected with the business, perhaps for investment in additional manufacturing capacity. Whatever the company's motives may be there are a number of basic questions which need answers to enable the company to assess the way in which the arrangement would work in practice and to compare the cost of factoring with other forms of borrowing or raising finance assuming that other methods were available.

A comprehensive factoring arrangement invariably requires the company to hand over responsibility for the maintenance and operation of its sales ledger to the factoring company together with the right to collect payments from customers direct. Although the company would continue to issue invoices, each invoice would show that payment was to be made to the factoring company, and this arrangement, with all that such disclosure would entail, may prove to be too difficult a pill to swallow. An arrangement on this basis is termed a 'disclosed service' whereas the undisclosed service does not require payment by customers to the factoring company but to the company itself.

A comprehensive factoring arrangement also usually includes the provision of some protection against bad debts. The cost and extent of such protection is variable and would depend on the usual criteria.

The factoring company may offer a non-recourse service which means that it would assume the credit risk or a recourse factoring service which would involve the company assuming the credit risk. Under a recourse factoring arrangement the value of any unpaid invoices would eventually be debited to the company.

In a number of situations, particularly in the case of a small or recently

Initial enquiry to factoring company

Dear Sir

This company is considering the possibility of entering into a factoring arrangement, but before any decision can be made we need to examine carefully the basis on which any prospective agreement with your company would operate. We enclose a copy of our most recent annual accounts which should give you sufficient background information about this company to enable you to make an initial assessment.

We should be grateful therefore if you could provide answers to the following specific questions:

1. How are your charges computed? In giving your reply could you please show the cost of providing the factoring services and the discount charge rate separately.
2. What percentage of the value of each invoice is payable on initial draw down and at what point and by what means would payment be made?
3. Is the retained percentage of the value of each invoice payable within a specified period from the date the invoice has been paid in full, or is the balance payable within a specific period whether or not the invoice has been paid?
4. Would you expect to take over responsibility for the administration and management of the sales ledger? We would much prefer for obvious reasons to retain this function ourselves. We consider that we have an efficient accounts department and, as you will see from the annual report, this company has been in existence for   years and has a good record so far as administrative and organisational matters are concerned.
5. What protection services do you offer with regard to bad debts? Fortunately few of our debts ever prove to be bad as we operate a stringent credit control policy. You will note that the bad debt provision shown in the accounts is minimal in relation to turnover.
6. We understand that you provide both recourse and non-recourse factoring services. Please let us know specifically the difference in cost between the two alternatives and explain what each service entails.

established company, the factoring company may require one or all of the directors to give personal indemnities, clearly an onerous requirement and one to be resisted if possible. Apart from the individual liability that would attach to the directors personally, complications would arise in the event that any of them wished to leave the company even if for valid reasons unconnected with the company's financial performance or position.

Factoring agreements usually run to a number of pages of fine print interspersed with a fair measure of legal jargon. It may be that legal advice will at some stage be required to explain the effect of some of the less obvious provisions. The point of writing a letter along the lines of the draft which follows is to simplify and perhaps speed up the process of finding out what exactly it is that a factoring company is willing to provide, and the cost of doing so. The alternative would be to write to obtain from the various factoring companies drafts of their standard agreements (and in some cases explanatory notes) and go through these to find out the answers, a procedure which would be quite time consuming.

7. Would you make it a requirement that your involvement is disclosed to our customers? Naturally, we would prefer an undisclosed factoring arrangement because we would not wish to give the wrong impression to our customers who may think that the reason why we have concluded a factoring arrangement is because the company's financial position is unsound. The main purpose for which we require the kind of facility offered by your company is to release cash to enable us to finance the acquisition of additional plant and machinery in order to increase production.

[Once you have replied to this enquiry and we have considered what you have to say, we will let you know if we wish to discuss with you our requirements in more detail.] [If before responding to this enquiry you would prefer to discuss our requirements with us we would be pleased to arrange a meeting at our office when you could also see how we operate our accounting procedures. You would also have the opportunity of seeing the way in which our products are manufactured and how the company generally is run.]

Yours faithfully

Commentary on letters of complaint to bank which has wrongfully failed to pay a cheque or cheques issued by company

Provided there are sufficient funds available or the company operates its accounts within an agreed overdraft facility (and there are no legal impediments to payment) a bank is obliged to pay cheques which are drawn on it within a reasonable period of time. Where a bank wrongfully fails to pay a cheque issued by the company the company has a claim for damages against the bank either on the ground of breach of contract or, very exceptionally, for libel.

The Courts draw a distinction between an ordinary 'domestic' customer and a trader. An aggrieved ordinary customer who brings an action for damages for breach of contract against the offending bank would receive only nominal damages unless he could prove that he had suffered actual damage or loss. There is no requirement in the case of a trader to prove actual damage or loss and although there may be some argument as to what constitutes a trader there is little doubt that a company would fall within this category. A company would therefore be entitled to recover damages of a reasonable amount for the impairment caused to its commercial credibility and it would not have to prove actual damage as such.

Although technically it would be possible for a company to claim damages for libel it is unlikely that it would do so. This option is usually an alternative course for an ordinary customer to pursue where he is unable to prove actual damage or loss.

It is not feasible to give a general indication of the level of damages which might be awarded if the matter came to Court, partly because much would depend upon the particular circumstances and partly because there do not appear to be any recently reported cases dealing with claims of this kind. The conclusion that can probably be drawn from this is that any claims which do arise are settled without Court proceedings being instituted or progressing too far.

To what extent a company would want to pursue any claim would depend on a number of factors, one of which would be the nature of its relationship with the bank. If the company relies heavily on the goodwill and co-operation of the bank in providing overdraft facilities the reaction of the company is likely to be governed accordingly.

The bank's action may, for example, have occurred because it had mistakenly credited a sum due to the company to the account of another customer with the result that the balance on the company's account was less than it should have

Complaint to bank which has wrongfully failed to pay a cheque issued by company

Dear Sir

Failure to pay cheque for £ dated
Name of payee:

We are writing to you in the strongest terms to inform you that the above mentioned cheque was not paid, even though the account on which it was drawn is, as you know, always in credit. This error by the bank has caused considerable embarrassment and threatens to undermine the confidence in the company on the part of not only the payee of the cheque but others who may learn of what has happened.

Would you therefore reply with a full explanation of how this error occurred and give an assurance that it will not happen again. We also require you to write to the payee of [address] apologising for the error. Please enclose a copy of such letter of apology with your reply.

Yours faithfully

been. Where, however, the economic situation is such that financial failures are occurring frequently, the viability of a company may be doubted if it becomes known that a company's cheques have been dishonoured. The consequences of this could be very damaging to the company.

On the other hand, the error may have been an isolated incident in which case the payee could be reassured that on representation the cheque would be met.

Whatever the circumstances, in principle the company would have the right to bring a claim for damages against the bank. However, the company may content itself with a letter of apology from the bank explaining the reasons why it dishonoured the cheque or cheques. The bank should also be required to write to the payee or payees apologising for the error. However, where the circumstances require, a company may consider that it is quite within its commercial rights to claim compensation as well. It is unlikely that the bank would want to be the subject of litigation for an unwarranted failure on its part and this fact may be used to advantage if the company decided to pursue a claim.

The company secretary should therefore, as a minimum, ask the bank to provide a letter of apology and explanation and also to write a letter of apology to the payee or payees. If the company decides to pursue a claim for damages the existence of the letter of apology and explanation from the bank would be a useful starting point, although if the bank refuses to confirm its error in writing it would not be fatal to any claim that the company may have as the bank's fault would be relatively easy to prove.

Two letters follow, the first short and fairly terse, the second more expansive.

Alternative letter of complaint to bank which has wrongfully failed to pay cheques issued by company

Dear Sir

Failure to pay cheques nos.

I refer to our telephone conversation today when I informed you that a number of this company's creditors had complained to me that their cheques had been returned to them following non-payment by the bank. As you acknowledged, this company operates well within its overdraft facility and consequently there was no reason why payment of these cheques should have been refused.

Following your enquiry within your branch you ascertained that a cheque for £50,000 payable to the company had been credited to another customer's account inadvertently. Even if that were the case I would have expected the bank to have taken a more cautious approach before refusing to pay so many of our cheques. After all, this company has been a customer of your bank for the last years without there having been any particular problems during that time.

The failure to credit a cheque for £50,000 to this company's account is a significant enough error but to compound it by the subsequent refusal to pay the various cheques without, I might say, reference to us before doing so constitutes a reckless disregard of the consequences and the effect which such failure was bound to have on the company's reputation and standing.

I therefore require that you let me have by return a letter giving your assurance that such an error will not be repeated and confirming that the bank has made the necessary adjustment to the company's account.

I also require you please to write to those payees listed in the enclosed schedule at their respective addresses confirming that the non-payment was entirely due to the bank's error. A number are threatening either to withhold further supplies of materials or to revise their terms of trade and it is therefore very important that such letters are sent immediately. In the meantime I have confirmed to each of the payees that they should re-present their cheques.

Yours faithfully

Commentary on request to bank for temporary increase in overdraft

Unexpected difficulties do arise and particularly where cash flow is restricted it may happen that receipts do not materialise in time for planned payments to be made, e.g. the payment of salaries at the end of a month. How such a problem is dealt with depends on the relationship between the company and its bankers. Nevertheless, if an overdraft limit is to be breached the bank should be notified as soon as the company becomes aware of the possibility. Just at that moment it may not be possible to contact the manager to agree a short term increase in the overdraft facility. This letter is the kind of letter to write in such circumstances.

Request to bank for temporary increase in overdraft

Delivery [by hand] [courier]

Dear

Request for a temporary increase in overdraft of £

Following my telephone conversation with your assistant today I am writing to you to let you know that despite our best efforts, we have not been able to secure the transfer of £ which was due to have been telegraphed to our account from our associated company's account with [name and address of bank]. I understand that the transfer has been delayed due to [set out reasons].

We had been relying on this transfer because the funds are required to pay our employees' salaries tomorrow.

It would be appreciated, therefore, if you would agree to an increase in our overdraft by £ until the expected funds have been received. I should be grateful if you could telephone me as soon as you can to confirm whether or not you are able to agree to this request.

Yours

CHAPTER 6

FREEHOLD AND LEASEHOLD PROPERTY

Commentary on request to chartered surveyor to carry out survey of freehold property to be purchased by company

The purchase of a property for commercial or manufacturing use represents a substantial investment. It is not the time to begrudge the payment of the additional cost of a full survey. A qualified surveyor who prepares a *full survey* on the company's behalf will provide a detailed report directly to the company, whereas a *valuation survey* will be comparatively less detailed (usually) and would be prepared for the prospective lender (albeit at the company's expense) for mortgage purposes. Even though a prospective lender may, if requested, provide the company with a copy of the valuation survey, it is still advisable for the company to commission its own survey notwithstanding the extra cost involved.

When instructing the surveyor the company secretary should ask for the report to include an assessment of the feasibility or otherwise of making additions or alterations to the property which the company would have to carry out for the purposes of its occupation.

Another potential benefit (although hopefully one which proves unnecessary to take up) is that if the surveyor instructed by the company is negligent and the company suffers loss or incurs expense as a result it would be able to sue the surveyor and recover damages. It may be possible to sue a negligent valuation surveyor even though the original contract to carry out the survey was between the lender and the surveyor but this principle has only been recently established by the Courts and it would not be possible to predict with certainty the outcome of any claim by an aggrieved company against a negligent valuation surveyor. It is far better to play safe so that if the company's own surveyor is negligent there would be direct recourse to the surveyor and through him to his insurers.

Request to chartered surveyor to carry out survey of freehold property to be purchased by company

Dear

Freehold property [address]

As I mentioned to you on the telephone today the company intends to purchase the above freehold property at a price of £ . I enclose a copy of the particulars of the property supplied by the estate agents.

Although the company will be buying the property partly with mortgage funds (and the prospective lender/mortgagee will be arranging for a valuation survey to be prepared for its own purposes), I think that it would be prudent for the company to obtain its own full structural survey and I should therefore be grateful if you would carry out such a survey on the company's behalf.

Could you please bear in mind that the company plans to construct a second storey to the single storey extension at the rear of the building, so you should include in your report an assessment as to whether the existing structure could support a second floor. Would you please also comment generally as to the feasibility or otherwise of this proposal.

Before you carry out the survey I should be grateful if you could please let me know, in writing, the basis on which your fee would be charged.

Yours

Commentary on request to chartered surveyor to carry out survey of leasehold property to be acquired by company

It can be just as important to instruct a qualified surveyor where the company is intending to acquire 'a secondhand' leasehold property, even though the acquisition price and other costs will probably not be so significant compared with the cost of a freehold purchase.

A copy of the lease should be obtained from the current tenant or the agents dealing with the disposal and sent to the surveyor for him to review. Although the company's solicitor will eventually prepare a full report detailing the tenant's obligations under the lease and point out other areas of potential liability, an initial appraisal by the surveyor would be helpful in that if there are any matters of real concern these can be identified at the outset before time is lost and further expense incurred in carrying out what would prove to be a wasted exercise.

The surveyor, for example, will be able to comment on the implications for the company so far as liability to contribute to the maintenance of the structure or fabric of the building or the premises generally is concerned and, importantly, should be able to give some guidance as to the likely level of the increase in rent at the next rent review.

The company secretary's letter should set out the company's proposals for the property, the intended use, and raise those points which are of interest or importance to the company. The letter should also include a request for the surveyor to advise if the lease contains any onerous covenants or obligations. In this way the possibility of the letter of instruction being construed against the company if there ever were a dispute as to the extent of the surveyor's remit should be reduced.

Request to chartered surveyor to carry out survey of leasehold property to be acquired by company

Dear

Leasehold property [address]

Further to our telephone conversation today I enclose a copy of the particulars of the property supplied by the estate agents. I also enclose a copy of the lease dated 19 and as you will see the term is for a period of twenty-five years of which approximately eleven years remain. You will note that the right to renew the lease at the end of the term under the Landlord and Tenant Act of 1954 has not been excluded.

The premium which the company has agreed to pay, subject to contract, is £ , which is more than had been expected. However, the premises are ideal in that they are situated close to the motorway. The company sees this acquisition as part of its expansion plans over the longer term and would expect to retain the premises indefinitely.

The company intends to refurbish fully the existing buildings to a modern standard and will borrow the amount required to carry out this work. Mortgage funds have been agreed in principle and the prospective lender will arrange for a valuation survey to be carried out on its behalf at the company's cost.

The company, however, considers that it would be prudent for an independent structural survey of its own to be carried out and I should be grateful if you would arrange to do this as soon as practicable subject please to your first letting me know in writing the basis on which your fee would be charged.

You will note that one of the provisions in the lease is that the tenant is responsible for keeping the building in a proper state of repair, and would you therefore include in your report an assessment of what this would mean in practice and what level of expenditure this is likely to involve in the immediate and the longer term.

Would you also please indicate what the increase in the rent is likely to be in a year's time when it is reviewed and whether the company's planned refurbishment work will have a bearing on the way in which the rent will be reviewed. If the fact that the refurbishment work has been carried out will result in an increase in the rent, some of the work can be delayed until after the review has taken place.

Please also include in your report any comments or advice on those provisions in the lease where you consider it appropriate.

Yours

Commentary on request/instructions to chartered surveyor to represent company in negotiations for rent review

If the premises, the subject of the rent review, form part of a larger building where a number of leases were granted at about the same time and for the same kinds of accommodation, the likelihood is that the various tenants will contact each other to discuss what stance should be taken prior to a rent review. It may be that one surveyor could act on behalf of the tenants as a whole in the negotiations with the landlord. That situation, however, does not occur very often and the individual tenant should consider taking action sooner rather than later to protect his position.

The wording of the rent review clause in the lease is the main determinant in deciding the basis on which the rent should be increased if at all. Modern rent review clauses are invariably 'upwards only' clauses, but it does not follow that the rent must be increased come what may. The effect of an 'upwards only' provision is that the rent can never decrease below that which was payable during the period immediately preceding the rent review. It may be helpful to look at the following typical rent review clause:

Rent review

1. The rent shall be
1.1 Until the first review date the initial rent, and
1.2 During each successive review period of five years of the Term the revised rent shall be the greater of the yearly rent payable under this lease immediately preceding the relevant review date and the open market rent of the demised premises at the relevant review date.
2. Procedure for determination of revised rent
2.1 The revised rent for the premises at the relevant review date will be the rent computed on the basis of making the Assumptions but disregarding the Disregarded Matters and having regard to the open market rental values current at the relevant review date.
2.2 The landlord and the tenant shall endeavour to agree the revised rent at any time within the period of nine months before the relevant review date but if they shall not have agreed the revised rent three months before the relevant review date the amount of the revised rent shall be determined by the Arbitrator who shall be appointed by agreement between the parties or in default of agreement by the President for the time being of the Royal Institution of Chartered Surveyors on the application of either party.
3. The Assumptions means the following Assumptions at the relevant review date
3.1 That the premises are fit for and fitted out and equipped for immediate occupation and

Request/instructions to chartered surveyor to represent company in negotiations for rent review

Dear

Leasehold premises [address]

As you know the company has a twenty-five year lease with approximately sixteen years remaining. A rent review is due in twelve months' time so we should start thinking now about what the new rent is likely to be, bearing in mind that the lease contains an 'upwards only' rent revision clause. The company has not yet received any communication from the landlord who is [name of landlord] but I think that it would be as well for us to have some idea of what the rent might reasonably be before the landlord lets us have his proposals. I also need to assess what impact there will be on the company's cash flow position following the rent review.

I enclose a copy of the lease so you can see the specific terms governing the basis on which the rent is to be reviewed. You will note in particular that improvements by the tenant are not to be taken into account, which is fortunate as a number of improvements to the premises have been made since the company commenced occupation.

I should mention that we have not always found the landlord a particularly easy person to deal with and I suspect that when we receive a letter from him or his surveyor suggesting the proposed increase it will be a much greater figure than is reasonable. Consequently, I doubt if it will be possible for us to be able to agree a new rent and I would therefore expect that you and the landlord's surveyor will become involved in the negotiations.

Once you have looked at the lease it may be useful for us to have a preliminary discussion here and perhaps you could let me know when you would be able to do so. In the meantime, however, could you please let me know the basis on which your fee would be charged.

Yours

use and that no work has been carried out on the premises by the tenant, its sub-tenants or their predecessors in title during the Term which has diminished the rental value of the premises and if the premises have been destroyed or damaged they have been fully restored.

3.2 That the premises are available to let by a willing landlord to a willing tenant as a whole without a premium but with vacant possession and subject to the provisions of this lease (other than the amount of rent but including these provisions for rent review) for a term equal to the Term.

3.3 That the covenants contained in this lease on the part of the tenant have been fully performed and observed.

4. Disregarded Matters mean:

4.1 Any effect on rent of the fact that the tenant, its sub-tenants or their respective predecessors in title have been in occupation of the premises.

4.2 Any goodwill attached to the premises by reason of the carrying on at the premises of the business of the tenant, its sub-tenants or their predecessors in title in their respective businesses.

4.3 Any increase in rental value of the premises attributable to the existence at the relevant review date of any improvement to the premises and carried out with consent where required otherwise and then in pursuance of an obligation to the landlord or its predecessors in title by the tenant, its sub-tenants or their respective predecessors in title during the term.

5. Time limits

Time shall not be of the essence in agreeing or determining the revised rent or of appointing an Arbitrator.

6. Adjustments to rent following revision at relevant review date

If the open market rent shall not have been agreed or determined in accordance with the provisions of this clause before the relevant review date, then until the open market rent shall have been so agreed or determined the tenant shall continue to pay on account rent at the rate payable immediately before the relevant review date, and when the open market rent shall have been agreed or determined the tenant shall forthwith pay to the landlord all arrears of the reviewed rent which shall have accrued together with interest upon the arrears.

7. Memorandum of rent review

When the rent shall have been ascertained in accordance with this clause memoranda shall be signed by or on behalf of the parties and annexed to this lease and its counterpart and the parties shall bear their own costs in doing so.

In particular it will be noted that in reviewing the rent certain matters should be disregarded. It is now usual for modern leases to incorporate a provision to the effect that time is not to be of the essence, which means that if the timetable or time limits are not rigidly adhered to it would not be fatal to the rent review procedure. The inclusion of such a provision is generally more for the benefit of the landlord who if he missed the opportunity to increase the rent under the lease initially will subsequently be able to do so out of time.

It may well happen that a rent review can be carried out with the minimum of hostility (sometimes very amicably) between the parties and the landlord and tenant may agree the rent between themselves even without reference to professional advice based on what both feel is reasonable and realistic when taking the rents of broadly comparable properties in the vicinity into account.

It does not pay, however, to be complacent and the company should take the precaution of instructing a chartered surveyor before the rent review process is due to commence.

There may also be other provisions in the lease which will have an effect on the rent. For example, if the use to which the premises can be put is unduly restrictive this may have a downward influence in determining the rent on the review.

Commentary on letter to valuation officer challenging the value ascribed to business premises in the uniform business rating list

The uniform business rating system came into effect on 1 April 1990 and as a result there are significant changes in the way in which an owner of non-domestic property, be he freeholder or tenant, can challenge the value shown in the rating list for his property, or to use the technical term 'hereditament'.

Under the old system if a rate payer wanted to appeal against the value attributed to his premises he had to submit a proposal to the local authority. Such a proposal could be submitted at any time but under the new system a proposal can now only be made in certain circumstances. A proposal under the new system must be addressed to the valuation officer and not, as was previously the case, the local authority.

The persons who are entitled to make a proposal are the occupier of the premises or anyone having a legal or equitable interest in the premises with the exception of a mortgagee. A proposal can only be made:

1. within six months of a material change in the circumstances relating to the premises;
2. where the premises are shown in the list as being occupied by one occupant when in fact the premises are occupied by several parties or the converse;
3. within six months of the Valuation and Community Charge Tribunal, the Land Tribunal or the Court of Appeal making a decision which is material in so far as it affects the property owned or occupied by the rate payer;
4. within six months of the rate payer commencing occupation of the premises provided that there has been no previous appeal on similar grounds in respect of the premises.

If the valuation officer agrees to accept the rate payer's proposal he is required to issue a notice of alteration and to serve the notice both on the rate payer and the local authority.

It should be noted, however, that if a proposal is accepted by the valuation officer any reduction will not necessarily be implemented with effect from the date on which the circumstances which prompted the making of the proposal occurred. If, for example, a material change in circumstances occurred in October but the rate payer does not submit his proposal until the following May, any reduction will only

Letter to valuation officer challenging the value ascribed to business premises in the uniform business rating list

The Valuation Officer

Dear Sir

Premises: [full description]

Current value: £

This company acquired the freehold of these premises ago. We understand that there has been no previous proposal or appeal in respect of the value ascribed to these premises in the valuation list. We consider that the value is too high for the following reasons:

1. The value ascribed to a virtually identical building [address] is only £
2. Since the rating list was compiled an order has been made prohibiting street car parking in the vicinity and this restriction causes considerable inconvenience to our visitors. The car parking which is available at these premises is barely sufficient to cater for the demand generated as a result of this company's occupation.

We therefore propose that the value shown in the rating list in respect of these premises should be reduced from £ to £ .

Yours faithfully, for and on behalf of Ltd/PLC

....

Company Secretary

take effect from 1 April not the preceding October. Consequently, it would generally be in the company's interest to submit a proposal as soon as it is practicable to do so.

A proposal does not have to be submitted in any prescribed form, although the new regulations do require that it must be in writing and that the name, address and capacity of the person making the proposal be stated. The property has to be clearly identified and the proposal must also state how the valuation list should be amended and the reasons why. The proposal must be addressed to and served on the valuation officer. The valuation officer has a six week period (which commences on the date the proposal was served on him) within which to serve a counter notice on the company if he does not agree with the proposal. In serving the counter notice the valuation officer is required to notify the company that it has a right of appeal. Should the company decide to exercise the right of appeal it must serve on the valuation officer a notice of disagreement within four weeks of the valuation officer's counter notice.

The right of appeal is to the Valuation and Community Charge Tribunal and if all parties agree the appeal can be determined by written representations without the need for a formal hearing. There is a prescribed procedure which has to be followed for the exchange of representations submitted by the parties and of any replies.

Commentary on request to landlord to allow additions or alterations to premises occupied by company

Leases invariably include a covenant in some form prohibiting a tenant from making additions or alterations to the premises. Typically, the covenant will distinguish between additions or alterations to the structure of the building (or the exterior of the premises as a whole) and non-structural interior additions or alterations. There will usually be an absolute prohibition against structural additions or alterations to the exterior of the premises but only a qualified prohibition in the case of interior additions or alterations. The usual wording in the latter case is that approval or consent is not to be unreasonably refused or withheld, although if these words have been omitted and the proposed additions or alterations constitute an improvement to the property then pursuant to the Landlord and Tenant Act 1927 it is implied that consent cannot be unreasonably withheld.

Even so, the application to the landlord for consent to allow additions or alterations is more than just a formality and the landlord is entitled to be supplied with sufficient information on which to be able to base his decision. The landlord would want, for example, to ensure that the proposals would not adversely affect the value of his reversionary interest or the appearance or the use of the premises or create adverse consequences for other occupiers in the vicinity or possibly his other tenants if parts of the premises have been let separately.

If the proposed additions or alterations relate to the structure of the building itself or the exterior of the premises as a whole and there is an absolute prohibition in the lease, it does not of course necessarily follow that the landlord would refuse consent if requested to give it.

If the additions or alterations require planning approval it would be sensible to request the landlord to give his consent in principle before the planning application has been submitted.

Leases do not always specify the mode in which the consent is to be given and if that is the case a letter from the landlord would be sufficient. On the other hand, the lease may prescribe that the landlord's formal licence is required and the production of such a licence can be a time consuming process with solicitors for the landlord and for the tenant becoming involved. The tenant will be required to meet all the legal costs.

If there is an absolute prohibition against an alteration or addition which would

Request to landlord to allow additions or alterations to premises occupied by company

Dear

Leasehold premises [address]

The company is proposing, subject to your consent, to carry out additions and alterations to the premises in order to improve and extend the toilet and washroom facilities.

We enclose a plan of the first floor which shows the position of the additional toilet and how the washroom area is to be enlarged. The company's architects will apply for any necessary consents from the local authority. However, before that application is made, we should be grateful if you would indicate whether or not you would approve what is proposed.

Clause   of the lease dated   provides that any additions or alterations to the premises require your prior written consent, such consent not to be unreasonably refused or withheld. We hope that you will agree that what is contemplated constitutes an improvement to the property and that accordingly you would be prepared to give your consent.

Yours

constitute an improvement and the landlord will not agree to the tenant's request for consent, the tenant may be able to implement the procedure under the Landlord and Tenant Act 1927 which is dealt with next.

Commentary on letter to landlord constituting notice of company's intention to make an improvement for which compensation will be claimed at the end of the tenancy

If the proposed works to be carried out by the company constitute any improvement to the premises, the company may, even though there is an absolute prohibition against any alteration or addition *or* the landlord's consent is not to be unreasonably withheld or delayed, consider it worthwhile making an application under the Landlord and Tenant Act 1927. If the application is successful the company would be entitled to claim compensation for the improvement at the end of the tenancy.

Such an application may be appropriate where the company wishes to carry out fairly substantial improvements to the premises (other than improvements which it is obliged to make under the terms of the lease) but there is a comparatively short period of time before the lease terminates and/or the right of renewal has been formally excluded under the Landlord and Tenant Act 1954 by Court order, although in the latter case there will be less chance of success. It is perhaps surprising that more tenants do not take advantage of the provisions of the 1927 Act, although it has to be said that the procedure is rather involved and takes time to implement.

The 1927 Act does not define specifically what constitutes an improvement but it would clearly have to be something that would add to the value of the landlord's interest in the premises. Repairs as such would not amount to an improvement, nor would the installation of a fixture or fitting which the tenant could remove at the end of the tenancy. The problem from the company's point of view, however, is that if the landlord does not co-operate and the Court has to be requested to certify that the improvement would constitute a proper improvement for the purposes of the Act many months will elapse before the improvement can be carried out and the delay may not be acceptable to the company. If the company wishes to preserve the right to compensation it should serve a notice on the landlord of its intention to make the improvement as soon as the first plans become available. The landlord has three months from receipt of the company's notice within which to object.

The notice does not have to be in any prescribed or particular form and a letter along the lines of the draft will suffice. The letter sets out the basic process governing the Court application. This is useful because it indicates to the landlord that the company secretary has done his homework and the Court application

Letter to landlord constituting notice of company's intention to make an improvement for which compensation will be claimed at the end of the tenancy

To be sent by Recorded Delivery

Dear

Leasehold premises [address]

The company is proposing to carry out alterations and additions to the premises in order to improve and extend the toilet and washroom facilities for the benefit of its employees. We enclose a copy of the plans which have been prepared by the company's architect showing what is intended.

The estimated cost of carrying out the proposed work is £ . As there is a period of only four years remaining under the lease and the benefit of the improvements will revert to you at that time, the company considers it reasonable to request you to pay compensation to the company equivalent to the cost of the work, at the end of the tenancy.

There are, as you may be aware, provisions under the Landlord and Tenant Act 1927 which govern a claim of this kind. This letter is proper notice to you for the purposes of the 1927 Act of the company's intention to carry out improvements to the premises. If, however, you decide to refuse the company's request for compensation you must respond to that effect within three months of the receipt of this letter.

If you do object the company will make an application to the Court for a certificate that the improvement is a proper improvement for the purposes of the 1927 Act. The Court, we are advised, will give such a certificate if it is satisfied that the effect of the improvement will be to add to the letting value of the premises at the end of the tenancy and that the improvement is reasonable and suitable to the character of the premises. In the circumstances the company considers that these criteria will be met and that such a certificate will be granted by the Court.

However, we consider that it would be in both our interests if you were to confirm in writing that compensation of £ will be paid to the company at the end of its tenancy without the need to apply to the Court for a certificate.

Yours

process has been seriously considered. This may perhaps persuade the landlord to be more responsive than he might otherwise be. If the landlord does not respond to the letter, or the response is negative in the sense that the landlord would not be prepared to pay compensation at the end of the tenancy, if the improvement is carried out the matter should be referred to the company's solicitors to prepare the application to the Court.

Even where an application to the Court has been instituted it would still be open to the landlord to agree to carry out the improvement himself and to charge a reasonable increase in the rent for doing so. Should this happen the Court would not then be prepared to grant a certificate permitting the improvement, the effect of which would be to disqualify the tenant from being able to claim compensation at the end of the tenancy. If, however, the landlord were subsequently to renege on his agreement to carry out the improvement the tenant could re-apply to the Court for the appropriate certificate.

Where the landlord has himself agreed to certify the improvement as an improvement eligible for compensation at the end of the tenancy, or the Court has certified the work to be an appropriate improvement, the company can carry out the work notwithstanding the fact that there may be an absolute prohibition in the lease. As already mentioned, it is sometimes the case that the procedure under the 1927 Act is implemented or threatened not in order to obtain compensation but to circumvent an absolute restriction in the lease against making any additions or alterations, structural or otherwise, to which the landlord was not prepared to consent when requested.

The compensation can only be claimed at the termination of the lease. Where the contractual tenancy is to cease as a matter of course at the end of the term the tenant must make a claim for compensation between three and six months before the term expires. Where the tenancy is terminated as a result of a notice to quit the tenant's claim must be made within three months of the date on which the notice to quit is served.

The amount of the compensation would not exceed the increase in the value of the landlord's reversionary interest in the premises and this may or may not be the amount incurred by the company in carrying out the improvement. The costs incurred will form the basis of the claim but the parties may have to resort to advice from a valuation surveyor or surveyors if agreement cannot be reached by negotiation.

No one should need reminding that wherever Court proceedings are involved there is always doubt as to the outcome. If the landlord intends to demolish the premises, or carry out major structural alterations himself at the end of the term, that fact would defeat an application by the company for compensation. Nevertheless, there will be situations where a company would find it worthwhile to consider an application under the 1927 Act to the landlord or to the Court for a certificate if the landlord refuses the request.

Commentary on request to landlord for permission to underlet the whole of premises occupied by company

Although there is usually an absolute prohibition against assigning, charging or underletting part of the premises, it is not unusual for the terms of a commercial lease to include a right on the part of the tenant to assign, charge or underlet the *whole* of the premises provided the landlord's consent or licence is first obtained by the tenant.

If there is an absolute prohibition against underletting and the tenant wishes to underlet, he will have to negotiate with the landlord for consent. The landlord in that situation will be under no obligation either to give consent or, for that matter, to act reasonably and it would not be open to the tenant to take any action to make the landlord do so.

However, there are statutory provisions which come to the aid of the tenant who wishes to underlet the whole where the lease provides that underletting may take place with consent but where the landlord is dilatory in co-operating. The Landlord and Tenant Act 1927 provides that if there is a covenant in the lease which states that an underletting can only take place with the consent of the landlord it is implied that the landlord's consent will not be 'unreasonably withheld'. These words are usually included in a commercial lease anyway and are amplified by the additional words 'or delayed'. There is normally little incentive for a landlord to act promptly when requested to give his consent to an underletting, even though his legal and surveyor's costs are, under the terms of the lease, the responsibility of the tenant. Delay by the landlord has in the past sometimes resulted in a prospective under tenant withdrawing to the consequent detriment of the existing tenant who, moreover, was denied any right to claim compensation or damages from the unco-operative landlord. True, an aggrieved existing tenant could have applied to the Court (and still can) for a declaration that the landlord's consent is unreasonably withheld but again, as with any other Court procedure, it takes time and can be costly.

To deal with the problem of delay on the part of a landlord the Landlord and Tenant Act of 1988 provides that where the consent of the landlord is not to be unreasonably withheld in respect of an underletting or assignment the landlord (which will include any superior landlord) must respond to the tenant's request within a reasonable time. The landlord must either give written consent which may

Request to landlord for permission to underlet the whole of premises occupied by company

Dear

Proposed underletting of

As you know this company occupies these premises under a lease dated 19 which is for a period of twenty-five years from 19 . Approximately eighteen years of the Term remain.

Clause of the lease provides that the tenant may underlet the whole of the premises subject to the landlord's consent which shall not be unreasonably withheld or delayed.

The company now proposes to underlet for a term of four years the whole of the premises to Ltd which carries on the business of . Three references have been obtained in respect of Ltd, one being a banker's reference and the other two trade references from companies with whom Ltd has dealt during the past three years. We consider that the three references are satisfactory and that the premises may safely be underlet to Ltd.

It is anticipated that the company's own business will expand during the next two to three years and therefore the company would want to be able to re-occupy the premises in about four years' time. Consequently, the proposed underletting to Ltd would be on the basis that the right of renewal at the end of the underlease would be excluded in accordance with the provisions of the Landlord and Tenant Act 1954 and the company would obtain the necessary Court order before the underlease was granted.

We should be grateful, therefore, if you would confirm that you will give your consent in writing as soon as practicable. We appreciate that a formal licence to the underletting will be required and that solicitors will be instructed on behalf of all the parties but it would be helpful at this stage if we could be certain that your consent would be forthcoming. Could you please pass on a copy of this request and of the references to any superior landlord if their consent is also required.

[You may or may not be aware that the Landlord and Tenant Act 1988 would apply to this request and that you are obliged to respond one way or the other within a reasonable time failing which it would be possible to bring a claim for incorporate conditions or he must state in writing why he refuses consent, and if he fails to do so within a reasonable time then the tenant may be in a position to claim damages, particularly if the delay leads to the withdrawal of the prospective under tenant. A landlord is also obliged to send a copy of any request in writing for consent within a reasonable time to any other party who may require to give consent also, for example a superior landlord.

Notwithstanding the 1988 Act a tenant who wishes to underlet the whole of the premises usually wants to ensure that the transaction proceeds to a conclusion as quickly as possible. If a company wishing to underlet waits until the proposed underletting has been formally agreed subject to contract through the agents and for the solicitors subsequently to be instructed, time will be lost and the company secretary should therefore take the initiative himself and write to the landlord direct in order to try to minimise any potential delay.

When the company secretary submits the request to the landlord he should state in his letter the nature of the business of the prospective under tenant and also enclose copies of any references which have been obtained. A prudent company secretary would have obtained references on behalf of the prospective under tenant anyway as the company secretary would want to satisfy himself as far as possible that the prospective under tenant is in a position (and was likely to remain so) to pay the rent and observe the terms of the lease. It should not be forgotten that the legal relationship between the landlord and the company will continue, notwithstanding any underletting, and in the event of the under tenant's default in paying the rent the company will have to make good the deficit when paying the landlord the rent due under the original lease.

If the prospective under tenant is itself a limited company the company granting the underlease would be advised to obtain from the directors of that limited company personal guarantees in favour of the underletting company to be incorporated in the underlease itself.

It would be open to the company, if it was considered desirable, to grant the underlease on the basis that any right of renewal which would arise at the end of the term be excluded, in which case an appropriate order from the Court would be required pursuant to the Landlord and Tenant Act 1954 before the underlease was completed. Reference is made in the draft letter as a reminder that this option is available.

Whether or not either of the alternative versions of the final paragraph of the letter should be included depends on the circumstances. If the company secretary has reason to believe, either from previous experience or the experiences of adjoining tenants, that the landlord is likely to be dilatory or unco-operative then the inclusion of a reference to the Landlord and Tenant Act 1988 may be appropriate.

damages against you if   Ltd were to withdraw from the proposed underletting as a result of your delay.]

[We should be grateful if you would respond one way or the other within a reasonable time as required by the Landlord and Tenant Act 1988.]

Yours

Commentary on request to landlord for permission to assign whole of premises occupied by company

In many respects the considerations which arise are similar to those where the company proposes to underlet the whole of the premises. For example the landlord is under the same duty to act promptly in response to a request for his consent to an assignment of a lease and to comply with the provisions of the Landlord and Tenant Act 1988. Clearly, an application to the Court for an order pursuant to the Landlord and Tenant Act 1954 excluding the right to renewal is not required as the company is parting with its entire interest in the lease although not, as will be seen, its financial risk.

Even though a company may assign a lease, it would still retain liability to the landlord in the event that the assignee failed to comply with the covenants of the lease and, in particular, pay the rent. That is so whether or not the company was the original tenant or an assignee itself. This fact should concentrate the company secretary's mind when it comes to deciding to whom an assignment of the lease should be permitted. Where the assignee is a limited company consideration should be given as to whether or not it would be prudent for the assigning company to extract from the directors of the proposed assignee the appropriate personal guarantees, although in practice it is unusual to do so. The lease itself may empower the landlord to require personal guarantees from the directors of the assignee company in his favour and this may provide some safeguard for the assigning company because if the assignee company defaults, the landlord will have direct recourse to its directors under their personal guarantees.

Request to landlord for permission to assign the whole of premises occupied by company

Dear

Proposed assignment of

As you know this company occupies these premises under a lease dated 19 which is for a period of twenty-five years from 19 . Approximately eighteen years of the Term remain.

Clause of the lease provides that the tenant may assign the whole of the premises subject to the landlord's consent which shall not be unreasonably withheld or delayed.

The company now proposes to assign the lease to Ltd. Three references have been obtained in respect of Ltd, one being a banker's reference and the other two trade references from companies with whom Ltd has dealt during the past three years. We consider that the three references are satisfactory and that the premises should be assigned to Ltd, which carries on the business of .

We should be grateful, therefore, if you would confirm that you will give your consent in writing as soon as practicable. We appreciate that a formal licence to the assignment will be required and that solicitors will be instructed on behalf of all the parties, but it would be helpful at this stage if we could be certain that your consent would be forthcoming. Could you please pass on a copy of this request and of the references to any superior landlord if their consent is also required.

[You may or may not be aware that the Landlord and Tenant Act 1988 would apply to this request and that you are obliged to respond one way or the other within a reasonable time failing which it would be possible to bring a claim for damages against you if Ltd were to withdraw from the proposed assignment as a result of your delay.]

[We should be grateful if you would respond one way or the other within a reasonable time as required by the Landlord and Tenant Act 1988.]

Yours

Commentary on request to landlord for permission to sub-let part of premises occupied by company in accordance with right contained in lease

In most commercial leases, certainly modern leases, there will be a prohibition against the creation of sub-leases of a part or parts of premises. As often as not, the prohibition will be absolute. Any sub-division of the premises will result in the creation of 'multiple occupation' which not only creates practical management problems but also may have adverse implications for the investment value of the landlord's reversionary interest. However, that is not to say that where there is an absolute prohibition a landlord would not be open to persuasion.

Where the premises comprise a number of 'self-contained' floors and there is suitable independent access to each floor it is quite feasible and practicable for the original lease of the premises as a whole to include the right to sub-let part. Leases of commercial premises containing such a right have been granted, particularly where the original developer, who either constructed the property or refurbished an existing property, found it impossible to find a single tenant to take the property as a whole.

As in the two preceding situations where the consent of the landlord is required the same comments relating to the provisions of the Landlord and Tenant Act 1927 and the Landlord and Tenant Act 1988 apply. The same general observations are also relevant.

Where a sub-tenancy of part of the premises is proposed it is probably advisable that a Court order be obtained under the Landlord and Tenant Act 1954 to exclude the sub-tenant's right of renewal at the end of the sub-tenancy. This is a relatively straightforward process and the company's solicitors will deal with the application in conjunction with the rest of the transaction in the usual way. If the Court order is to be obtained the prospective sub-tenant should be notified at the outset of the negotiations.

Request to landlord for permission to sub-let part of premises occupied by company in accordance with right contained in lease

Dear

Proposed sub-letting of part of

As you know this company occupies the whole of the premises under a lease dated 19 which is for a period of twenty-five years from 19 . Approximately eighteen years of the Term remain.

Clause of the lease provides that the tenant may sub-let part of the premises provided that the sub-letting relates to at least one complete floor. The third floor is at the moment surplus to our requirements and consequently the company's proposal is that this floor should be sub-let to Ltd for a period of eight years. There is a reasonable prospect that the company's business will expand during the course of the next eight years and we would therefore want to be in a position to reclaim possession of the third floor at that time. Consequently, the proposed sub-letting to Ltd would be on the basis that the right of renewal at the end of the sub-lease would be excluded in accordance with the provisions of the Landlord and Tenant Act 1954 and the company would obtain the necessary Court order before the sub-lease was granted.

We enclose three references relating to Ltd which carries on the business of . One of the references is a banker's reference and the other two are trade references from companies with whom Ltd has dealt during the past three years. We consider that these three references are quite satisfactory.

We should be grateful, therefore, if you would confirm that you will give your consent in writing as soon as practicable. We appreciate that a formal licence to the sub-letting will be required and that solicitors will be instructed on behalf of all the parties but it would be helpful at this stage if we could be certain that your consent would be forthcoming. Could you please pass on a copy of this request and of the references to any superior landlord if their consent is also required.

[You may or may not be aware that the Landlord and Tenant Act 1988 would apply to this request and that you are obliged to respond one way or the other within a reasonable time failing which it would be possible to bring a claim for damages against you if Ltd were to withdraw from the proposed sub-letting as a result of your delay.]

[We should be grateful if you would respond one way or the other within a reasonable time as required by the Landlord and Tenant Act 1988.]

Yours

Commentary on complaint to adjoining tenant or owner alleging nuisance

The tort or civil wrong of Nuisance is committed when there is an interference with a person's use or enjoyment of land or some right over it. 'Enjoyment' in this context means undisturbed occupation.

Examples of nuisance include interference with the use and enjoyment of land or property by water, fire, smoke, smell, fumes, gas, noise, heat, electricity, disease or anything else which may cause inconvenience or material discomfort to an occupier.

Consequently, an owner or occupier of land who is subjected to nuisance caused as a result of the negligence or omission or lack of consideration on the part of some other owner or occupier of land is entitled to apply to the Court for an injunction and can additionally claim damages, although a claim for damages will rarely be appropriate unless the nuisance has resulted in physical damage to the property of the plaintiff.

A significant factor which the Court will take into account in deciding whether or not interference constitutes nuisance is the nature of the locality in which the alleged nuisance occurs. Where commercial and business activities take place the Court will consider that adjoining owners and occupiers accept that there will be some degree of discomfort as a result. In other words, the standards that might be appropriate to a residential neighbourhood are not necessarily the same as would be expected to apply in a business or industrial area.

The facts described in the following letter are probably on the border line of what would constitute an actionable claim for nuisance. The nature of the locality would be very relevant. Nevertheless, the circumstances described do constitute a *prima facie* case and the fact of writing the letter may result in some remedial or corrective action being taken. The reason why this topic is included is to demonstrate that it is not necessary for the owner or occupier of premises to continue to accept without complaint the inconsiderate behaviour of the owners or occupiers of premises in the vicinity and that in some situations the civil law may provide a remedy.

As an alternative to civil proceedings the company should consider making a request to the local authority that the local authority should take action under the public health legislation. The conditions existing at the adjoining premises may amount to a statutory nuisance. If the local authority considers that a statutory

Complaint to adjoining tenant or owner alleging nuisance

Dear Sir

We regret that we have to write to you to complain about the way in which you operate your restaurant which is causing us considerable nuisance and discomfort for the following reasons:

1. The two large dogs which you keep at your premises in a confined space in the rear garden bark very loudly, particularly when pedestrians pass by. The rear garden is only a few yards away from the boundary of our offices and a number of our office windows open out on to your premises. During the last week there have been various occasions when both dogs have been barking for long periods during the morning when it would appear your premises are left unattended. Consequently, a number of our employees have found it difficult to concentrate on their work. We must ask you therefore to make proper arrangements to keep the dogs under control or, if that is not possible, remove them from your premises.
2. From the middle of each morning until late afternoon there are unpleasant cooking smells emanating from your premises and this causes considerable discomfort to our employees. We assume that the arrangements which you have installed to prevent the escape of unpleasant cooking smells are either inadequate or faulty. We must ask you therefore to take immediate action to reduce the emission of the smells from your premises and would you please let us know how you propose to deal with this problem.

If you are unable or not prepared to take the necessary steps to deal with these two matters we will be contacting our solicitors to instruct them to issue Court injunction proceedings the cost of which will be claimed against you.

It may of course be that you are unaware of the impact of these matters on, not only ourselves but other occupants of properties in the vicinity. We hope that in the interests of good neighbourliness you will be able to prevent further repetition in the future.

Yours faithfully

nuisance does exist it can issue an abatement notice on the owner or occupier of the offending premises. If the abatement notice is ignored the local authority then has the option of making an application to the Magistrates' Court. If such application is successful the Court may impose a fine on the owner or occupier creating the statutory nuisance. An alternative option open to the local authority is to institute injunction proceedings in the High Court and should the injunction be ignored the owner or occupier of the offending premises runs the risk of imprisonment.

Commentary on threat to adjoining occupier of premises to make a complaint under the Control of Pollution Act 1974 – Noise Abatement

The 1974 Act enables a local authority to designate all or part of its area as a noise abatement zone. Once an area has been so designated the local authority will proceed to measure the level of noise emanating from the premises affected by the order and the results will then be recorded in a register to be maintained by the local authority.

The local authority has to notify each owner or occupier in writing of the noise level measured in respect of their premises. There is a right of appeal to the Secretary of State if an owner or occupier considers the measurement to be too high and this appeal has to be brought within twenty-eight days of notification. If the owner or occupier does not make an appeal within the twenty-eight-day period the validity or accuracy of the measurement cannot be challenged.

If an adjoining owner considers that the registered noise level is being exceeded he can inform the local authority and ask the local authority to investigate and, if necessary, issue a noise abatement notice. If, as a result of the reference to the local authority, it does issue a noise abatement notice the occupier or owner on whom notice is served can appeal to the Magistrates' Court.

An aggrieved adjoining owner can independently take action himself by making an application to the Magistrates' Court instead of asking the local authority to do so. Some local authorities are more inclined to enforce observance of permitted noise levels in an abatement zone than others. Generally, however, it would be the more sensible course to notify the local authority in the first instance. The local authority may by the very fact of contacting the offender produce the appropriate response without the need for Court action, either by itself or the complainant.

Threat to adjoining occupier of premises to make a complaint under the Control of Pollution Act 1974 – Noise Abatement

To be delivered by hand

Dear Sir

Excessive noise level

As you will know this area has been designated by the local authority as a noise abatement zone. We have checked the register maintained by the local authority and the noise level permitted in respect of your premises is not to exceed decibels. We believe, however, that the noise level presently emanating from your premises exceeds this permitted level and during the past few days in particular the noise level has caused considerable discomfort to members of our staff.

We understand that you have recently installed a new machine and we can only assume that the noise attenuation measures that should have been incorporated have either been omitted or are insufficient or have been incorrectly or inadequately installed.

We regret that when we telephoned earlier today and spoke to your Mr his reaction was unhelpful. We are not prepared to allow the present situation to continue for any longer than is necessary and unless immediate steps are taken to deal with the problem to our satisfaction we will have no option but to notify the local authority and request that the noise level be measured and if it exceeds the permitted level to serve on you a noise abatement notice.

Unless we hear from you within the next twenty-four hours confirming that you are prepared to deal with the problem as requested we will proceed to notify the local authority.

Yours faithfully

CHAPTER 7

EMPLOYMENT CONTRACTS AND TERMINATION

Commentary on offer of employment

The letter which follows is generally intended for use in connection with the employment of a senior employee, although it could be amended or adapted for any salaried employee. How detailed the letter needs to be will depend on how far the company considers it is necessary to go in order to obtain the prospective employee's acceptance of the offer. A prospective employee will usually require the reassurance of a written offer letter from the new employer before terminating his current employment but if the terms of the offer letter appear to be onerous or unreasonable the prospective employee may decline to accept.

Alternatively, the offer letter could be less detailed but enclosed with it would be a copy of the company's terms and conditions of employment which incorporate the obligatory statutory particulars to be given by the employer. The abridged letter, together with the terms and conditions, would then constitute the employment contract without the need for a formal written contract between employer and employee to be entered into at a later date.

This letter, however, has been drafted on the assumption that a formal contract of employment will be concluded following the satisfactory completion of the probationary period by the employee. Not only does the letter set out the basic information which the employee would want the company to confirm but it includes some of the less palatable elements which the company will require the employee to agree to include in the subsequent contract. If these matters are not drawn to the employee's attention until after the completion of the probationary period and only when he is requested to enter into the formal contract of employment, difficulty will arise if the employee is not prepared to accept, for example, the restraint conditions. A prospective employee may more readily agree to accept such restrictions if these are brought to his attention and agreed to by him at the time the offer is made. A prospective employee may already have made the decision mentally to leave his current employment and therefore be more receptive.

The other important element in the letter of offer is to incorporate clearly the basis on which the probationary period will operate so that there is no misunderstanding should the company wish to terminate the employment prior to the completion of the probationary period.

Offer of employment

Dear

Job description/title

I am now able to confirm the company's offer of employment following our meeting in this office and subsequent telephone conversation. As I mentioned, the offer is subject to the following:

1. Your undergoing a medical examination to be carried out by the company's nominated doctor and the result of the examination being satisfactory to the company.
2. The receipt of satisfactory references from the [ ] persons whom you have nominated and your present employer. As I mentioned on the telephone we will now be writing to your referees and your present employer and perhaps, if you have not already done so, you could let them know that we will be making contact.

The following matters will apply to your employment with the company from the date of commencement which we agreed will be

1. Although you have received a written job description which sets out your basic duties you would, as discussed, be expected to take on such additional duties as the company required you to do as circumstances warranted.
2. Your hours of work will be between 9 a.m. and 5.30 p.m. with 1 hour for lunch. We will expect you to devote the whole of your time and attention to the company's business during those hours from Monday to Friday. We would also expect you to work such additional hours within reason as the company may require from time to time [and if that does occur then you will receive payment at an appropriate rate to be agreed]. [If the company operates a flexi time scheme details should be inserted at this point.]
3. The first [six] months of your period of employment will be a probationary period and for the duration of the probationary period either of us may terminate your employment on giving [two] weeks' notice in writing to the other. After the satisfactory conclusion of your probationary period the

Reference should also be made to the commentary on the contract of employment for senior/salaried personnel precedent on page 218 as the two precedents are complementary.

length of written notice required to be given by either of us will be [one] month.

4. Your initial salary will be £ a year. The company's policy is to review salaries [two] months [or thereabouts] after the conclusion of its financial year which is . The review will take into account the company's financial position as well as your performance but there is no obligation on the part of the company to increase your salary as a result of a review. Salaries are paid at the end of each calendar month, usually by way of direct payment to your bank, and if you accept this offer of employment could you please let me know your bank details including the branch sort code.
5. Your entitlement to holiday is [ ] days per year which of course is in addition to public holidays. [Entitlement to holiday accrues at the rate of [ ] days for each completed month worked in each calendar year, which means that in the current year your entitlement to holiday will be [ ] days.] [We did discuss your planned holiday arrangements for this calendar year and as agreed these will be honoured.] If holiday entitlement is not taken during the calendar year to which it relates, the company may at its discretion make a payment in lieu.
6. You will be provided with a company car [on the satisfactory completion of your probationary period]. At the moment the company bears the cost of the maintenance of the cars which it provides to its employees as well as meeting the running expenses although employees pay for petrol privately used. This policy is always subject to review and can be varied at the company's discretion at any time.
7. In the event that you are absent as a result of sickness or injury you will be entitled to receive full pay for the first [three] months. Thereafter, payments will be made at the company's discretion. The payments will, however, be calculated net of any sickness benefit to which you may be entitled.
8. The company operates a pension scheme and you will become eligible to participate following the satisfactory completion of your probationary period. There is of course no obligation on your part to become a member of the scheme. Details of the scheme will be given to you for you to consider at the appropriate time.
9. During the course of your employment you will have access to and be able to use for the benefit of the company's business certain information relating to the company's customers and suppliers, its finances, production methods and its pricing policies. In the event that your employment with the company is terminated for whatever reason, you will be required to continue to keep such information confidential and not to divulge it to any other person, firm or company. Furthermore, the company prohibits the removal by any employee from the company's premises of any of the company's records or

copies unless these are required for use in connection with the promotion of the company's business.

10. In the event that your employment with the company is terminated for any reason you would not for a period of [two] years following such termination be able either on your own account or on behalf of any other business entity to deal with or solicit any of the clients or customers of this company who were clients or customers during the [two] years prior to the termination of your employment and who are located within a radius of [twenty] miles of the company's premises.
11. In the event that your employment with the company is terminated for any reason you would not be permitted to work for or be employed by any company or entity whose business competes with the business of this company and which is located within a [twenty] mile radius of the company's premises. This limitation will apply for a period of [twelve] months following the termination of your employment with this company.

[12. Should you have any complaint concerning your employment, or any grievance, this will be dealt with in accordance with specific procedures which the company has established for dealing with such matters. These procedures are reviewed periodically [and I enclose separately details of the grievance procedure which is currently in force and which is relevant to an employee of your status within the company. I also enclose a note of the disciplinary procedures operated by the company which again are reviewed periodically].]

[13. [I enclose a copy of the company's employment rules which include disciplinary and grievance procedures and which apply to all of the company's employees.]

The above is not exhaustive but it includes the more significant provisions of the company's contract of employment for senior personnel which you will be required to sign on the satisfactory conclusion of your probationary period.

I very much hope that you are able to accept this offer of employment and if you wish to do so could you please sign the enclosed copy of the letter and return it to me as soon as possible.

Yours

Company Secretary

[illegible]

To be typed on copy letter:

I accept the terms and conditions set out in this letter.

Signed________________________

Date ________________________

Commentary on letter varying terms of contract of employment

Not all employees will have a written contract of employment, although the nature of the employer/employee relationship is essentially contractual. The only obligation on the part of an employer is to provide the employee within thirteen weeks of the commencement of the employment the statutory particulars pursuant to the Employment Protection (Consolidation) Act 1978, and not all employers do even that.

Where a company enters into formal written contracts with its employees, varying those contracts may present problems because it is not open to one party to a contract to change its terms unilaterally. An attempt to do so may constitute a breach and enable the employee to bring an action for damages, although to make such a claim worthwhile the employee would need to show sufficient economic loss.

If the proposed variation is sufficiently substantial it may amount to a repudiation of the whole contract and consequently an aggrieved employee may be in a position to bring either a civil action in the Courts for wrongful dismissal or an unfair dismissal claim to an Industrial Tribunal.

A company proposing to make a variation will therefore need to consider the likely reactions of the employees and may as part of that process consult with the employees' representative or the employees directly before reaching a conclusion. Where, however, the proposed variation is minor its imposition, with or without previous consultation, may be accepted without complaint if a reasonable period of notice is given by the company together with an explanation.

If a company wishes to retain some flexibility so that it can vary its contracts of employment as circumstances change, one method it may consider is to issue a formal contract to each employee containing a clause which reserves to the company the right to make minor variations unilaterally on notice and to make more significant variations on giving to each employee a period of notice within which the employee may object, failing which the variation will be deemed to have come into effect automatically. Such a clause is included in the contract of employment for senior salaried personnel precedent on page 225.

If it is considered appropriate that the consent of an employee should nevertheless be obtained to any proposed variation he should be asked to sign and return a copy of the letter notifying him of the variation.

Letter varying terms of contract of employment

Dear

The directors have decided [in consultation with your Union representative] that as from 19 , clause of your contract of employment will be varied to the extent that bonus payments which up to now have been paid on a fortnightly basis will in future be paid on a monthly basis. One of the reasons for introducing this variation is to reduce the administrative costs of making bonus payments at such frequent intervals.

[Enclosed is a copy of this letter which you should please sign and return to me within seven days of receipt.]

[Clause of your contract of employment provides that the company has the right to make any reasonable changes to your conditions of employment and in the company's opinion the proposed variation is reasonable.]

Yours

Commentary on letter confirming reasons for summary/ immediate dismissal of employee

A contract of employment can be terminated at common law where there is a breach of the contract sufficient to justify dismissal without notice, which also means without payment of salary in lieu of notice. For example, gross negligence or serious incompetence on the part of an employee would justify summary dismissal, as would proven dishonesty. Where dismissal is for what would be regarded as a first offence the misconduct committed must be gross. Theft or violence would be sufficient in certain circumstances. In order to defend successfully a claim which may be made to the Industrial Tribunal an employer would have to pass the reasonableness test which has two limbs, firstly that the procedure he followed or used was reasonable and, secondly, that the dismissal would be judged to fall within the range of reasonable responses in the circumstances, which means that some reasonable employers would dismiss in the same situation, and for the same reasons, although others may not.

There has been a considerable number of decisions as to what does or does not constitute unfair dismissal and it is beyond the scope of this book to discuss the effects of such decisions as a specific topic. The point of including this letter is to remind company secretaries that in certain circumstances it may not be necessary to comply with the usual procedure of issuing formal written warnings to the miscreant employee. If the employee's conduct is sufficient (and demonstrably so) to justify instant dismissal the appropriate action can be taken immediately.

Letter confirming reasons for summary/immediate dismissal of employee

Dear

Dismissal due to your conduct

This letter constitutes notice to you of the termination with immediate effect of your employment with the company. The reason for your dismissal is, as you know, due to your admitted theft of the company's property and your violent assault on Mr   in the course of your attempt to leave the company's premises when apprehended. You were given the opportunity to explain the reason for your conduct in the discussions which took place in your supervisor's office this morning shortly after these events occurred but you declined to do so other than to admit both offences.

In view of the gravity of these two offences the company has decided that no payment of wages should be made to you in lieu of notice. Consequently, your only entitlement to payment is for three days' accrued wages and a cheque will be sent to you for the amount due as soon as practicable.

Yours

Commentary on letter terminating contract of employment due to frustration as a result of employee's inability to carry out the requirements of his employment

Employers tend to focus their attention on the consequences that follow as a result of the dismissal of an employee and which may lead to an application to the Industrial Tribunal claiming unfair dismissal.

There is more to employment law than the employment protection legislation. It is the product of the law of contract and the common law generally, as well as various statutes and statutory instruments. If an employee is in breach of the provisions of his contract to a material extent and to take an extreme example, should he be sent to prison, the contract is frustrated. The ability of the employee to perform his duties may, for example, depend upon his retention of a licence of some form and once that licence is lost, forfeited or suspended, the employee can no longer fulfil his part of the contract. Many employees require a driving licence in order to perform the work for which they are employed.

Even where the circumstances constitute frustration of the contract sufficient to result in its termination, it may nevertheless be open to an employee who has two years' continuous employment to apply to the Industrial Tribunal claiming unfair dismissal. The employer would then be subject to the reasonableness test referred to in the commentary on the previous letter.

If the capacity to drive is an essential requirement for the job and an employee loses his licence an employer would be justified in terminating the contract and paying the appropriate amount in lieu of notice, although if the circumstances leading to the loss of the licence constitute gross misconduct an employer would be entitled to regard the contract as terminated with immediate effect and not be obliged to pay wages or salary in lieu of notice.

If, however, it would be possible to employ the employee in another capacity, albeit at a different rate of pay and perhaps on the basis of different conditions, this option should be considered in order to thwart a possible claim for unfair dismissal to the Industrial Tribunal.

Letter terminating contract of employment due to frustration as a result of employee's inability to carry out the requirements of his employment

Dear

The loss of your driving licence

Following your conviction for driving with excess alcohol and disqualification from driving for a period of eighteen months, the company has no alternative but to treat your contract of employment as being determined with immediate effect.

As you will appreciate, as the sole sales representative of the company, the company is very much dependent upon your ability to travel and to visit the company's customers who are numerous and located in many different parts of the country. The company would not be able to finance any other means for you to be able to continue to visit the company's customers and it will have to employ a replacement representative immediately.

The directors have considered whether or not it is or will be possible to employ you elsewhere in the company but there is no suitable position currently which you could fill and there is no prospect of one arising in the foreseeable future.

Although the loss of your licence as a result of a conviction for driving with excess alcohol in the course of your employment constitutes in our view gross misconduct which would entitle the company to dismiss you summarily without payment in lieu of notice, the directors have decided that the company should still make such payment to you and a cheque in respect of your accrued pay together with two months' payment of salary in lieu of notice is enclosed.

The directors very much regret that this situation has arisen and that you have to leave the company's employment in these circumstances.

Yours

Commentary on letter to spouse/next of kin following death of employee

Many companies, particularly the larger ones with fully constituted personnel departments, will have their own procedures for dealing with the aftermath of the death of an employee. Other companies will take differing approaches. Some will feel that they do not have the necessary experience or resources to be able to help whereas others will feel that it is something that they would want to be able to do for a variety of reasons.

However, the family of the deceased employee may resent the involvement of or interference by the company, either for their own personal reasons or where possibly the employee died during the course of his employment as a result of an accident which in the family's opinion was avoidable or due in some way to the fault of the company.

Having established that the family would want the company's assistance the question then arises as to what form this assistance might take. Sometimes it will amount to not much more than just being available and willing to listen and at other times the assistance may be more tangible. The draft letter sets out some areas where assistance might be provided.

Letter to spouse/next of kin following death of employee

Dear

As I mentioned on the telephone we would very much like to help you if you would want us to do so by providing some practical assistance as follows:

1. One of the company's retired employees, Mr of has said that he would be available to provide transport for you and your family for the next few weeks the cost of which would be paid by the company. If you want to take up this offer please either get in touch with Mr direct [Tel. no., address] or, if you would prefer, through me.
2. You will need to obtain copies of the death certificate and I can arrange to do this for you if you would like.
3. If you do not have a solicitor I can introduce you to the company's solicitors who would be able to deal with any of the legal formalities. [The company will meet [half] the solicitor's costs.]
4. I confirm that the company would be prepared to pay the funeral expenses. If you agree to the company doing so I will contact the undertaker to confirm this.
5. There are two employees of the company who have had similar experiences recently who would be very willing to talk to you about what is involved. If you would like either of them to do so, please let me know.

Finally, I have made arrangements for the immediate payment of [your husband's] accrued wages and any other amounts which were due to [him] [her] to be paid directly to you within the next few days, although I appreciate that this is the last thing you would want to be concerned about at the present.

Please do not hesitate to let me know if we can help.

Yours

CHAPTER 8

WRONGFUL INTERFERENCE WITH COMPANY'S BUSINESS BY THIRD PARTIES

Commentary on complaint to third party alleging breach of secrecy and confidentiality agreement (written or oral) entered into when joint venture or merger negotiations were being held but which were not concluded

Where several parties commence discussions which are intended to lead to a long term mutually beneficial arrangement or amalgamation it is quite common for them to enter into a secrecy or confidentiality agreement either in writing or orally. In the course of the discussions each will divulge to the other sensitive commercial information which could be used by the recipient to its advantage. A secrecy and confidentiality agreement ideally should be drawn up by the company's solicitors so that in the event of a breach by the other party the appropriate action can be readily taken or threatened. If there is a breach the aggrieved company should act promptly by writing the first letter which follows. If such a letter does not produce the required response the matter should immediately be passed to the company's solicitors with instructions to write a letter stating that Court proceedings will be instituted if the requested undertaking is not received from the offending party. The initial letter from the company and the further letter from the solicitors, following one after the other may convince the other party to abide by the agreement without the need for further action to be taken. It is the same in principle if the agreement was oral or had been contained in correspondence between the company and the other party(ies). However, if the agreement was oral only the position would not be so clear cut because the other party(ies) may deny that such an agreement had been made although it might be implied.

In some cases the breach may be of such significance that the aggrieved company would want to take Court action not only to prevent repetition but in order to obtain damages for economic or financial loss. The second letter describes circumstances where such loss is very likely to have occurred, although the extent would depend on how much business was actually lost or reasonably expected to be lost. The assessment of economic or financial loss is very difficult in practice and would depend upon a number of factors. It may also be some time before the true consequences and effect of the disclosure of the information could be assessed. It is important, though, for the company to take the necessary action in order to prevent any further disclosure of information which if made would also adversely affect the company's business. The second letter is drafted on the assumption that the company considers it crucial that the other party should be prevented from continuing to disclose the restricted information to other competitors.

Complaint to third party alleging breach of secrecy and confidentiality agreement (written or oral) entered into when joint venture or merger negotiations were being held but which were not concluded

Dear Sir

Breach of secrecy and confidentiality agreement

We understand from one of our customers that your company has made an approach offering to supply products which this company supplies. The prices quoted by you are at slightly cheaper rates than the prices which we quote.

Although it is now more than a year ago since we were negotiating a [joint venture arrangement] [the possibility of merger] with you the secrecy and confidentiality agreement [contained in correspondence between us] [which is dated] [which was made orally at the time] continues to be effective and enforceable. The customer who has notified us of your approach is one whose identity and other contractual information appeared in the schedule which we gave to you. This customer is located some distance away and the general nature of its business would not give the impression that it would be a purchaser of our products.

The only conclusion, therefore, which we can draw is that you have approached this customer knowing that it is a customer of this company and in breach of the secrecy and confidentiality agreement. We therefore request your undertaking in writing that you will not breach the terms of the agreement again. If we do not receive your unequivocal written undertaking by we will immediately request the company's solicitors to institute injunction proceedings to restrain you from committing any further breaches.

You will be aware that should we obtain such an injunction you will be liable for the legal costs involved.

Yours faithfully

It might be asked why should the company write either of the two letters when, in the normal course of events, the company's solicitors would also write a formal 'letter before action'. The reason is simply that by the time the company has notified the solicitors that a breach has occurred and has supplied the solicitors with sufficient information on which to base their own letter there will be inevitable delay. The company secretary is in the best position to be able to draw together the facts which could well be more complicated or detailed than those described in either of the letters. The only obvious comment by way of warning is that the company secretary must be absolutely sure of his facts before committing any accusations to print.

Alternative letter of complaint to third party alleging breach of secrecy and confidentiality agreement (written or oral) entered into when joint venture or merger negotiations were being held but which were not concluded

Dear Sir

Breach of secrecy and confidentiality agreement

Disclosure of confidential information to

It has come to our notice that you have disclosed information concerning the business of this company to Ltd, a direct competitor. The information relates not only to the volume of our sales in Wessex but includes details of our customers in that area and the value and type of goods supplied to each customer.

We would refer you to the terms of the secrecy and confidentiality agreement [contained in correspondence between us] [dated and concluded] [which we made orally] at the time we were negotiating [a joint venture arrangement with you] [the possibility of merger] and which continues to be effective and enforceable.

In view of the gravity of your breach we have already instructed the company's solicitors to issue injunction proceedings immediately and to claim damages based on the loss to this company of that part of its business in Wessex as a result of your action in divulging the information.

Yours faithfully

Background note to the tort or civil wrong of passing off

Immediately a company becomes aware that a competitor is trading in such a way as to represent to the public that the competitor's goods or services are either those of the company or in some way connected with it the company must consider taking appropriate action to curtail or prevent repetition by the competitor. The immediate remedy which may be open to an aggrieved company in a passing off action is to apply for and obtain what is known as an interlocutory injunction, the effect of which would be to restrain the offending competitor from continuing to trade in the way complained of. The chances of obtaining such an injunction may, however, be jeopardised if the company does not take swift action.

Injunction proceedings are costly, although if the company is successful some part, if not most, of its legal costs would normally be payable by the other party. The company's course of action (and whether it considers the risk of litigation worth running) will depend on the circumstances and the extent to which it regards the activity of the competitor as a threat to its business.

Even if the decision is taken to instruct solicitors quickly there will inevitably be a delay of some days before the solicitors can be properly informed as to the nature and extent of the alleged passing off by the competitor and to have collated sufficient facts on which to base their own initial letter of complaint. The company secretary with his knowledge of the company's business should be able to act that much more quickly even if immediately following the writing of a letter the matter is then referred to the company's solicitors with instructions to institute the Court proceedings in conjunction with counsel.

The law relating to passing off has developed in a fairly haphazard way since the beginning of the nineteenth century culminating in the leading modern case of *Warnink* v. *Townend 'the Advocaat case'* in 1979 in which Lord Diplock identified five characteristics which must be present in order to create a valid cause of action for passing off:

1. a misrepresentation;
2. made by a trader in the course of trade;
3. to prospective customers of his or ultimate consumers of goods or services supplied by him;

Complaint by company to third party alleging passing off

Dear Sir

Use by you of the name [Mikrosell]

You will note from this letterhead that one of the operating divisions of this company uses the trade name [Mikrocell].

We enclose a current copy of XYZ publication which carries your company's advertisement in the name of [Mikrosell] describing your products, which, although designed for a different area of the computer market, have a number of features which would reasonably lead existing and potential customers to confuse your products with those of this company. In fact we have already received a number of letters from our customers inquiring about your products believing that we are the manufacturers.

This company has been manufacturing and trading in computer goods since 19 and has used the name [Mikrocell] continuously since 19 . It has established a reputation during that time and has acquired a distinctive trading style. The use by you of the above name in the marketing of your products constitutes a misrepresentation that your goods are in fact those of this company.

Clearly the continuing use by you of the name [Mikrosell] has caused and will continue to cause damage to this company's business. We therefore require from you an undertaking that you will cease to use the name with immediate effect. Unless we have such an undertaking in writing from you by 19 we will instruct our solicitors to institute Court proceedings for an interlocutory injunction. We are confident that we will be granted an injunction together with an order against you to pay the legal costs involved.

Yours faithfully

4. which is calculated to injure the business or goodwill of another trader (in the sense that this is a reasonably foreseeable consequence); and
5. which causes actual damage to the business or goodwill of the trader by whom the action is brought or will probably do so.

These five characteristics can be reduced to three broad facets, *each* of which has to be proved if the company is to be successful:

(i) A reputation attaching to the company

As the reason for taking the action is to protect the company's goodwill it must show that it has developed a reputation and carried on business such that a particular section of the population, which may be quite local, identify the company's products specifically with the company. If the word used to denote the product or mark is an invented word then it is more straightforward for the company to prove its reputation in the word or mark. Although there is no specific requirement that the company should have been using the distinctive name, mark or distinguishing indicia for any particular period of time, it follows that the longer there has been the use the more likely it will be that the company can prove that its reputation is well founded and substantial. A good example is the House of Lords decision in *Reckitt & Colman* v. *Borden* 1990. In this case Borden began selling their lemon juice in yellow plastic lemon shaped containers and even though the containers bore a different brand name and a different label it was held that this was insufficient to prevent confusion in the minds of customers who associated (and had done so for many years) lemon juice sold in lemon shaped containers with the product manufactured by Reckitt & Colman.

(ii) Misrepresentation by the defendant

The company will have to prove that the defendant has misrepresented that its goods or business are those of the company.

It is not necessary that the public at large should be proved to be confused but that a significant part of the public has been misled by the conduct of the defendant. The question to be answered is whether or not consumers or customers generally are likely to be confused by the defendant acting in such a way.

(iii) Damage or potential damage to the company

In addition to establishing its own reputation and demonstrating misrepresentation on the part of the defendant the company must be able to prove actual damage. Where the company and defendant are competitors in the same type of business or goods the Court will infer that there is potential damage to the company's goodwill. There has to be a common field of activity which would create the potential for the

business of the defendant to overlap, even if only marginally, with the business of the company.

If the company was unable to prove actual damage or the prospect of actual damage the Court may instead find that there has been or there is likely to be damage to the company's goodwill.

This review of the basic elements of the law of passing off is intended to give the company secretary some idea of what is involved and what has to be proved or shown. The impression is that in recent years there has been an increase in the number of situations in which passing off has occurred and will continue to do so, particularly in those areas of business where a 'no holds barred' philosophy prevails. A company should therefore be ever vigilant and be prepared to take the appropriate action necessary to protect its brand names or, as in the case of *Reckitt & Colman* v. *Borden*, the design or distinctiveness of the packaging or to use an old but judicially approved phrase 'the get-up' of its products.

A letter to the offending competitor may produce the desired effect and persuade him that it would be in his interests to change the way in which he conducts his business. The competitor may consider that the cost of an unsuccessful defence of an application for an interlocutory injunction would be prohibitive and may also consider the executive time that would be spent in having to respond to such proceedings unwarranted. If the letter does produce the appropriate response the company will save itself a significant amount in legal costs and fees. The letter will also constitute evidence that the company acted as promptly as it could once it became aware of the behaviour of the competitor.

Commentary on response by company to allegation of passing off

There are several ways in which the recipient of the last letter may respond. The complainant company may perhaps in reality be reluctant to institute Court proceedings. There are always risks in litigation and none more so where, as in cases of this kind, the quality of the evidence presented and the way in which it is presented counts heavily in determining the outcome not only so far as the initial injunction proceedings are concerned but more particularly in the assessment of damages by the Court. A reasoned response without going into too much detail may therefore have the required effect of discouraging the complainant company from carrying out its threat.

The second approach is to regard the response as a way of buying time. The detail to be included should be sufficient to stall the complainant company from issuing Court proceedings immediately. Before it could do so it would have to spend a considerable amount of time in consulting its solicitors who would then have to prepare in detail the necessary evidence in order to be in a position to instruct counsel. Not only will counsel have to advise as to the merits of the complainant company's case but also prepare in conjunction with its solicitors the lengthy statement of claim to be set out in the writ. If the Court proceedings were to be delayed for sufficiently long a period the Court may hold that a longer period of delay than was necessary had occurred and would refuse to grant the injunction. A refusal to grant an injunction would not mean that the proceedings would be terminated there and then. The complainant company could proceed to a full hearing of its claim but it would be many months before the Court would find time to deal with it and there is the chance that the complainant company would in the meantime decide to discontinue its action. As time goes on the amount of executive effort which will be taken up in progressing the Court action will begin to tell.

Whichever approach is taken, it is important to deny the allegations made by the complainant company. The suggestion that there should be discussions to see to what extent the apparently conflicting positions of the parties could be resolved may be a useful tactic because, not only will time be continuing to run but there may be a chance that in a face to face encounter a more conciliatory attitude will prevail. In fact it is not unknown for parties who have found themselves in this sort of situation to conclude that they should exploit to their mutual advantage a common area of business or potential business in the form of a joint venture or similar arrangement.

Response by company to allegation of passing off

Dear Sir

Use by this company of the name of [Mikrosell]

We acknowledge your letter of the requesting an undertaking that this company should cease to use the name [Mikrosell].

We have considered all the points which you make in your letter and respond with the following conclusions.

Firstly, your company's reputation has been acquired in the micro computer business and there is nothing we believe in the way in which you conduct your business to suggest that you intend or are likely to expand into the main frame computer market. This company's products have been developed for the main frame computer market and, moreover, are directed at a particular segment of that market as specified in our advertisements and publicity material.

Secondly, we refute your contention that there has been misrepresentation on our part. In our view it is inconceivable that any of your customers would be deceived or confused. Our advertisements and promotional material clearly show that the products described are manufactured by this company.

Thirdly, for the reasons mentioned above, we deny that there is any common field of activity between us or that our respective activities overlap, or will overlap in the future.

We consider that we deal in distinct and separate markets. We have invested a great deal of time and money in the research and development of our products and in devising the promotional literature. We therefore would oppose any application made by you for an interlocutory injunction.

However, without prejudice, it would perhaps be sensible for representatives of both companies to discuss possible ways in which we could both operate in the future so as to preserve the separate identities and characteristics of our respective businesses and products and which in the process may allay any fears which you have that your business will be adversely affected by us.

Yours faithfully

Commentary on complaint to former employee who is canvassing or dealing with the company's customers

The legal position is dealt with more fully in the explanatory notes to the directors' service agreement precedent on pages 202 and 203. The assumption which is being made in drafting this letter is that the employee was not particularly senior but that he knew the identity of the company's customers, the prices charged and the type of goods and products which were supplied to those customers, and had either memorised this information or had taken copies of some of the company's records relating to its customers.

The purpose of restating the covenants in the letter is twofold. Firstly, the employee may genuinely or conveniently have forgotten that such clauses had been incorporated in his contract of employment. Secondly, although it is probable that the former employee will take the letter to a solicitor he may not take his contract of employment. The inclusion of the covenants in the letter would therefore enable the solicitor to advise the former employee more promptly without the need to arrange another appointment which would possibly lead to a further delay before the former employee ceased acting in the way complained of.

Complaint to former employee who is canvassing or attempting to deal with the company's customers

Dear Sir

It has come to our notice that on two occasions within the last month you have contacted customers of this company with the express intention of supplying [specify items] which this company has supplied to those customers for some time. We also understand that the prices which you have quoted are only slightly less than the prices charged by this company and therefore the only conclusion which can be drawn is that you have intentionally approached these customers with a view to acquiring their business.

You will recall that in your contract of employment clauses prohibited you from soliciting business from this company's customers or from using any of the information which you obtained during your employment with this company which was confidential to the company. The relevant clauses in full are as follows:

Clause

'Not for a period of [twelve] months beginning with the termination of your employment directly or indirectly to solicit or procure orders or attempt to do so from any person or business entity located within a radius of [twenty] miles of the company's premises and who was a customer or client of the company during the period of [two] years prior to the date of termination of your employment'

Clause

'Not for a period of [twelve] months beginning with the termination of your employment, to use private and confidential information belonging to the company, including in particular information concerning any customer or client of the company located within a [twenty] mile radius of the company's premises and who had been a customer or client of the company during the period of [two] years prior to the date of termination of your employment'.

We consider that you are in breach of these covenants which, in the company's

view, are reasonably necessary for the protection of its business, not only in their scope but because the restrictions only apply for a [twelve] month period commencing on the date your employment ceased. The restrictions only apply to those customers who are located within a [twenty] mile radius of the company's premises and who had been customers or clients of the company during the [two] year period prior to your leaving the company. You left the company's employment just over [three] months ago and the two customers (who are local) whom we know you have approached were customers of this company during the preceding [two] years.

This letter is being delivered by hand to your home address, such is the seriousness with which the company regards your action. Unless we receive within forty-eight hours your written undertaking to comply with the covenants we will instruct the company's solicitors to issue injunction proceedings in order to restrain any breach by you in the future. You will be aware that should the company obtain such an injunction, and it is confident that it will do so, you will become liable for the legal and Court costs involved.

Yours faithfully

Commentary on complaint to another company using the same or a similar name to that of the company

Prior to the Companies Act 1981 the Registrar of Companies carried out a review of the names submitted for use by companies to be incorporated, and if the Registrar considered that the proposed name was too similar to a name that was already in use the Registrar would notify the promoters of the new company and request that a different name be adopted.

Now, so long as the name of a prospective company is not identical to the name of an existing company (or the name incorporates a sensitive word) the Registrar will allow the new company to be incorporated. If there is a possibility of any confusion, then it is up to the objecting original company to take two possible courses of action, both of which could be pursued together if the circumstances warranted.

The first option is to complain to the directors of the newly registered company that a passing off situation may arise and that if the new company does not change its name Court injunction proceedings will be instituted. The second option is to write to the Registrar requesting that the newly registered company be ordered by the Secretary of State to change its name. Such an application has to be made to the Registrar within twelve months of the date of incorporation of the other company. If the Secretary of State is persuaded to make the necessary order the period within which the change has to be made will be specified in the order.

It should be noted that the twelve month period commences with the date of incorporation not the date the existence of the newly registered company comes to the knowledge of the objecting company. To avoid being caught out it would be prudent for a company secretary to retain one of the various agencies who offer a name watching or check service so that if a new company is formed with a similar name to his company he can be notified immediately.

The company secretary would find it helpful to obtain a company search in respect of the newly registered company using a name which may pose a threat to his own company, not only in order to obtain the address of the registered office but also to check on the names and addresses of the directors and the shareholders so as to be able to assess how straightforward it would be for the newly registered company to pass the necessary special resolution to change its name.

Complaint to another company using the same or a similar name to that of the company

Dear Sir

Similarity of your company's name with this company's name

We are writing to you to complain that the name of your company is so similar to the name of this company that confusion, which will be detrimental to this company, will inevitably arise. Your company's name   Limited is, as you will see from this letterhead, virtually identical to the name of this company. We assume that the choice of the name for your company is coincidental and that there has been no deliberate intention to register such a name in order to take advantage of this company's reputation.

There is every likelihood that the continued use by your company of its present name will cause inconvenience and expense. For example, correspondence addressed to you may come to us by mistake and vice versa. We consider that it would be in both companies' interests for your company to change its name so that there is no room for confusion between the two.

Would you please therefore confirm that you will make the necessary arrangements to change your company's name as quickly as it is practicable to do so. The result of our company search shows that you, and your co-director, are the only two shareholders and consequently there would be no difficulty in passing the requisite special resolution changing the company's name.

As you may be aware, we could apply to the Registrar of Companies requesting the Secretary of State to make an order that your company should change its name but before we do so we would prefer to give you the opportunity of making the change voluntarily.

Yours faithfully

Commentary on application/request to Registrar of Companies requesting order/direction that other company changes its name

The Companies Registration Office has issued notes for guidance on company names and in the introduction to the notes there is a clear statement that the onus is on persons forming companies to satisfy themselves in advance on the acceptability of the proposed name, bearing in mind that an objection might be received which could result in the company being directed to change its name. The Secretary of State has power to direct a company to change its name within twelve months of its registration if it is 'the same as' or in the opinion of the Secretary of State 'too like' a name appearing in the index of names at the time of registration. Requests for such a direction are normally expected to be brought as a result of objections from a company which considers that the name of the newly registered company is 'too like' or the same as that of the objecting company.

In practice what this appears to mean is that any name will be registered except a name which is exactly the same as a name already appearing on the index of company names.

Examples of names which are 'too like' existing names are set out in the notes for guidance. Before the Secretary of State is prepared to make an order an objecting company is required to give reasons in full and include any evidence of confusion which has arisen. If, for example, names are phonetically identical the Secretary of State may consider that as sufficient reason for making an order. If a company secretary does need to write a letter to the Registrar he would be well advised to obtain a copy of the notes for guidance (which are readily available) from the Registrar beforehand.

Application/request to Registrar of Companies requesting order/direction that other company changes its name

Dear Sir

Limited [company number]

We understand that a new company has been registered with the above name. It is self-evident in our view that the name is phonetically similar to the name of this company. This company was incorporated on .

We have also obtained a copy of the memorandum and articles of association of the new company and the main objects clause states that the purpose of the company is to carry on the business of , which is an area of activity in which this company [operates] [proposes to operate shortly]. We have already written to the directors of Limited at the company's registered office address requesting them to arrange for the company to change its name but we have not received any acknowledgment or response to that letter which was sent three weeks ago by recorded delivery.

Accordingly we would ask the Secretary of State to conclude that Limited is a name which is 'too like' the name of this company and accordingly direct that Limited changes its name in such a way as to remove any similarity. If you require any further information in support of this application would you please let us know.

Yours faithfully

CHAPTER 9

DISPUTES WITH DEBTORS AND CUSTOMERS

Commentary on request for payment of overdue account

A letter of this kind is usually the culmination of many attempts by telephone or perhaps personal calls to the debtor's place of business to obtain payment. Such a letter is not intended to be too aggressive in tone and in fact is more in the way of a plea. It may be that the intended recipient has been a good customer in the past but has met with temporary difficulties, in which case it would be counterproductive for the company to alienate the customer and destroy any chance of a continuing business relationship in the future. If that is not the case the letter should be cut short after the word 'immediately' in the first paragraph.

Request for payment of overdue account

Dear

Date of invoice
Amount of debt
Date payment due

We have not yet received payment from you although, as you know, we have telephoned you on several occasions requesting payment to be made. The latest payment date was as shown above and a further seven days have now elapsed. Would you please arrange to make payment immediately, failing which we regret that we will be unable to make any further deliveries to you in response to a number of orders which you have recently submitted.

It is unfortunate that we have to write to you in these terms but, as you will appreciate, we will only be able to carry on our business satisfactorily if payments by customers are made promptly.

Yours

Commentary on threat to instruct solicitors to issue proceedings to recover a debt

This is a standard letter, but it is surprising how often such a letter is not written with the precision that it deserves. Although it may prove necessary to instruct solicitors to issue the Court proceedings, having first written to the debtor before doing so, a letter from the company may produce payment.

It is important that the letter should include in the heading the relevant information so that the recipient cannot respond with the excuse that he is not sure which payment is being requested, or that the invoice has been lost, or any one of the many different reasons, some original and some not so, which are given for non-payment.

If the conditions of contract provide that interest is to run from a specific date then the letter should say so, stating how interest is computed, the total to date, and the rate per day at which it will continue to accrue. The defaulting debtor will then know exactly the amount to pay at any one time. If the conditions of contract do not provide for the payment of interest, the company will only be able to claim interest from the date the payment was due once a Summons or Writ has been issued. The 'statutory' rate of interest can vary from time to time and a check should be made with the local County Court.

The recovery of legal and Court costs from a defaulting debtor can often be a problem, especially where the amount claimed is less than £500. Rather than state that the debtor will become liable for the cost of any legal proceedings it is more correct to say that an application will be made for an order that the debtor pays the costs of the proceedings.

Threat to instruct solicitors to issue proceedings to recover a debt

Dear Sir

Date of invoice
Amount of debt
Date payment due

Although we wrote to you on the requesting immediate payment of the amount due which was then [ ] weeks in arrears, you have ignored our request and have failed to contact us to discuss any arrangements for settlement.

[Condition of our terms and conditions of sale provides that interest at 3 per cent above bank base rate will be incurred if payment is not made on the prescribed date which is [twenty-eight] days from the date of our invoice. The interest that has accrued to date is £ and the daily rate at which it will continue to accrue is £ .]

Consequently, we are now writing to you to inform you that, unless payment in full [together with accrued interest] is received immediately, we will request our solicitors to issue Court proceedings to recover the amount due. [If Court proceedings are issued, then, as you will be aware, we will be entitled to include in the [Writ] [Summons] a claim for interest at the rate of per cent per annum from the date that the payment was due.] In addition application will be made for an order that you should pay the costs of the Court proceedings.

Yours faithfully

PART II

AGREEMENTS

Introduction to the agreements

General

As with the draft letters where square brackets appear in the precedents it is to indicate that the words, phrases or clauses contained within the brackets are alternatives or suggestions or may otherwise require completion or adaptation in some way. Each precedent has its own commentary which sets out the main considerations which should be borne in mind in its use.

Some of the precedents are designed primarily for use by the employed company secretary, in particular the agreements in Chapters 11, 12 and 14. The first of the director's service agreements in Chapter 10 will be useful for the employed company secretary although a director would probably want to take separate legal advice on some of the provisions. In any event, the company should also request its own solicitors to vet a director's service agreement before it is signed.

The second of the director's service agreements in Chapter 10 and the shareholders' agreements in Chapter 13 are more likely to be of use to professional advisers, for example accountants, solicitors or chartered secretaries acting for a private company or an unquoted PLC.

Arbitration

A number of the precedents incorporate arbitration clauses. Arbitration can only take place as a result of agreement by the parties either before or at the time a dispute arises. There are some advantages in resorting to arbitration rather than instituting Court proceedings. A judge is an expert in the law but he may not necessarily have a particular knowledge of the parties' business. On the other hand, an arbitrator who is appointed to deal with a dispute arising out of a commercial business contract will usually have some knowledge of the business of the parties.

The arbitration procedure commences with a meeting at which the main points of contention are established and at this preliminary meeting the arbitrator will draw up a programme stipulating, among other things, the time scale within which pleadings, expert reports and witness statements are to be submitted by both sides. The arbitrator may also decide that representations by either party will be dealt with in writing and that consequently there will not be a need for a full scale hearing before him at a later date. It may also happen that at the preliminary meeting the arbitrator will identify the main issues dividing the parties and it is not unknown for a dispute to be settled by discussion at the meeting.

Unlike Court proceedings there is some room for manoeuvre in arbitration proceedings in that the parties may agree that some of the formal rules of evidence be dispensed with. The parties can also decide the time and place to suit themselves which they would not be able to do if the dispute had been referred to the Court. Parties involved in litigation have very little control over the timing and venue of the proceedings which may cause them considerable inconvenience and expense.

Another advantage of arbitration is that the hearing and outcome are not made public and where commercial issues have to be decided that consideration may be important.

Arbitration, however, is not a satisfactory forum if one party has a very strong case against the other because the Court procedures for dealing with cases of that kind can be invoked quickly and at comparatively little cost. Contrary to what may be imagined, the arbitration procedure is not necessarily a cheaper method of dispute resolution.

Even though a contract or agreement includes an arbitration clause an aggrieved party is not prevented from instituting Court proceedings in respect of any dispute which may arise, although in most cases it would be pointless to do so as the Court will, unless there were substantial grounds for not doing so, stay the proceedings on the basis that as the parties had agreed to resort to arbitration they should follow that course.

Careful consideration thus needs to be given as to whether an arbitration clause should be included in an agreement or not.

Execution of agreements

Few agreements entered into by companies require sealing, the more obvious examples being conveyances and leases relating to land and deeds of guarantee. Rarely would agreements in Chapters 12 or 14 require to be executed as deeds. The way in which the agreements in Chapters 10, 13 and 14 should be executed is discussed in the introduction to each agreement and where an agreement can be executed as a deed the attestation clauses are set out alternatively depending on whether or not the company has taken advantage of section 130 of the Companies Act 1989 and has dispensed with the use of its seal.

CHAPTER 10

DIRECTOR'S SERVICE AGREEMENTS

Introduction to director's service agreement where a director has a nil or minor shareholding in a company (including a listed PLC)

Many companies enter into formal service agreements with their executive directors; others do not. There is no legal requirement for a company and a director to conclude a written service agreement but it is usually advisable for both parties to do so. The company is, however, obliged to provide a director who is an employee (whether there is a written agreement or not) with certain information in accordance with the Employment Protection (Consolidation) Act 1978, as mentioned below. Although, technically, the status of a director is that of an officer of the company, he may also be an employee which will invariably be the case if he is a full time director. A non-executive director is an officer of the company only; he is not an employee.

If the company's articles incorporate the provisions of Table A, a director will be entitled to such remuneration as the company may by ordinary resolution determine and unless the resolution provides otherwise the remuneration shall be deemed to accrue from day to day. The payment of remuneration or fees on this basis is more appropriate in the context of a part time non-executive director, but it is an outmoded concept in the case of a full time executive director who will expect the way in which he is to be remunerated to be clearly defined.

A director's service agreement which is comprehensively drawn will, however, contain many other provisions apart from remuneration. From the company's point of view there are a number of benefits to be gained by incorporating not only the usual employment terms and the obligatory statutory information in a formal agreement, but also by placing certain restraints on the director which apply both during his employment and after its termination. Such restraints which can be imposed to protect the company's legitimate business interests will normally be greater than the law would necessarily imply. The very fact that the restrictions are spelt out in an agreement may also encourage the director to observe them more readily.

Another advantage of having a formal service agreement is that in the event of a dispute there would be no doubt as to what was or was not included and this would be of evidential value if it were necessary for the company (or the director) to enforce the terms of the agreement.

A director may require a formal service agreement because he considers it to be commensurate with his status and the level of his responsibility within the company. If the director has been recently recruited to the company in that capacity he will require the security which a service agreement would provide.

The Companies Act 1985 makes specific reference to director's contracts of service. Section 318 provides that where such an agreement is in writing a copy must be kept in an appropriate place which in practice means the company's registered office or principal place of business. If the contract of service is not in writing and there is only an oral agreement then a written memorandum setting out its terms must be kept on the same basis as a contract which is in writing. A written contract or memorandum is open to inspection by any member of the company without charge and if there is default in complying with the requirements of section 318, a criminal offence is committed.

Section 319 provides that where a company enters into a contract with a director and there is a provision to the effect that the employment is to continue for at least five years, such a provision will be void unless it has first been approved by resolution of the shareholders and this is so whether the company is a private company with a few shareholders or a listed PLC.

As mentioned above, a full time director who is an employee is entitled under the terms of the Employment Protection (Consolidation) Act 1978 to receive a written statement from the company detailing certain specified information relevant to his employment. Contrary to what is often thought to be the case, there is no statutory obligation on an employer and employee to enter into a *written* contract pursuant to the 1978 Act. The only obligation which the employer has to fulfil is to provide the employee with the specified information in writing – the statutory particulars – not later than thirteen weeks after the beginning of the employee's employment with the employer. The statutory particulars are all included or referred to in the precedent.

A service agreement should be prepared in duplicate and in most cases the agreement can be signed by a director on behalf of the company and by the appointee with each of them retaining one complete document. Occasionally, it will be necessary for the agreement to be executed as a deed which again should be done in duplicate with each party retaining a complete copy. Some provisions would only be enforceable if contained in a document executed as a deed but few such provisions are likely to be included in a director's service agreement. The only item included in the precedent is in clause 13.3 in which the director irrevocably appoints the company to be his attorney to sign documents and the like in connection with vesting the benefit of an invention in the company. In the majority of cases therefore a service agreement need not be executed as a deed as clause 13 would be excluded as not being relevant.

Director's service agreement where a director has a nil or minor shareholding in a company (including a listed PLC)

Date 19 .

The Parties:

LTD/PLC whose registered office is at ('the Company') (1)

of ('the Director') (2)

IT IS AGREED as follows:

1. Definitions and interpretation

1.1 These terms and expressions shall have the following meanings in this Agreement:

Note A (see p.196)

'ASSOCIATED COMPANY' means any company which is a holding company or a subsidiary company as defined in sections 736 and 736A of the Companies Act 1985 as substituted by section 144 of the Companies Act 1989.

'THE BOARD' means the Board of directors as constituted from time to time of the Company.

1.2 The clause headings do not form part of this Agreement and do not affect its construction or interpretation and are for reference purposes only.

Note B (see p.197)

2. Commencement and duration of employment

The Company shall employ the Director and the Director shall serve the Company as [Managing Director] [Executive Director] [Chief Executive] [other title or description] and subject to the provisions for termination of his employment contained in this Agreement such employment [shall commence with immediate effect] [commenced] [shall commence] on [date] and

[shall continue until determined by either party giving to the other [ ] [weeks] [months] notice in writing] or

[shall continue until either party gives to the other notice in writing which if given before the 19 shall be not less than [ ] [weeks] and if given after that date shall be [ ] [months]] or

[be for an initial period of [ ] [years] and then to continue until such time as this Agreement is terminated by either party giving to the other not less than [ ] [weeks] [months] notice in writing].

3. Duties and obligations of the director

Note C (see p.198)

The Director shall for so long as his employment continues:

3.1 Undertake and perform such duties and exercise such powers and functions in relation to the Company and its business as the Board shall from time to time assign to or vest in him in his capacity as [Managing Director] [Executive Director] [Chief Executive] [other title or description] and do so for any Associated Company and [without further remuneration unless otherwise agreed] accept such appointments in any such Associated Company as the Board may from time to time require.

3.2 Devote [the whole of his time] [sufficient of his time], ability and attention to the performance of his duties.

3.3 Do everything that is within his capacity to promote and develop the business, reputation and interests of the Company and of any Associated Company [provided, however, the Director shall not enter into any contracts on behalf of the Company or any Associated Company other than contracts in the ordinary course of the business of the Company or any Associated Company].

3.4 Comply with all proper and reasonable requirements and directions of the Board.

3.5 Perform his obligations jointly with any other person of director status if required by the Board so to do.

[3.6 Comply with the provisions of the employment description and specification set out in the [letter] [document] dated 19 .]

4. Location

Note D (see p.198)

The Director shall:

4.1 Carry out his duties at such place or places as the Board shall require.

4.2 Perform his duties in whole or in part on behalf of any Associated Company at its place or places of business as the Board shall require.

5. Salary

Note E (see p.199)

5.1 The Company shall pay to the Director during the course of his employment a salary commencing at the rate of £ per annum payable in arrear by twelve equal instalments [on the [day] of every month] [on the dates salaries are paid to the Company's employees generally] and the salary shall accrue from day to day.

[5.2 The salary shall be inclusive of any fees otherwise payable to the Director in accordance with the articles of association of the Company and any Associated Company.]

5.3 The rate of salary shall be reviewed on or about the [specify] each year by [an independent remuneration committee comprising the Chairman and the non-executive directors of the Company] [the Board] [the managing director], and any consequent increase in the rate of salary shall be paid by the Company with effect from that date [provided that in any event the rate of salary shall be increased by the same percentage increase by which the retail price index has risen since the date of the last review].

[5.4 If at any review date the basis of computation of the retail price index has altered and a new basis introduced then any official reconciliation between the two bases of computation published by the appropriate government department shall be binding on the Director and the Company.

5.5 If no official reconciliation has been published, then an adjustment shall be made to the latest index figure to make it so far as is practicable comparable with the previous method of computation.

5.6 In the event of any dispute between the Company and the Director regarding the calculation of any increase in the rate of salary in consequence of any rise in the retail price index pursuant to sub-clauses 5.3, 5.4 and 5.5 such dispute shall be referred to the Company's auditors to resolve acting as experts and not as arbitrators and their decision shall be final and binding on the Company and the Director.]

Note F (see p.199)

6. Additional payments

The Company shall pay to the Director a [bonus] [commission] during the course of his employment in respect of each complete accounting reference period of the Company [other than the first such period expiring after the commencement of the Director's employment and the final such period in which this Agreement is terminated by either party for whatever reason] computed as follows:

6.1 The [bonus] [commission] payment shall be limited to a maximum of [£] [a specified proportion of current annual salary].

6.2 The [bonus] [commission] payable shall be per cent of the amount by which the [aggregate of the] net profits [as defined in clause 6.3] of the Company [and any Associated Company] exceeds £ .

6.3 The [aggregate of the] net profits of the Company [and any Associated Company] [is] [are] the amount shown in the audited profit and loss account[s] of the Company [and any Associated Company whether consolidated or not] computed after deducting:

6.3.1 all liability to taxation;

6.3.2 all director's fees and salaries;

6.3.3 any income attributable to fixed assets or arising from trade investments;

6.3.4 depreciation of all plant and equipment and any other assets;

6.3.5 any capital profits or losses;

6.3.6 such amount as the directors consider is appropriate to transfer to the reserves of the Company [or any Associated Company] in respect of any anticipated requirements for working capital and/or any other purpose;

6.3.7 any income or profit attributable to extraordinary items;

6.3.8 any income or profit attributable to any business or Company acquired during the particular accounting reference period to which the [bonus] [commission] payment relates.

6.4 Within [ ] month[s] of the approval of the annual [consolidated] accounts by the Board and the signing of the annual [consolidated] accounts by a director or directors the auditors shall be requested by the Company to compute [acting as experts and not as arbitrators] the additional amount (if any) payable by way of [bonus] [commission] to the Director, and the certificate of the auditors shall be conclusive and binding on the Company and the Director.

6.5 The Company shall make the payment of such [bonus] [commission] as certified by the auditors to the Director within [twenty-eight] days of receipt of the auditors' certificate.

7. Other benefits

Note G (see p.199)

7.1 The Company shall:

7.1.1 provide life insurance cover for the Director at the rate of [ ] times his annual salary from time to time [and shall procure that the proceeds of such insurance shall be paid to the Director's spouse [and/or other dependants] as the Company in its absolute discretion shall determine] on condition that the Director shall at least once in every year attend for a medical examination and permit in writing a report of the examination to be sent in confidence to the company;

7.1.2 provide private medical insurance cover in accordance with the scheme (if any) operated by the Company from time to time subject to the Director attending any annual medical examination on the same basis as provided in clause 7.1.1;

7.1.3 provide accident insurance cover at the rate of [ ] times the Director's annual salary from time to time;

7.1.4 make contributions on behalf of the Director to a pension scheme operated by the Company subject to the rules of such scheme as amended from time to time [conditional upon the Director making as required all contributions due from him in accordance with the provisions of such scheme];

7.1.5 provide Director's liability insurance cover in the sum of at least £ to be increased from time to time as agreed between the parties.

7.2 Any other benefits provided by the Company for the Director or his family are provided at the Company's discretion and do not form part of any contractual entitlement arising out of the Director's employment under this Agreement.

Note H (see p.200)

8. Car

8.1 The Company shall:

8.1.1 for so long as the Director is qualified to drive, provide [a car reasonably suitable for the performance by the Director of his duties having due regard to his position and status within the Company] [specify make of car and model];

8.1.2 meet the cost of insurance, maintenance and all running expenses of the car [except fuel consumed during private use of the car];

8.1.3 replace such car when it is [ ] years old or has been driven more than [ ] thousand miles.

8.2 The Director shall take proper care of the car and ensure that it is correctly maintained and where appropriate shall do so in accordance with the terms of the manufacturer's warranty and will observe all provisions and conditions relating to the insurance policy.

8.3 The Director shall immediately on the termination of this Agreement, for whatever reason, return the car together with its keys to the Company at such place as the Company may require.

9. Expenses

The Company shall:

9.1 Procure the repayment to or reimburse the Director all travelling accommodation and other expenses reasonably incurred by him in the proper performance of his duties provided that the Director shall produce to the Company sufficient evidence of the payment by him of such expenses as the Company or its auditors may require.

9.2 Reimburse the Director the cost of subscriptions to all professional bodies to which he may belong.

9.3 Meet the cost of the Director's home telephone rental and the cost of such calls as he may make in carrying out his duties under this Agreement.

Note I (see p.200)

10. Holidays

10.1 The Director shall be entitled to [ ] working days' holiday in each year [set out dates of holiday year] to be taken at such time or times as the [chairman] [managing director] [Board] shall consider most convenient having regard to the requirements of the business of the Company or any Associated Company. [The Director shall not be allowed to carry forward any holiday entitlement not taken to a subsequent year and such entitlement shall accordingly be lost although at the Company's discretion it may make payment in lieu of such unused holiday entitlement.]

10.2 In respect of the holiday year in which the Director commences his employment he shall be entitled to [[ ] working days for each completed month worked during that year] [such proportion of his annual entitlement as his initial period of employment bears to one calendar year].

11. Incapacity, illness and sick pay Note J (see p.200)

11.1 If the Director shall at any time be incapacitated or prevented by illness, injury, accident or any other circumstances beyond his control from performing his duties under this Agreement for a total of up to [specify number of working days or weeks] absence in any period of [twelve] months the Company shall for such period continue to pay the Director his current level of annual salary [such payment to be inclusive of any statutory sick pay or social security benefits] [and any entitlement to [bonus] [commission] payments].

11.2 If the Director shall continue to be absent and unable to perform his duties beyond the period of absence referred to in clause 11.1 the Company may at its discretion discontinue payment in whole or part of his current level of annual salary [and any entitlement to [bonus] [commission] payments] until the incapacity or illness shall cease or the Company may at its option determine this Agreement by notice in writing specifying in such notice the date of termination of the Director's employment.

12. No conflict of interest Note K (see p.201)

The Director shall not be directly or indirectly engaged, concerned or interested in any other business or be involved in any way in competition with the business of the Company or any Associated Company or any business which is involved in the supply of goods or services to the Company or any Associated Company or is a customer of the Company or any Associated Company provided that nothing in this clause shall prevent the Director from holding [directly or through nominees] not more than [ ] per cent of the issued shares of securities of any Company whose shares are listed on the International Stock Exchange or similar capital market.

[13. Inventions Note L (see p.201)

13.1 In the event that the Director makes or participates in making any discovery or invention which directly or indirectly affects or relates to the business of the Company or any Associated Company, or if the discovery or invention is capable of being used by the Company or any Associated Company, the discovery or invention shall belong to the Company and the Director shall immediately provide full details in writing to the Board and shall give assistance as may be necessary to enable the Company to benefit from the discovery or invention.

13.2 The Director shall when requested by the Company apply or join in applying for patent registration or such other protection as may be appropriate at the Company's expense.

[13.3 The Director irrevocably appoints the Company to be his attorney in his name and on his behalf to sign, execute or do any such instrument or thing and generally to use his name for the purpose of giving to the Company [or its nominee] the full benefit of the provisions of this clause and a certificate in writing signed by any director or the company secretary shall so far as any third party is concerned be conclusive evidence that any instrument or act falls within the authority conferred by this clause.]

Note M (see p.201)

14. Confidentiality

Except as may be necessary for the proper performance of his duties the Director shall not either before or after the termination of his employment disclose, divulge or communicate to any person, firm or company any trade secret, manufacturing process or information relating to the business methods, customers or suppliers or finances or any other confidential information relating to the Company or any Associated Company which the Director has obtained during his employment provided that this clause shall not apply to any information which becomes public knowledge other than directly or indirectly through the default of the Director.

[15. Dealings in shares or securities

The Director shall observe all rules and regulations of the International Stock Exchange in relation to any dealing by him in the shares or other securities of the Company or any Associated Company and will also abide by any regulations which the Company makes or any code of conduct which it may issue from time to time relating to dealings in shares or other securities of the Company or any Associated Company.]

Note N (see p.202)

16. Termination of directorship

This Agreement shall terminate automatically in the event that the Director:

16.1 Reaches the age of [ ].

16.2 Is disqualified from being a director or is prohibited by law.

16.3 Resigns as a director.

[16.4 Is not re-elected as a director at an Annual General Meeting of the Company.]

16.5 Is removed as a director by the Company in General Meeting.

Note O (see p.202)

17. Summary dismissal

The employment of the Director may be terminated by the Company without prior written notice (the Company reserving the right to pay the Director his current level of annual salary for the appropriate period in lieu of notice) if the Director shall at any time:

17.1 Commit or be guilty of any serious or persistent breach or non-performance of any of his obligations under this Agreement.

17.2 Become bankrupt or make any composition or enter into any general arrangement with his creditors.

17.3 Be guilty of any [gross] [serious] misconduct however arising which in the opinion of the Board reflects adversely on the Company or any Associated Company.

17.4 Become of unsound mind or become a patient under the Mental Health Act 1983.

17.5 Be convicted of any criminal offence which in the opinion of the Board impairs the fitness of the Director to carry out his duties under this Agreement.

17.6 Be unable for any reason to carry out his duties under this Agreement.

18. Consequences of termination Note P (see p.202)

In the event that this Agreement is terminated for any reason:

18.1 The Director shall immediately upon the request of the Company resign without any claim for compensation from all offices held by him in the Company and any Associated Company and in the event of his failure to do so the Company is irrevocably authorised to appoint some person in his name and on his behalf to execute any documents and to do all things that may be necessary to give effect to any such resignation.

18.2 The Director shall immediately deliver to the Chairman or other representative of the Company all documents (together with any copies) including notes, records, accounts, memoranda or papers and any other items or property relating to or concerning the business of the Company and any Associated Company or any of its or their suppliers, agents, distributors or customers.

18.3 The Director shall not, if resolved by the Board, continue to work on behalf of the Company or any Associated Company during a period of notice and if the Board so resolves the Company shall continue to pay the Director his current level of annual salary. The Director shall not for the duration of the notice period be employed or act in any capacity for any other person, firm or company, except with the consent of the Board in writing.

19. Non-solicitation Note Q (see p.202)

The Director shall not within [describe area or specific radius] and for a period of [ ] [months] [years] after ceasing his employment under this Agreement however caused directly or indirectly whether on his own account or on behalf of another business entity:

19.1 Solicit or procure business from any person, firm or company who or which within a period of [ ] year[s] preceding the termination of this

Agreement was a customer or client of the Company or any Associated Company or who dealt generally or occasionally with the Company or any Associated Company.

19.2 Solicit the services of or endeavour to encourage any person who shall have been a director, officer, employee or consultant of the Company or any Associated Company within the period of [ ] year[s] preceding the termination of this Agreement, to leave the employment of the Company or any Associated Company.

Note R (see p.203)

20. Non-dealing

The Director shall not within [describe area or specific radius] and for a period of [ ] [months] [years] after ceasing his employment under this Agreement however caused directly or indirectly carry on business or deal with any person, firm or company who or which within a period of [ ] years preceding the termination of this Agreement was a customer, client, supplier, agent or distributor of the Company or any Associated Company.

Note S (see p.203)

21. Non-competition

The Director shall not within [describe area or specific radius] and for a period of [ ] [months] [years] after ceasing his employment under this Agreement however caused be engaged or assist in carrying on any business which competes with the business of the Company or any Associated Company or otherwise be interested or concerned either directly or indirectly whether as a consultant, employee, director, partner, adviser, agent or in any other capacity in or with any person, firm or company whose business competes with any business of the Company or any Associated Company.

Note T (see p.203)

22. Declaration of reasonableness of clauses 19, 20 and 21

The parties declare that they consider the application of the restrictions imposed by clauses 19, 20 and 21 to be reasonable and no greater than is necessary for the protection of the business of the Company and any Associated Company but in the event that unforeseen changes occur or Court judgments are delivered which would render any of the provisions invalid or void the parties declare that each of the covenants are to be regarded as separate and severable and where appropriate a covenant shall be amended to the extent necessary to make such covenant as amended or modified effective and enforceable.

23. Disciplinary rules and procedure

The Company's disciplinary rules and procedure details of which [have been given to the Director] [are available for inspection on request to the company secretary] shall [not] apply to the Director.

24. Grievance procedure

The Director shall initially refer any grievance which he may have arising out of his employment under this Agreement to [the chairman] [the non-executive directors] and in the event that the grievance is not resolved to the Director's satisfaction, he shall refer the matter to the Board as a whole to determine.

25. Employment Protection (Consolidation) Act 1978 statutory particulars Note U (see p.204)

The particulars which are required to be given pursuant to section 1 of the Act and which have not already been given are:

25.1 Contracting out certificate under the Social Security Pensions Act 1975.
A certificate is [not] in force in respect of the employment of the Director.

[25.2 Continuous employment
The employment of the Director with the Company prior to the date specified in clause 2 of this Agreement forms part of the Director's continuous employment with the Company and his continuous employment therefore commenced on .]

25.3 Hours of work
[There are no specific hours of work.] [The Director's normal hours of work are from a.m. to p.m. Monday to Friday.] [The Director shall spend such time as is necessary to enable him to carry out his duties properly in accordance with clause 3 of this Agreement.]

26. Reconstruction or amalgamation

In the event of the liquidation of the Company for the purpose of reconstruction or amalgamation which results in the termination of the employment of the Director under this Agreement and the Director is offered employment on terms and conditions which are broadly similar to the terms of this Agreement, with any Company or undertaking resulting from the reconstruction or amalgamation then the Director shall have no claim against the Company in respect of such termination.

27. Notices

Any notices, instruction or communication shall be sent by ordinary first class post or by such other means as may be appropriate in the circumstances and in the case of a notice served by first class post it shall be deemed to have been received by the party to whom it was sent forty-eight hours after posting and in the case of any other form of transmission on proof of receipt.

28. Law

This Agreement shall be governed by English law.

THE COMMON SEAL of LTD/PLC was hereunto affixed in the presence of:

Director

Secretary

or

EXECUTED AS A DEED by and on behalf of LTD/PLC by

Director

Secretary

or

SIGNED for and on behalf of LTD/PLC by

Director

EXECUTED AS A DEED by the Director in the presence of:

or

SIGNED by the Director

Explanatory notes on director's service agreement where a director has a nil or minor shareholding in a company (including a listed PLC)

A. Definition of associated company (see p. 186)

Reference to associated companies should be made in the agreement even if there are none at the time the agreement is entered into. Situations do change and if any associated companies are formed or acquired, the director will be contractually bound to discharge his responsibilities in relation to those companies if the board requires him to do so. With the advent of the Companies Act 1989 the definition of what may constitute an associated company has become more difficult in that in addition to the amendments (introduced by section 144 of the Companies Act 1989) to section 736 of the Companies Act 1985 which re-define holding and subsidiary companies the category of business undertakings which are now to be included within group accounts has been enlarged. The definition should therefore be looked at in the context of the company's present and projected structure to make sure that the definition of an associated company is sufficient or whether a variation would be more appropriate.

B. Commencement and duration of employment (see p.186)

If the director is an existing employee or has been a director for some time the agreement will be the subject of negotiation 'across the table'. If, however, the director has been recently recruited to the company in that capacity, he will have received an initial offer of employment the terms of which may have incorporated a provision to the effect that during the initial period of employment (to be defined) the agreement can be terminated on either party giving to the other a shorter period of notice.

It is good practice to enclose with the initial letter of offer of employment a draft of the proposed form of service agreement and to have obtained the prospective director's written approval of its terms at the time he accepts the offer of employment so that the agreement cannot subsequently be re-negotiated by him.

The point at which the term of employment commences and its duration will depend on what is agreed between the parties. The various alternatives are as follows:

1. The agreement continues indefinitely until such time as either party gives to the other a specified period of notice in writing. How long the period of notice should be will depend on a number of factors. If the period is a long one, perhaps a year or more, the company would be faced with the prospect of paying the appropriate amount of salary in lieu if the decision is taken by the company to terminate the agreement and dispense with the director's services immediately. If the director is obliged to give a long period of notice it is questionable as to how effective he would be during the notice period. The length of the period of notice to be given by the company or the director could be different if it is either necessary or appropriate.
2. This alternative is a variation of (1) except that there is provision for shorter notice to be given by either party during what is in effect an initial probationary period which would probably be for a period of between three and twelve months.
3. In this alternative the period of the employment is for an initial fixed period of years and is expressed to continue after that period until the agreement is

terminated by either party giving a specific period of notice. This gives the new director some security in that if the company sought to determine the agreement within the initial fixed period the director could claim damages for wrongful dismissal.

There is a fourth alternative which is not included in the precedent. The term of employment could be expressed as a fixed term with or without any provision for renewal. If the fixed term expires but continues for a time without agreement for a specific period of renewal the director would then be entitled to a reasonable period of notice from the company. In addition, where a contract provides for a fixed term of employment of one year or more and the employee has agreed in writing to exclude his statutory rights under the Employment Protection (Consolidation) Act 1978 not to be unfairly dismissed, he would accordingly lose his statutory rights under the Act. It is unlikely that such an arrangement would be acceptable to a prospective director. Nevertheless, it should be borne in mind as an option to be considered if appropriate.

C. Duties and obligations of the director (see p. 187)

The provisions of this clause range between the specific and the general and give the company a certain amount of flexibility. Although many of the duties are self-evident or would be implied the scope is expanded to include the obligation on the part of the director to perform the duties for associated companies and, should it be appropriate, either at the outset or in the future, to do so jointly with some other person.

As drafted the clause is quite onerous so far as the director is concerned and it may be appropriate for some of the obligations to be diluted slightly by the occasional insertion of the word 'reasonable'.

Any duties or functions which are specific to the director should be included as additional clauses although if there is a separate job description or specification it would be advisable for this to be included by direct reference as suggested in clause 3.6.

D. Location (see p. 187)

If the company requires the director to relocate the director would in the absence of such a clause be within his rights to decline such a request and invariably this would have adverse practical and financial consequences for the company. Although a certain degree of flexibility on the part of the director would be implied, in the absence of such a clause it is unlikely that he could be required to move to an entirely different location.

In some cases a director would only be able to carry out his duties properly if he lived within a certain distance of the office or factory and if so an additional clause to that effect would be inserted.

E. Salary (see p. 187)

It will be noted that this clause provides that any director's fees which would or may be payable in accordance with the articles of association of the company or any associated company are not payable in addition to the annual salary. Although the company is obliged to review the director's salary it is implied that such a review would be carried out properly and in good faith by the company or the parties nominated on its behalf. There is, however, no obligation to increase the salary although the clause includes the option to bring it into line with any increase in the RPI. The inclusion of an RPI related increase would be solely for the benefit of the director because his salary would automatically increase by the proportionate amount regardless of the company's financial position or performance.

F. Additional payments (see p. 188)

In addition to the director's basic annual salary there will probably be some agreement entitling the director to additional profit or performance related pay. Consequently, it would be necessary to agree the formula which would determine the additional amount payable and, where such payment is related to the net profits of the company, how those net profits would be defined or computed. The definition of net profit can be one of a number of almost infinite variables depending not only on the nature of the company's constitution and its business but also on what the parties negotiate and what the auditors may advise. It may not always be appropriate for the bonus or commission payment to be calculated on the profits of any associated company, even though the director may perform some function on their behalf, and that is why all references to associated companies in the clause are in parentheses.

G. Other benefits (see p. 189)

The inclusion of the obligation to fund life insurance cover and the other insurances as an express term of the agreement may be of doubtful value so far as the company is concerned. Should the company and the director part in other than amicable circumstances such provision may rebound on the company in that the value of these benefits would be taken into account in assessing the level of compensation that may be payable to the director. It will be noted that clause 7.2 expressly declares that any other payments or benefits which the director or members of his family may receive are not to be regarded as contractual. The benefits mentioned are those which would normally be included in a director's service agreement.

As section 137 of the Companies Act 1989 has amended section 310 of the Companies Act 1985 it is now lawful for a company to pay premiums to insure directors against liability for breach of duty, negligence and default but not in respect of any claim arising out of the director's dishonesty or the imposition of fines or other penalties.

It will be noted that the provision of life insurance and private medical insurance is subject to the director undergoing a medical examination each year and, moreover, agreeing to authorise the doctor in writing to send the result to the company. The inclusion of this requirement in writing is necessary if the company wishes to insist that the director attend a periodic medical examination.

Any provision obliging an employee to become a member of a company pension scheme is void as a result of the Social Security Act 1986.

H. Car (see p.190)

The essential points are dealt with, although there are a number of other options which could be incorporated. It may perhaps have been agreed that the director should be able to use a particular car in which case this should be stipulated. Another option would be simply to say that the director is entitled to use a car made available to him in accordance with the company's general scheme which may be varied or suspended from time to time at the company's discretion.

If the company does not provide the director with a car and the director has to use his own car in the course of the company's business a specific provision should be included stating that the company will pay the director an amount for each mile travelled, at a rate to be determined by the company from time to time.

I. Holidays (see p.190)

As often as not where a director commences his employment any existing holiday arrangements will be honoured by the company notwithstanding any other considerations. If that is so then clause 10.2 can be deleted.

J. Incapacity, illness and sick pay (see p.191)

This is a difficult aspect to resolve, especially if the ability of the director to continue working is crucial to the company's performance. The provision of a 'key man' insurance arrangement is unlikely to be entirely satisfactory if the director is incapacitated for a significant period of time and there are relatively few individuals (even if available) who have the requisite experience and are of suitable calibre.

It is important from the company's point of view that there should be a provision enabling the company to terminate the agreement in the event that the director is absent for too long. Even though termination for this reason would not be a breach of contract giving the director a right to sue for damages for wrongful termination it may nevertheless give rise to a claim for unfair dismissal. Such a claim would not necessarily be successful. On balance the risk of a claim for unfair dismissal being brought is worth running when compared with the practical difficulties which would arise if there were no mechanism enabling the company to bring matters to a head. Otherwise the situation would be allowed to drift and the uncertainty damaging to the company's business.

K. *No conflict of interest (see p.191)*

Although to some extent the provisions of this clause would be implied, nevertheless it would be as well to include it so that the company can point to the specific prohibition if a problem or dispute should arise.

L. *Inventions (see p.191)*

The inclusion of this clause is optional and there will be relatively few agreements in which it would be relevant but it is good practice to include the clause if there is a remote possibility of a director making such an invention, even though the company could rely on the provisions of the Patents Act 1977.

M. *Confidentiality (see p.192)*

In the relationship between a company and a director the law implies a number of duties on the part of the director, one of which is a general duty of good faith. It would be a breach of this implied term if the director were, during the course of his employment, to disclose confidential information, whether or not for his benefit, and if following the termination of his employment he were to disclose particularly confidential information or the company's trade secrets.

The law in this area has only recently been clarified in the case of *Faccenda Chicken Ltd* v. *Fowler* in 1986. In seeking to restrain the actions of Mr Fowler following the termination of his employment with Faccenda Chicken Ltd, the company could not rely on any relevant clause in a service agreement or contract of employment (as none existed) and was left to pursue its action on the basis of what the law implied. The company was unsuccessful in restraining Mr Fowler from setting up business in competition with it because the information which he used and which he had obtained during the course of his employment was not regarded by the Court as highly confidential, nor had the company expressly stated that such information should be regarded as confidential. The lesson to be learned from this case so far as any employer is concerned is that if it wishes to prohibit an employee from using what it would consider to be private commercial information relating to its business it should enter into an agreement with the employee incorporating an appropriate confidentiality clause preferably tailored to suit the particular employee concerned. The inclusion of the clause should also discourage an employee from acting in contravention of it.

N. Termination of directorship (see p. 192)

It should be noted that if a director is not re-elected at the company's AGM or is removed as a director he may still be able to bring an action against the company for damages for wrongful termination and breach of contract. The inclusion of clause 16.4 in most cases will not be appropriate as the articles of many companies will specify that certain directors, for example the managing director, for the time being is not to be subject to rotation.

O. Summary dismissal without notice (but with option to pay salary in lieu) (see p. 192)

What would constitute a serious or persistent breach or non-performance of any of the director's obligations would be a question of fact and would therefore be open to interpretation by the Court or Tribunal if there was litigation or a claim for unfair dismissal. Not all breaches would be sufficiently material to enable the company to treat the agreement as terminated without notice.

The reservation of the right of the company to pay the director's salary in lieu of notice is a device which would permit the company to terminate, without being itself in breach of contract, so that the obligations and covenants on the part of the director which are intended to continue after termination would remain in effect and be enforceable.

P. Consequences of termination (see p. 193)

It will be noted that the director is not only obliged to return all documents and the like but is not entitled to retain any copies.

Q. Non-solicitation (see p. 193)

This is another difficult area and something of a minefield for the unwary. A major obstacle to overcome is that conditions in restraint of trade are *prima facie* void as being contrary to public policy. If such a condition is to be effective and capable of being enforced then it must be reasonable in duration, subject matter and geographical area, and limited to what is necessary to protect the company's legitimate business interests. The law requires that the market must be kept open, free from unwarranted restrictions and competition encouraged. With the effect of EC legislation this principle is more likely to broaden than narrow.

As a covenant restraining the solicitation of the company's customers can only be effective for a reasonable period of time, what that period should be would depend to some extent on the seniority of the director. If the covenant were to be enforced, a Court would also take into account how long the director has been employed and as that would not be known at the time the agreement is entered into, there inevitably will be some risk in a Court deciding that the length of time for which the restriction is expressed to continue after termination of the agreement is unreasonable and therefore the clause is unenforceable. In the case of a director a period not exceeding two years would probably be appropriate. It is better to err on the side of caution so as not to prejudice the chances of a clause being enforced at all in the event that the Court has to decide. Although the company could rely on the provisions of clause 22 of the precedent the effectiveness of this clause can not be guaranteed.

Another consideration to be borne in mind is that if the clause refers to any customer or client of the company (which the clause in the precedent does), the period of time for which it is expressed to be effective should be shorter rather than longer and perhaps as short as nine to twelve months. If, however, the clause is limited to customers or clients with whom the director personally dealt the period of time could be longer, perhaps up to two years. Reference should be made to clause 21.1 of the contract of employment for a senior salaried employee which is drafted on this alternative basis.

A non-solicitation clause is to some extent defective in principle and practice anyway as there could be a problem of proving who made the approach – the former director or the company's customer. If it were the company's customer who approached the former director this would not constitute a breach of the clause.

R. Non-dealing (see p. 194)

A more effective alternative clause would perhaps be a non-dealing clause in the sense that any breach could more easily be proved as a question of fact. Again, however, if the clause came to be tested in Court the question of reasonableness would have to be resolved and therefore the period and the geographical area should be no greater than is reasonably necessary to protect the company's business.

S. Non-competition (see p. 194)

The same general observations apply to this clause as to the previous two clauses in that there is the risk that if the restricted area is too wide or the period too long the clause will not be enforceable, although again clause 22 may be sufficient to save it.

T. Declaration of reasonableness of clauses 19, 20 and 21 (see p. 194)

As has already been mentioned the effectiveness of this clause cannot be guaranteed but at least it would be demonstrated to the Court that the parties did consider the implications of what they were agreeing to.

The Courts have shown some inclination to severing parts of restraint clauses by removing the offending part and leaving the rest to operate. Amending as opposed to severing a restraint clause, however, is a different matter and generally Courts have been reluctant to rewrite. The approach to be adopted therefore seems to be that all three clauses should be included separately, drafting each clearly with the intention of doing what is reasonable and on the basis that if the effectiveness of the clauses was ever subject to Court scrutiny the Court would either enforce one or more of the clauses considered to be reasonable or delete the clause or clauses deemed to be more widely drawn than was reasonably necessary.

U. Employment Protection (Consolidation) Act 1978 particulars (see p.195)

Although the agreement contains most of the statutory particulars required to be given in accordance with the Act, those which remain to be given are included in this clause.

Introduction to director's service agreement suitable for managing or executive director of private company or 'unquoted' PLC where the director has less than a 50 per cent shareholding

This service agreement requires a different and individual approach to that of the previous precedent, although there are a number of similarities in principle. This precedent is intended for use where the number of shareholders is relatively small, perhaps up to fifty in total, and the director is one of those shareholders with a stake in the equity of between 10 per cent and 45 per cent. The director may well be the mentor and founding force of the company but lacks the necessary capital. The shareholders contributing the capital will be interested in receiving dividends with the possibility in the longer term of capital growth, either because the company becomes an unlisted or listed PLC or it is acquired by a third party. In the meantime the company will be run by the director and one or two other directors who may in effect be employees or who may perform a non-executive role.

As the director holds less than 50 per cent of the share capital he could be removed as a director by ordinary resolution passed by the remaining shareholders and it is partly in order to deal with such a possibility that it would be advisable for the director to have a service agreement.

It is also important from the company's point of view that there should be a service agreement with the director so that restrictions can be placed on him, some of which will operate during the course of his employment and some which will come into effect following the termination of the agreement. As the director is the guiding force, much of the value of the company would be represented by his capacity, experience and know how. However, the extent to which restrictions can be imposed on the director will be a matter for negotiation between the director and the rest of the shareholders or their representatives at the time the financing arrangements are being discussed.

Reference should be made to the commentary on the previous precedent as many of the points in that commentary and the references to the various legal requirements are also relevant here.

One of the main differences between the two precedents is that in this precedent there is no provision for summary dismissal. Consequently, the employment of the director cannot be terminated immediately if the director commits any of the various offences set out in clause 17 of the previous precedent. The reason for this is that if the shareholders as a whole decide that the behaviour of the director justifies dismissal they can remove him by ordinary resolution. This is considered to be more appropriate than to give the power of dismissal to the board of directors which because of its likely constitution would be unable to deal with the situation effectively.

Where a director has a controlling shareholding in the company the position is clearly different. As the director is in effect the owner of the company and manages it on his own behalf and the behalf of the minority shareholders, many of the provisions in this precedent are not relevant. Where, however, the influence of the minority shareholders is such that they can require the director to enter into an agreement in order to impose restraints this precedent, suitably adapted, could be used for the purpose.

If the director is likely to make inventions, a clause similar to clause 13 in the previous precedent should be included, in which event the agreement should be executed as a deed.

Director's service agreement suitable for managing or executive director of private company or 'unquoted' PLC where the director has less than a 50 per cent shareholding

Date 19 .

The Parties:

LTD/PLC whose registered office is at ('the Company') (1)

of ('the Director') (2)

IT IS AGREED as follows:

1. Definitions and interpretation

1.1 These terms and expressions shall have the following meanings in this Agreement:

Note A (see p.212)

'ASSOCIATED COMPANY' means any company which is a holding company or a subsidiary company as defined in sections 736 and 736A of the Companies Act 1985 as substituted by section 144 of the Companies Act 1989.

'THE BOARD' means the Board of directors as constituted from time to time of the Company.

1.2 The clause headings do not form part of this Agreement and do not affect its construction or interpretation and are for reference purposes only.

Note B (see p.212)

2. Commencement and duration of employment

The Company shall employ the Director and the Director shall serve the Company as [Managing Director] [Executive Director] [Chief Executive] and subject to the provisions for termination of his employment contained in this Agreement such employment [shall commence with immediate effect] [commenced] [shall commence] on [date] and

[shall continue until determined by either party giving to the other [ ] [weeks] [months] notice in writing]; or
[be for an initial period of [ ] [years] and then to continue until such time as this Agreement is terminated by either party giving to the other not less than [ ] [weeks] [months] notice in writing].

Note C (see p.212)

3. Duties and obligations of the director

The Director shall for so long as his employment continues:

3.1 Exercise such powers and perform such duties in relation to the business and affairs of the Company as may from time to time be reasonably required for the furtherance of the business of the Company or any Associated Company provided, however, the Director shall not enter into any contracts on behalf of the Company or any Associated Company other than contracts in the ordinary course of the Company's business or the business of any Associated Company.

3.2 Devote the whole of his time, ability and attention to his duties on behalf of the Company and of any Associated Company during normal working hours Monday to Friday inclusive and shall in addition, as may be required, work outside or beyond normal working hours or at weekends or during holidays if reasonably required to do so for the furtherance of the business of the Company or any Associated Company.

4. Location

Note D (see p.2

The Director shall carry out his duties at [such place or places as may be necessary] [specify particular location].

5. Salary

Note E (see p.2

5.1 The Company shall pay to the Director during the course of his employment a salary commencing at the rate of £ per annum payable in arrear by twelve equal instalments on the last working day of every month.

5.2 The salary shall be [exclusive] [inclusive] of any fees otherwise payable to the Director in accordance with the articles of association of the Company and any Associated Company.

5.3 The rate of salary may be reviewed from time to time on such basis as the Board and the Director shall agree [following consultation by the other members of the Board with the shareholders of the Company other than the Director].

6. Other benefits

Note F (see p.2

The Company shall:

6.1 Provide life insurance cover for the Director at the rate of [ ] times his basic annual salary from time to time [and shall procure that the proceeds of such insurance shall be paid to the Director's spouse [and/or other dependants]].

6.2 Provide private medical insurance cover in accordance with the scheme [if any] operated by the Company.

6.3 Provide accident insurance cover at the rate of [ ] times the Director's annual salary from time to time.

[6.4 Make contributions on behalf of the Director to a pension scheme operated by the Company subject to the rules of such scheme as amended from time to time [conditional upon the Director making as required all contributions due from him in accordance with the provisions of such scheme].]

6.5 Provide director's liability insurance cover in the sum of at least £ to be increased from time to time as may be agreed between the parties.

7. Car

7.1 The Company shall:

7.1.1 for so long as the Director is qualified to drive, provide a car reasonably suitable for the performance by the Director of his duties having due regard to his position and status within the Company;

7.1.2 meet the cost of insurance, maintenance and all running expenses of the car [except fuel consumed during private use of the car];

7.1.3 replace such car when it is [ ] years old or has been driven more than [ ] thousand miles.

7.2 The Director shall take proper care of the car and ensure that it is correctly maintained and where appropriate shall do so in accordance with the terms of the manufacturer's warranty and will observe all provisions and conditions relating to the insurance policy.

8. Expenses

The Company shall:

8.1 Procure the repayment to or reimburse the Director all travelling, hotel and other expenses reasonably incurred by him in the proper performance of his duties provided that the Director produces to the Company sufficient evidence of the payment by him of such expenses as the Company or its auditors may require.

8.2 Reimburse the Director the cost of subscriptions to all professional bodies to which he may belong.

8.3 Meet the cost of the Director's home telephone rental and the cost of such calls as he may make in carrying out his duties under this Agreement.

9. Holidays

The Director shall be entitled to [ ] working days' holiday in every calendar year to be taken at such time or times as may be approved by the Board.

Note G (see p.213)

10. Incapacity, illness and sick pay

If the Director shall at any time be incapacitated or prevented by illness, injury, accident or any other circumstances beyond his control from performing his duties under this Agreement for a total of up to [specify number of working days or weeks] absence in any period of [twelve] months the Company shall for such period continue to pay the Director his current level of annual salary [such payment to be inclusive of any statutory sick pay or social security benefits].

Note H (see p.214)

11. No conflict of interest

The Director shall not be directly or indirectly engaged, concerned or interested in any other business or be involved in any way in competition with the business of the Company or any Associated Company or any business which is involved in the supply of goods or services to the Company or any Associated Company or is a customer of the Company or any Associated Company.

12. Confidentiality

Except as may be necessary for the proper performance of his duties the

Director shall not either before or after the termination of his employment disclose or divulge to any person, firm or company any trade secret, manufacturing process or information relating to the business methods, customers or suppliers or finances or any other confidential information relating to the Company or any Associated Company which the Director has obtained during his employment provided that this clause shall not apply to any information which becomes public knowledge other than directly or indirectly through the default of the Director.

13. Termination of directorship Note I (see p.214)

This Agreement shall terminate automatically in the event that the Director:

13.1 Is disqualified from being a director or is prohibited by law.

13.2 Resigns as a director.

[13.3 Is not re-elected as a director at an Annual General Meeting of the Company.]

13.4 Is removed as a director by the Company in General Meeting.

14. Consequences of termination

In the event that this Agreement is terminated for any reason:

14.1 The Director shall immediately upon the request of the Company resign without any claim for compensation from all offices held by him in the Company and any Associated Company and in the event of his failure to do so the Company is irrevocably authorised to appoint some person in his name and on his behalf to execute any documents and to do all things that may be necessary to give effect to any such resignation.

14.2 The Director shall immediately deliver to the Chairman or other representative of the Company all documents (together with any copies), including notes, records, accounts, memoranda or papers and any other items or property relating to or concerning the business of the Company and any Associated Company or any of its or their suppliers, agents, distributors or customers.

15. Non-solicitation Note J (see p.214)

The Director shall not within [describe area or specific radius] and for a period of [ ] [months] [years] after ceasing his employment under this Agreement however caused, directly or indirectly whether on his own account or on behalf of another business entity:

15.1 Solicit or procure business from any person, firm or company who or which within a period of [ ] year[s] preceding the termination of this Agreement was a customer or client of the Company or any Associated Company or who dealt generally or occasionally with the Company or any Associated Company.

15.2 Solicit the services of or endeavour to encourage any person who shall have been a director, officer, employee or consultant of the Company or any Associated Company within the period of [ ] year[s] preceding the termination of this Agreement, to leave the employment of the Company or any Associated Company.

Note J (see p.214)

16 Non-dealing

The Director shall not within [describe area or specific radius] and for a period of [ ] [months] [years] after ceasing his employment under this Agreement however caused, directly or indirectly carry on business or deal with any person, firm or Company who or which was a customer, client, supplier, agent or distributor of the Company or any Associated Company during the Director's term of employment under this Agreement.

Note J (see p.214)

17. Non-competition

The Director shall not within [describe area or specific radius] and for a period of [ ] [months] [years] after ceasing his employment under this Agreement however caused be engaged or assist in carrying on any business which competes with the business of the Company or any Associated Company or otherwise be interested or concerned, either directly or indirectly, whether as a consultant, employee, director, partner, adviser, agent or in any other capacity in or with any person, firm or company whose business competes with any business of the Company or any Associated Company.

18. Declaration of reasonableness of clauses 15, 16 and 17

The parties declare that they consider the application of the restrictions imposed by clauses 15, 16 and 17 to be reasonable and no greater than is necessary for the protection of the business of the Company and any Associated Company but in the event that unforeseen changes occur or Court judgments are delivered which would render any of the provisions invalid or void the parties declare that each of the covenants are to be regarded as separate and severable and where appropriate a covenant shall be amended to the extent necessary to make such covenant as amended or modified effective and enforceable.

Note K (see p.215)

19. Employment Protection (Consolidation) Act 1978 statutory particulars

The particulars which the Company is required to give pursuant to section 1 of the Act and which are not otherwise contained in this Agreement are as follows:

19.1 Grievance procedure. The Director shall initially refer any grievance which he may have in respect of this Agreement and his employment to [the chairman] [the Board] [the shareholders].

19.2 Disciplinary rules and procedure. The Company has not issued any disciplinary rules nor does it operate any disciplinary procedure relevant to the Director's employment under this Agreement.

19.3 Contracting Out Certificate under the Social Security Pensions Act 1975. A certificate is [not] in force in respect of the employment of the Director.

19.4 Hours of work. [The Director's normal hours of work are from a.m. to p.m. Monday to Friday.] [The Director shall spend such time as is necessary to enable him to comply with his obligations specified in Clause 3 of this Agreement.]

20. Notices

Any notices, instruction or communication shall be sent by ordinary first class post or by such other means as may be appropriate in the circumstances, and in the case of a notice served by first class post it shall be deemed to have been received by the party to whom it was sent forty-eight hours after posting, and in the case of any other form of transmission on proof of receipt.

21. Law

This Agreement shall be governed by English law.

THE COMMON SEAL of LTD/PLC was hereunto affixed in the presence of:

Director

Secretary

or

EXECUTED AS A DEED by and on behalf of LTD/PLC by

Director

Secretary

or

SIGNED for and on behalf of LTD/PLC by

Director

EXECUTED AS A DEED by the Director in the presence of:

or

SIGNED by the Director

Explanatory notes on director's service agreement suitable for managing or executive director of private company or 'unquoted' PLC where the director has less than a 50 per cent shareholding

A. Definition of associated company (see p.206)

Refer to note A. on page 196. The possibility of an associated company being acquired or formed is perhaps less likely in this case, although it would be as well to include a definition.

B. Commencement and duration of employment (see p.206)

It is inappropriate to include a notice period that is less during the initial period of employment and longer during the subsequent period as the director will not be subject to a trial or probationary period. The duration should either be open ended with a specified period of notice to be given by either party or be for an initial fixed period with notice subsequently to be given by either party.

C. Duties and obligations of the director (see p.206)

These are less expansive than in the previous precedent. For example there is not a requirement on the part of the director to perform his obligations jointly with any other person. There is no reference to compliance with the directions of the board as it is unlikely that, given the circumstances, this would be a satisfactory arrangement. The director will be able to carry out his duties on a day to day basis on a fairly loose rein and only be answerable to the rest of the shareholders at intervals. Their control lies in their ability to remove the director by passing an ordinary resolution to that effect, subject, however, to the possibility that the director could bring a claim for damages for wrongful termination of the agreement.

As the director will be a free agent there is a proviso prohibiting him from entering into any contracts other than contracts in the ordinary course of the company's business. Whether or not this restriction should be included is a matter for negotiation but it would remind the director that he should be circumspect in his dealings on behalf of the company with outside parties if his capacity to enter into contracts is limited in this way.

It will also be noted that there is no reference to an employment description or job specification which in this context would generally be inappropriate.

D. Location (see p.207)

It is questionable whether or not there needs to be any reference to location at all. Again, it depends on the nature of the business and to what extent flexibility on the part of the director is a requirement.

E. Salary (see p.207)

This clause provides only for the payment of an annual salary. Whether or not directors' fees which might be payable in accordance with the articles of association should be inclusive or exclusive of the annual salary is a question to be resolved. There is no requirement that the salary should be reviewed, although there is provision for the company and the director to review the salary from time to time if that was agreed. However, it might be appropriate to include an RPI increase formula in which case reference should be made to clause 5 of the previous precedent.

There is no formula in the clause relating to the payment of a bonus or commission in addition to the director's annual salary. The fruits of the director's efforts will be represented by the increase in the value of his shareholding in the company and the payment of dividends. Entitlement to a commission or bonus payment may work against the interests of the other shareholders since the payment would give the director an enhanced return ahead of the other shareholders and this may adversely affect the company's ability to finance its operations or expansion plans.

F. Other benefits (see p.207)

Entitlement to life insurance and private medical insurance cover does not depend on the director undergoing an annual medical examination as it is considered that the imposition of such an obligation would in the circumstances be inappropriate. It may be that the inclusion of any reference to a pension scheme would not be relevant as in the formative stage the company may not be able to operate such a scheme nor may such a scheme be contemplated, in which case clause 6.4 should be deleted and the director left to make his own private arrangements.

G. Incapacity, illness and sick pay (see p.208)

This clause provides for the payment of sick pay during a specific period of illness.

There is no provision for the company to terminate the agreement in the event that the period of illness continues beyond the specified period. If the company wishes to take action to determine the agreement because the director's absence is prolonged the shareholders would be able to pass the necessary ordinary resolution to remove the director. If that happened the company may have to pay compensation for wrongful termination of the agreement. If the director was incapacitated to the extent that he was unable to carry out his duties under the agreement it may be possible for the company to show that the agreement was terminated due to frustration of contract. If that could be proved it would have the effect of limiting the director's ability to bring Court action against the company, claiming compensation for alleged wrongful termination of the agreement. If the shareholders are minded to remove the director the implications of doing so must be carefully considered.

H. No conflict of interest (see p.208)

As the director is the mainstay of the company and its driving force it is important that his efforts should be employed fully on behalf of the company for the benefit of the other shareholders. Although the director has a fiduciary duty to the company which requires him to apply his efforts and his time for the benefit of the company as a whole the agreement should nevertheless contain a specific prohibition against the director putting himself into a position where a conflict of interest could arise. The very fact of the inclusion of such a clause may discourage the director from taking any action which may lead to a conflict of interest.

I. Termination of directorship (see p.209)

The effect of this clause is that should the directorship be terminated the agreement itself is terminated. It may not be relevant to include as one of the reasons for termination the fact that the director is not re-elected at an annual general meeting. If the company's articles include a paragraph in terms similar to regulation 84 of the Companies (Tables A to F) Regulations 1985, a managing director or a director holding any other executive office is not required to retire by rotation.

It would also follow that if the director is removed by resolution of the shareholders in general meeting and the agreement is terminated the removal and termination may, in the absence of compelling reasons justifying such action, have been carried out wrongfully and the director would accordingly be able to claim damages from the company in compensation for loss of office.

There is no provision for the director to retire at a specific age.

J. Non-solicitation, non-dealing and non-competition (see p.209, 210)

Reference should be made to the notes on equivalent clauses in the previous precedent where the drafting problems and the enforcement uncertainties are discussed. The inclusion of these provisions in this precedent is for the protection of the other shareholders. The director may well attempt to resist the inclusion of any such clauses within the agreement, not necessarily because he wants to be able to abuse his position but because he believes that the imposition of such clauses is wrong in principle.

It is debatable whether the shareholders would be able to insist on the inclusion of these clauses anyway. If the prospects for the company look particularly favourable, which presumably they would do if external shareholders were prepared to invest in it, they may take the view that it would be better to be involved than not and consequently they may take a fairly relaxed attitude to the imposition of any restraints on the director. If a prospective shareholder were to take too hard a line he may find himself excluded from the invitation to subscribe for shares in the company.

K. Employment Protection (Consolidation) Act 1978 (see p.210)

This is a sweeping-up clause to include those matters required to be notified by a company in accordance with the Act. For obvious reasons it would be inappropriate to define any grievance procedure to be followed or define what disciplinary rules or procedures should apply to the director in the situation envisaged in this precedent.

CHAPTER 11

CONTRACT OF EMPLOYMENT AND CONSULTANCY AGREEMENT

Introduction to contract of employment for senior salaried employee

The content of this precedent is a halfway house between a full director's service agreement and a basic contract of employment for general employees. Senior employees will require an individual contract of employment, firstly as a statement of what it is they are employed to do and what emoluments they will receive, and secondly as being commensurate with their status.

Senior employees, although not all, are likely to be involved in formulating part of a company's strategy and policy and will therefore obtain a fairly detailed knowledge of the company's business which could be useful to a competitor or which they could exploit for their own benefit. Consequently, provisions with regard to confidentiality should be included as should other restraints to protect the company's legitimate business interests for the duration of the employment and following its termination.

There is no requirement that the prior approval of shareholders of the terms of an employee's contract under section 319 of the Companies Act 1985 shall be obtained, nor do such contracts have to be made available for inspection by the company's shareholders as in the case of a director's service agreement, unless the employee is sufficiently senior and his role is tantamount to that of a shadow director. In that case his contract of employment would be subject to the same regime as a director who has been formally appointed. Listed companies are only obliged to disclose the remuneration paid to some employees within defined bands and to do so anonymously.

The precedent refers to 'the employee' which may be considered in some cases to be impersonal. The alternative would be to describe the employee as Mr   wherever the words 'the employee' appear and to make the minor changes to the wording that would be required if this redesignation was made, or substitute the word 'you' for the words 'the employee' and make the necessary consequential amendments.

Contract of employment for senior salaried employee

Date   19

The Parties:

          LTD/PLC whose registered office is at   ('the Company') (1) of ('the Employee') (2)

IT IS AGREED as follows :

1. Commencement of employment [and probationary period] Note A (see p.226)

1.1 The employment commenced on . [The subsequent [ ] [weeks] [months] shall constitute the probationary period and during the probationary period the employment may be terminated by either party giving to the other [ ] weeks' notice in writing.]

[1.2 On the satisfactory completion of the probationary period the employment shall be confirmed in writing and shall continue until either party gives written notice of [ ] months to the other.]

2. Duties and requirements of the employee Note B (see p.227)

The Employee shall:

[2.1 Be employed as [ ] and in that capacity shall [specify work to be performed].]

[2.1 Be employed as [ ] and in that capacity shall fulfil the requirements specified in the employment description set out in the [letter] [document] [annexed] [dated 19].]

2.2 Comply with the reasonable directions of [the head of department] [other designated person] [the Company] which may involve the Employee in carrying out some work in addition or which is different to that specified or referred to in clause 2.1.

2.3 Work at such place or places as the Company shall require and to travel to such designated locations.

3. Normal hours of work Note C (see p.227)

The normal hours of work are from a.m. to p.m. Monday to Friday. In addition, the Employee may be required to work outside or beyond normal working hours or at weekends or on holidays if reasonably required to do so for the furtherance of the business of the Company [for no additional payment] [and if extra payment is to be made for such work then such payment will be agreed at the time].

4. Salary Note D (see p.227)

4.1 The Company shall pay to the Employee a salary commencing at the rate of £ per annum payable in arrear by twelve equal instalments [on the [day] of every month] [on the date salaries are paid to the Company's employees generally].

4.2 The rate of salary shall be reviewed on or about the [specify] in each year.

Note E
(see p.227)

5. Bonus payments or commission

5.1 In addition to the annual salary the Company shall pay [at its discretion] [subject to satisfactory completion of the probationary period] a [bonus] [commission] computed on the following basis:

5.1.1 the [bonus] [commission] payment shall be limited to a maximum of [£] [a specified proportion of the current rate of annual salary];

5.1.2 the [bonus] [commission] payable shall be [ ] per cent of the amount by which the aggregate of the net profits of the Company as certified by the Company's auditors [who shall act as experts and not as arbitrators] exceeds £ in any one complete accounting reference period of the Company;

5.1.3 the [bonus] [commission] payments shall be paid within [twenty-eight] days of the receipt of the auditor's certificate;

5.1.4 the Company reserves the right to vary the basis on which [bonus] [commission] payments are made on giving [twenty-eight] days' notice to the Employee, and also reserves the right to cease making [bonus] [commission] payments on giving such period of notice to the Employee as it considers appropriate.

Note F
(see p.227)

6. Other benefits

The Company shall [subject to satisfactory completion of the probationary period]:

6.1 Provide life insurance cover for the Employee at the rate of [ ] times his basic annual salary from time to time [and shall procure that the proceeds of such insurance shall be paid to the Employee's spouse [and/ or other dependants] as the Company in its absolute discretion shall determine] on condition that the Employee shall as often as required, but not more than once in every year, attend for a medical examination and permit in writing a report of such examination to be sent in confidence to the Company.

6.2 Provide private medical insurance cover in accordance with the scheme [if any] operated by the Company from time to time subject to the Employee attending any medical examination on the same basis as in clause 6.1.

6.3 Provide accident insurance cover at the rate of [ ] times the Employee's annual salary from time to time.

6.4 Make contributions on behalf of the Employee to a pension scheme operated by the Company subject to the rules of such scheme as amended from time to time [conditional upon the Employee making as required all contributions due from him in accordance with the provisions of such scheme].

Note G
(see p.227)

7. Car

7.1 The Company shall [subject to satisfactory completion of the probationary period]:

7.1.1 for so long as the Employee is qualified to drive, provide a car reasonably suitable to enable the Employee to carry out his duties under this Agreement;

7.1.2 meet the cost of insurance, maintenance and all running expenses of the car [except fuel consumed during private use of the car].

7.2 The Employee shall take proper care of the car and ensure that it is correctly maintained and where appropriate shall do so in accordance with the terms of the manufacturer's warranty and will observe all provisions and conditions relating to the insurance policy.

8. Expenses

Note H (see p.228)

The Company shall:

8.1 Procure the repayment to or reimburse the Employee all travelling, accommodation and other expenses reasonably incurred by him in the proper performance of his duties provided that the Employee shall produce to the Company sufficient evidence of the payment by him of such expenses as the Company or its auditors may require.

[8.2 Reimburse the Employee the cost of subscriptions to all professional bodies to which he may belong.]

9. Holidays

9.1 The Employee shall be entitled to [ ] working days' holiday in each holiday year [set out dates of holiday year] to be taken at such time or times as shall be agreed and which shall be considered as the most convenient having regard to the requirements of the business of the Company. The Employee shall not be allowed to carry forward any holiday entitlement not taken to a subsequent year and such entitlement shall accordingly be lost, although at the Company's discretion it may make payment in lieu of such unused holiday entitlement.

9.2 [In respect of the holiday year in which the Employee commences his employment he shall be entitled to [ ] working days for each completed month worked during that year.] [In respect of the calendar year in which the Employee commences his employment he shall be entitled to such proportion of his annual holiday entitlement as the initial period of his employment bears to one calendar year.]

10. Incapacity, illness and sick pay

Note I (see p.228)

10.1 If the Employee shall at any time be incapacitated or prevented by illness, injury, accident or any other circumstances beyond his control from performing his duties under this Agreement for a total of up to [specify number of working days or weeks] absence in any period of [twelve] months the Company shall for such period continue to pay the Employee his current level of annual salary [such payment to be inclusive of any statutory sick pay or social security benefits] [and any entitlement to [bonus] [commission] payments].

10.2 If the Employee shall continue to be absent and unable to perform his duties beyond the period of absence referred to in clause 10.1 the Company may at its discretion discontinue payment in whole or part of his current level of annual salary [and any entitlement to [bonus] [commission] payments] until the incapacity or illness shall cease or the Company may at its option determine this Agreement by notice in writing specifying in such notice the date of termination of employment.

[10.3 If the Employee is unable to attend for work due to illness, injury or accident or for any other reason and he has not received permission to be absent he must notify or arrange to notify [designate department or person to be notified] by midday on the first day of his absence.]

[10.3 The procedure which the Employee will be required to follow where his absence is due to illness, injury or accident or any other reason is set out in the employment procedures handbook issued by the Company from time to time.]

11. Gifts and inducements offered by third parties

The Employee is prohibited from accepting any payment, gift or other inducement from any existing or prospective supplier to or customer of the Company.

12. Retirement age

Currently the retirement age for all of the Company's employees is [ ] years but is subject to alteration at the Company's discretion.

13. No conflict of interest

The Employee shall not:

13.1 Be directly or indirectly engaged, concerned or interested in any other business or be involved in any way in competition with the business of the Company or any business which is involved in the supply of goods or services to the Company or is a customer of the Company.

13.2 Carry out any other work or activities during the normal hours of work or any other time spent on the Company's premises outside the normal hours of work.

Note J (see p.228)

14. Inventions

14.1 In the event that the Employee makes or participates in making any discovery or invention which directly or indirectly affects or relates to the business of the Company or if the discovery or invention is capable of being used by the Company, the discovery or invention shall belong to the Company and the Employee shall immediately provide full details in writing to the Company and shall give assistance as may be necessary to enable the Company to benefit from the discovery or invention.

14.2 The Employee shall when requested by the Company apply or join in applying for the patent registration or such other protection as may be appropriate at the Company's expense.

14.3 The Employee irrevocably appoints the Company to be his attorney in his name and on his behalf to sign, execute or do any such instrument or thing and generally to use his name for the purpose of giving to the Company [or its nominee] the full benefit of the provisions of this clause, and a certificate in writing signed by any director or the company secretary shall so far as any third party is concerned be conclusive evidence that any instrument or act falls within the authority conferred by this clause.

15. Confidentiality

Note K (see p.228)

Except as may be necessary for the proper performance of his duties the Employee shall not either before or after the termination of his employment disclose, divulge or communicate to any person, firm or company any trade secret, manufacturing process or information relating to the business methods, customers or suppliers or finances or any other confidential information relating to the Company which the Employee has obtained during his employment provided that this clause shall not apply to any information which becomes public knowledge other than directly or indirectly through the default of the Employee.

[16. Dealings in shares or securities

The Employee shall observe and abide by any regulations which the Company makes or any code of conduct which it may issue from time to time relating to dealings in shares or other securities of the Company.]

17. Disciplinary rules and procedure

The Company's disciplinary rules and procedures which are available for inspection on request to the company secretary shall apply to the Employee.

18. Grievance procedure

The Employee shall initially refer any grievance [in writing] which he may have arising out of his employment under this Agreement to [designate person] who will determine what action, if any, should be taken in response to the Employee's grievance. In the event that the Employee is dissatisfied with the response and action (if any) taken by [designate person] he shall refer his grievance [in writing] to the managing director to determine.

Note L
(see p.228)

19. Termination and summary dismissal

The employment of the Employee may be terminated by the Company without prior written notice [the Company reserving the right to pay the Employee his current level of annual salary for the appropriate period in lieu of notice] if the Employee shall at any time:

19.1 Commit or be guilty of any serious or persistent breach or non-performance of any of his obligations under this Agreement.

19.2 Be guilty of any [gross] [serious] misconduct however arising which in the opinion of the Company reflects adversely on the Company.

19.3 Be convicted of any criminal offence which in the opinion of the Company impairs the fitness of the Employee to carry out his duties under this Agreement.

20. Consequences of termination

In the event that this Agreement is terminated for any reason:

20.1 The Employee shall immediately deliver to the nominated representative of the Company all documents (together with any copies) including notes, records, accounts, memoranda and papers and any other items or property relating to or concerning the business of the Company or any of its suppliers, agents, distributors or customers.

20.2 The Employee shall immediately return the car (if any) allocated to him to such location as the Company shall nominate and hand over the keys to a representative of the Company.

Note M
(see p.228)

21. Non-solicitation

The Employee shall not within [describe area or specific radius] and for a period of [ ] [months] [years] after ceasing his employment under this Agreement however caused, directly or indirectly whether on his own account or on behalf of another business entity:

21.1 Solicit or procure business from any person, firm or company who or which within a period of [ ] year[s] preceding the termination of this Agreement was a customer or client of the Company or who dealt generally or occasionally with the Company and with whom or which the Employee was personally concerned during the term of his employment under this Agreement.

21.2 Solicit the services of or endeavour to encourage any person who shall have been a director, officer, employee or consultant of the Company within the period of [ ] year[s] preceding the termination of this Agreement, to leave the Company's employment.

Note M
(see p.228)

22. Non-dealing

The Employee shall not within [describe area or specific radius] and for a period of [two] years after ceasing his employment under this Agreement however caused, directly or indirectly carry on business or deal with any person, firm or company who or which was a customer, client, supplier, agent or distributor of the Company and with whom or which the Employee was personally concerned during the term of his employment under this Agreement.

23. Non-competition

Note M (see p.228)

The Employee shall not within [describe area or specific radius] and for a period of [ ] [months] [years] after ceasing his employment under this Agreement however caused be engaged or assist in carrying on any business which competes with the business of the Company or otherwise be interested or concerned either directly or indirectly whether as a consultant, employee, director, partner, adviser, agent or in any other capacity in or with any person, firm or company whose business competes with the business of the Company.

24. Declaration of reasonableness of clauses 21, 22 and 23

The parties declare that they consider the application of the restrictions imposed by clauses 21, 22 and 23 to be reasonable and no greater than is necessary for the protection of the business of the Company but in the event that unforeseen changes occur or Court judgments are delivered which would render any of the provisions invalid or void the parties declare that each of the covenants are to be regarded as separate and severable and where appropriate a covenant shall be amended to the extent necessary to make such covenant as amended or modified effective and enforceable.

25. Variation in the terms of this agreement

Note N (see p.229)

The right is reserved to the Company to make changes to any of the provisions of this agreement and the Employee shall be notified of such changes in writing. Where a proposed change is not material the Company shall notify the Employee of the date on which the change is to become operative. Where a proposed change is material the Company shall give the Employee at least [twenty-eight] days' written notice of the proposed change and unless the Employee objects in writing within the period specified in the notice, the Employee shall be deemed to have accepted such change.

26. Employment Protection (Consolidation) Act 1978 statutory particulars

The particulars which are required to be given pursuant to section 1 of the Act and which have not already been given are:

A contracting out certificate issued under the Social Security Pensions Act 1975 is [not] in force in respect of the employment.

THE COMMON SEAL of LTD/PLC was hereunto affixed in the presence of:

Director

Secretary

or

EXECUTED AS A DEED by and on behalf of LTD/PLC by

Director

Secretary

or

SIGNED for and on behalf of LTD/PLC by

Director

EXECUTED AS A DEED by the Employee in the presence of:

or

SIGNED by the Employee

Explanatory notes on contract of employment for senior salaried employee

A. Commencement of employment (and probationary period) (see p.219)

The contract must state the date on which the employment commences or commenced. The letter of offer of employment on page 135 is drafted on the basis that no formal contract of employment would be concluded until the probationary period had been satisfactorily completed. The alternative would be to conclude the contract at the commencement of the employment but to incorporate provisions relating to the probationary period. This clause therefore provides for either alternative. If the contract is to be coupled with the offer of employment on the basis set out in the precedent offer letter this clause will simply read 'the employment commenced on '.

B. Duties and requirements of the employee (see p.219)

A definition of the job title or duties to be performed can either be set out in a separate letter or other document or in the agreement itself. Although it would be implied that a senior employee would be flexible in the range of duties which he would undertake, nevertheless it would be as well to include a provision to the effect that he is obliged to carry out some work which is different or in addition to that specified if the company from time to time requests him to do so.

C. Normal hours of work (see p.219)

If the company operates a flexi time system then the rules governing its operation should be set out here. Any period for lunch should also be specified.

D. Salary (see p.219)

This clause does not include any provision for increasing the salary in accordance with RPI. If it is appropriate that it should do so then the relative clauses in the director's service agreement precedent on pages 187–188 can be incorporated.

E. Bonus payments or commission (see p.220)

What constitutes net profits for the purpose of computing the bonus or commission depends on what the auditors certify. There is no formula to which the auditors need adhere and to that extent the company and the auditors have considerable flexibility. Payment should be subject to the satisfactory completion of the probationary period if this is relevant.

If the employee is a sales manager the clause can be amended to include reference to sales targets and the like but such provisions will vary considerably from one company to another depending on the nature of the company's business and its products.

F. Other benefits (see p.220)

The provision of the benefit should be subject to the satisfactory completion of the probationary period if this is relevant.

G. Car (see p.220)

There is no obligation in the clause as drafted to replace the car at any particular point or to provide the employee with a specific car and model.

H. Expenses (see p.221)

There is no provision for reimbursement of telephone charges incurred by the employee when using his telephone from home. If it is appropriate for this to be included then it should be.

I. Incapacity, illness and sick pay (see p.221)

Although in general terms the clause is similar to clause 11 in the director's service agreement precedent on page 191 the employee is additionally subject to a requirement to report his inability to attend for work within a specified time or to do so by reference to any employment procedures handbook or rule book which the company may issue.

J. Inventions (see p.222)

The inclusion of this clause is not likely to be relevant in many situations but where there is any prospect that the employee will make any invention or other discovery it is good practice to include the clause even though the company could rely on the provisions of the Patents Act 1977. Where the clause is included, the agreement should be executed as a deed.

K. Confidentiality (see p.223)

In view of the status of the employee and the degree of knowledge which he will acquire it is important to include a confidentiality provision, even though to some extent the obligations would be implied.

L. Termination and summary dismissal (see p.224)

There could be a conflict between the provisions of this clause and the requirements of the company's own disciplinary procedures. The disciplinary procedures, if any, will be publicised and up-dated from time to time and will specify how alleged disciplinary breaches will be investigated, dealt with and how the appeals machinery will operate. The rules may also include definitions of what constitutes ordinary misconduct and serious misconduct and incapacity or incapability. If such procedures have been formulated it would be necessary to comply with them even though the agreement provides for summary dismissal in certain circumstances, otherwise the employee may be entitled to bring a claim for unfair dismissal to an Industrial Tribunal.

M. Non-solicitation, non-dealing and non-competition (see pp.224–225)

Reference should be made to the notes on these clauses on pages 202–203. It will be noted that the non-solicitation and non-dealing clauses are qualified and apply only to those customers, clients, suppliers, agents or distributors with whom or which the employee was personally concerned during the term of his employment. It is considered that there is a greater chance of the clauses being enforceable if challenged if their effect is restricted in this way. The period for which all three clauses should be expressed to operate should be no more than two years in each case.

N. Changes to terms of employment (see p.225)

Although the company would want to retain flexibility there is a limit to which it can go in the sense that one party to a contract cannot unilaterally change its terms unless provision to that effect is contained within the contract and then only so far as is reasonable. There is the risk that such a clause could fall foul of the Unfair Contract Terms Act of 1977 but so long as it is applied reasonably it should be upheld if challenged.

Introduction to agreement with business consultant

This precedent is for use where a company wishes to obtain the services of a business consultant either on an *ad hoc* basis or for a determinable period of time. The company may, for example, require a marketing consultant to devise a marketing plan or strategy for its products, or it may need to make a temporary appointment to replace the finance director or financial controller who is absent or incapacitated but is expected to be able to return to work eventually.

There are a number of consultants who, for one reason or another, operate on a freelance basis as a way of professional life and, consequently, a consultant may offer his own terms and conditions as part of the proposed arrangement. If the need to secure the services of, say, a financial controller arises, there may be some urgency and a temporary replacement will have to be found quickly. Unless the company secretary has access to a precedent of a suitable agreement the chances are that he may feel more inclined to accept the terms and conditions of the consultant which may be more onerous than would normally be acceptable.

The use of this precedent should help to put the company secretary 'in the driving seat' in the negotiations with the consultant, although there is no provision for some of the consultant's own terms and conditions to be incorporated. In that way it should be possible to strike a balance which is satisfactory to both parties. It would also mean that all the arrangements are embodied in the one document rather than in correspondence. If the consultant does not have his own form of agreement or terms and conditions or they are not to be used, then the definition in clause 1.1 should be deleted as should clause 2 and the remaining clauses renumbered accordingly.

Although the precedent is drafted on the basis that the consultant is an individual it could be used where the consultant operates through the medium of a limited company, in which case the necessary amendments can be made, for example, by substituting 'he' with the word 'it'. Appropriate amendments should also be made if the consultant is female.

This kind of agreement is a contract *for* services rather than a contract *of* service. The distinction is important because if the agreement were to be construed as a contract of service it would put the company and the consultant in an employer–employee relationship which neither would want. It is important, therefore, that the agreement be clearly framed as a contract for services. One element in determining whether a contract is one of service or for services is the degree of control exercised by the party requiring the services over the party providing them. Control, however, is only one aspect to be considered. Other factors which would point to the contract being one for services are where the provider assumes some financial risk or if he supplies and uses his own equipment or he is not and could not be regarded as part of the organisation retaining him.

The nature of the relationship also has a particular bearing on the way in which the payments made to the consultant will be taxed and whether they fall to be taxed under schedule D or schedule E. There is also a tax impact from the company's point of view in that where the relationship is one of a contract for services the company would not be required to pay employer's National Insurance Contributions. If the Inland Revenue were to examine an arrangement to see what the reality of the situation is it is more likely to come to the conclusion that it is one of part time employment and not a genuine contract for services unless the consultant has more than one source of income and can clearly demonstrate that he has freedom of movement. In practice, most consultants that a company would be likely to retain should be able to demonstrate that they are consultants to a number of different clients apart from the company.

The consultant will want to ensure that any risk of a contract of employment arising inadvertently is minimised. On the other hand, as the consultant will learn a great deal about the way in which the company operates, its products, markets, finances, trade secrets and the like, some provision should be included to restrain the consultant from divulging or using such information, either for the duration of the arrangement or after its conclusion. The company should therefore impose a confidentiality covenant in order to protect its legitimate business interests.

It should be noted that the Supply of Goods and Services Act 1982 applies to a contract where a supplier of services has agreed to provide those services. The 1982 Act implies certain terms; for example there is an implied term that the supplier will carry out the services with reasonable care and skill and will do so within a reasonable time if no time for doing so is stated in the contract. These matters are specifically included or dealt with in the precedent and there would consequently be no need to rely on the provisions of the 1982 Act.

Agreement with business consultant

Dated 19 .

The Parties:

LTD/PLC whose registered office is at ('the Company') (1)

whose address is ('the Consultant') (2)

IT IS AGREED as follows:

1. Definitions and interpretation Note A (see p.235)

1.1 These terms and expressions shall have the following meanings in this Agreement:

'CONSULTANCY SERVICES' means [describe specifically or incorporate by reference to separate document or schedule if applicable].

'CONSULTANT'S TERMS AND CONDITIONS' means the Consultant's terms and conditions attached to this Agreement.

'DAY' means the period between the hours of 9 a.m. and 5.30 p.m., where appropriate for the purposes of clauses 5 and 6.

1.2 The headings to the clauses are for convenience and reference only and shall not affect their interpretation.

2. The consultant's terms and conditions

Only conditions [refer to specifically by numbering or other means] of the Consultant's Terms and Conditions shall apply to this Agreement and be incorporated.

3. Appointment of consultant

The Company appoints the Consultant who shall provide the Consultancy Services in accordance with the provisions of this Agreement.

4. Duration Note B (see p.235)

This Agreement shall commence [with immediate effect] [on] and shall continue [for a period of [months] [years] [or] until the Consultancy Services have been rendered by the Consultant [whichever shall first occur] [until terminated by either party giving written notice to the other of not less than [ ] complete calendar month[s]].

Note C (see p.235)

5. The consultant's duties and obligations

The Consultant shall:

[5.1 Provide the Consultancy Services [for as many hours] [on as many days] per [week] [month] as may be necessary at such times and at such venues as the Company may reasonably require, although the Consultant shall not be obliged to spend more than [ ] [hours] [days] per [week] [month] in doing so unless the parties shall otherwise agree in writing.]

[5.1 Provide the Consultancy Services on [ ] days per [week] [month] at such venues as the company may reasonably require.]

5.2 Provide the Consultancy Services with care and in a proper and professional manner.

[5.3 [Arrange] [Maintain] professional negligence insurance cover in the minimum sum of £ to cover the liability of the Consultant in respect of any default, negligence or omission by him in the course of providing the Consultancy Services and shall within [seven] days of being requested to do so provide the Company with a copy of such policy and written confirmation showing that such policy is still in force and effect.]

5.4 Comply with the reasonable requirements of the Company as may be requested from time to time by [named individual or title of Company's nominee] provided that in doing so the Consultant shall not be subject to the direction or control of the Company.

Note D (see p.235)

6. The company's obligations

The Company shall:

[6.1 Pay a fee of £ together with VAT if applicable to the Consultant payable as follows [set out frequency and method of payments].]

[6.1 Pay the Consultant at the rate of £ per [hour] [day] [week] [month] together with VAT if applicable within [fourteen] days of receipt of the Consultant's invoices which he may render at any time after the last working day of each calendar month.]

6.2 Reimburse the Consultant all travelling expenses [and other expenses] incurred by him in carrying out his obligations under this Agreement provided he shall produce receipts or other evidence of such expenditure to the Company.

6.3 Provide the Consultant with sufficient office accommodation [and secretarial assistance], including the use of a telephone to enable the Consultant to perform the consultancy services.

6.4 Provide the Consultant with all necessary information in connection with the Company's business that he may reasonably require.

7. Confidentiality

The Consultant shall not disclose or divulge or allow to be disclosed or divulged to any person, firm or company (other than as may be permitted in accordance with clause 16) any information which he receives or obtains relating to the Company's business, finances, trade secrets, manufacturing methods and processes, technology, or any other information relating to the Company including the names and addresses of any customers or clients of or suppliers to the Company, and shall keep confidential all such information both during the period of this Agreement and after its termination however caused.

8. **Termination** Note E (see p.236)

The Company may at its sole discretion terminate this Agreement in writing immediately or on giving such period of notice in writing as the Company considers appropriate if the Consultant:

8.1 Is in breach of the terms of this Agreement where although such breach is capable of remedy, it has not been so remedied by him within twenty-one days of receipt of the notice from the Company specifying the breach and requiring its remedy.

8.2 Is incompetent or guilty of gross or serious misconduct or negligence in providing the Consultancy Services.

8.3 Fails or refuses to carry out any requirement reasonably and properly requested of him by [named individual or title of Company's nominee].

8.4 Is unable to provide the Consultancy Services for a period of [ ] weeks due to illness, injury or other incapacity.

9. **Rights and obligations prior to termination**

On the termination of this Agreement all pre-existing rights and obligations which have accrued to or by either of the parties under this Agreement shall continue in full force and effect.

10. **Delivery and return of documents and other property on termination**

The Consultant shall at the expiration or termination of this Agreement however caused immediately deliver to the Company or return to it all documents and any copies, including memoranda, notes, accounts, records, specifications and papers and any other items or property relating to or belonging to the Company which the Consultant may have in his possession or be under his control.

11. **Arbitration**

All differences or disputes which may arise in connection with this Agreement, or its construction or effect shall be referred to a single arbitrator to be agreed upon by the parties but in default of their agreement the President for the time being of the Chartered Institute of Arbitrators shall nominate an arbitrator in accordance with the

Arbitration Acts 1950–1979 or any statutory modification or re-enactment for the time being in force.

12. Notices

Any notice or communication shall be sent by ordinary first class post, telex, facsimile transmission or by such other means as may be appropriate in the circumstances, and in the case of a notice served by first class post it shall be deemed to have been received by the party to whom it was sent forty-eight hours after posting and in the case of any other form of transmission twenty-four hours after sending.

13. Entire agreement

This Agreement constitutes the entire agreement between the parties with respect to the matters dealt with and supersedes any previous agreement between the parties in relation to such matters.

Note F (see p.236)

14. Tax status of consultant

The Consultant acknowledges that he is an independent contractor and not an employee of the Company and that he shall personally meet all liability for income tax, VAT, national insurance contributions and the like.

15. Restriction on assignment by consultant

This Agreement cannot be assigned by the Consultant.

16. Sub-contracting by consultant

The Consultant shall be personally responsible for providing the Consultancy Services, although he may delegate in part to members of his staff or to another party with the consent of the Company provided such other party enters into an appropriate confidentiality agreement with the Company in terms similar to those contained in clause 7.

17. Law

This Agreement shall be governed by English law.

SIGNED by
on behalf of the Company

SIGNED by the Consultant

Explanatory notes on agreement with business consultant

A. Definitions and interpretation (see p.231)

As mentioned in the introduction, if the consultant does not have his own terms and conditions then the reference should be deleted as should clause 2 and the remaining clauses renumbered accordingly. It is important to define what constitutes a day for the purposes of clause 5. The hours stated are arbitrary and do not include any provision for lunch and there is no distinction between weekdays and weekends or bank holidays. The definition may therefore need modification.

B. Duration (see p.231)

The duration of the agreement can be for a specific period of time which may be weeks, months or years or for so long as it takes the consultant to render the consultancy services, or it can continue for so long as it suits both parties.

C. The consultant's duties and obligations (see p.232)

Clause 5.1 is in the alternative. The first version is more appropriate where an overall fee is to be paid and the consultant has to provide the services within that figure, although he may be entitled to reimbursement of travelling expenses (and other expenses) in addition. If, however, the fee is all inclusive clause 6.2 should be deleted.

The second alternative is for use where some continuity is required and the services are to be provided on a regular basis.

Although the consultant will retain control over the way in which he provides the services there will be situations in which it would be reasonable for the company to be able on occasion to make requests or suggestions to him as to the way in which he organises or carries out his work. The company may, for example, wish to relocate the consultant to another office or require him to participate in a practice evacuation of the building. The company must not, however, reserve the right to direct or control the consultant.

Although it may not always be appropriate or practicable to require the consultant to arrange professional negligence insurance cover, where it is prudent to do so the company should make it a requirement if it can be agreed.

D. The company's obligations (see p.232)

It will depend upon the nature of the services to be provided as to what office accommodation and back-up facilities the consultant can reasonably expect the company to provide in addition to making the payments to him. Some consultants will have their own office facilities and will only need to visit the company's premises to attend meetings and report to members of the company's personnel from time to time.

E. Termination (see p.233)

Termination is expressed to be at the option and discretion of the company only. The consultant may require that he has the option to terminate the agreement in certain circumstances, particularly if payment is not made by the company in accordance with the agreement. This is something to be negotiated at the time.

F. Tax status of consultant (see p.234)

There should be a statement confirming that the consultant acknowledges that he is an independent contractor and not an employee of the company, although in the absence of such a declaration a contract for services would be implied in most cases. However, where the situation is border line this provision must be included even though it may not be conclusive. If the Inland Revenue were to query the nature of the arrangement it would look to the substance of the relationship rather than the way in which it is described.

CHAPTER 12

OTHER SPECIFIC AGREEMENTS

Introduction to agreement for the development and evaluation of a prototype or pre-production item of equipment

Companies, particularly in the engineering and related industries from time to time require experimental or pre-production prototypes or equipment to be assessed and evaluated but may not have the specialist capacity to be able to carry out the function internally. It may therefore be necessary to contract out this work to a third party which has the requisite technical skills and resources. The precedent which follows will need to be adapted to take account of the particular characteristics of the prototype or equipment which is to be evaluated, improved or developed but it does provide the basic structure for this type of arrangement and attempts to strike a reasonable balance between the interests of the company on the one hand and the development/evaluating company (referred to as 'DE' in the precedent) on the other.

The way in which the payment arrangements will be structured will also depend on the nature and the technical complexity of the prototype or equipment, the length of time which the evaluation process is expected to take, the projected financial outlay of DE and the relative bargaining position of the two parties.

Many of the details to be incorporated into the agreement will be of a practical rather than a legal nature. In some cases the company will have considerable input into the way in which the evaluation or development programme is formulated and is to be carried through and in other cases the company will have little input, leaving it to the discretion of DE but preferably within certain financial limits and time constraints.

The precedent is drafted on the basis that the company is not in a position to define a programme at the outset and requires DE to carry out an initial assessment of the prototype or equipment and to prepare and submit a report within a specific period of time. In the light of that report the company can either decline to continue with the arrangement or, if it considers that the initial results are promising, it can discuss with DE a further programme of work but will not be committed to pay for the further work if the likely costs are prohibitive or as a result of further consideration the expected financial return is only marginal.

If there is not to be a two stage arrangement, refer to explanatory note B on page 244 which sets out the replacement clause to be used in that situation.

If DE does not have its own form of agreement or terms and conditions or they are not to be used then the definition in clause 1.1 should be deleted as should clause 2 and the remaining clauses renumbered accordingly.

Agreement for the development and evaluation of a prototype or pre-production item of equipment

Dated 19

The Parties:

LTD/PLC whose registered office is at ('the Company') (1)

LTD/PLC whose [principal place of business] [registered office] is at ('DE') (2)

IT IS AGREED as follows:

1. Definitions and interpretation

1.1 These terms and expressions shall have the following meanings in this Agreement:

'DE's TERMS AND CONDITIONS' means DE's terms and conditions attached to this Agreement.

'THE PROTOTYPE OR ITEM OF EQUIPMENT' means [define, or if more appropriate include by reference to separate document to be annexed].

1.2 The headings to the clauses are for convenience and reference only and shall not affect their interpretation.

2. DE's terms and conditions

Only conditions (refer to specifically by numbering or other means) of DE's Terms and Conditions shall apply to this Agreement and be incorporated.

3. Appointment of DE

The Company appoints DE to carry out its obligations in accordance with the provisions of this Agreement.

4. Duration

This Agreement shall commence [with immediate effect] [on] and shall continue [for a period of [ ] months] [years] [until DE has fulfilled its obligations to the satisfaction of the Company] [until terminated by either party giving written notice to the other of not less than [ ] complete calendar month[s]]. Note A (see p.24

Note B
(see p.244)

5. DE's duties and obligations

5.1 DE shall:

5.1.1 carry out electrical, mechanical, engineering and other tests and make an initial evaluation of the Prototype/Equipment and provide a report of such evaluation in writing to the Company within [ ] [weeks] [months];

5.1.2 conduct the tests to be carried out in the course of the initial evaluation in such manner as DE considers to be appropriate although it shall take into account any proposal or request which may be made by [the Company's nominated engineer[s]] [specify person or persons by name] to the extent which it is reasonably practical to do, but where such proposals or requests are rejected or not acted upon DE shall state the reasons in its initial evaluation report;

5.1.3 in the event that a further programme is agreed between the Company and DE following the Company's appraisal of the initial evaluation report, carry out modifications and improvements to the Prototype/Equipment and conduct such further tests as may be required in accordance with the further programme and in consultation with the Company's nominated engineer[s] and shall comply with the appropriate standards of current practice and such regulations as may be applicable;

5.1.4 provide comprehensive interim reports within [seven] days of the end of each month in which testing and evaluation work has been done describing in sufficient detail the nature of the work that has been carried out to the Prototype/Equipment during that month to enable the Company to assess and review the progress which has been made;

5.1.5 allow the Company's personnel to attend at its premises for the duration of this Agreement in order to review and assess progress at times to be agreed but at least once in each [week] [month] and make available qualified members of its staff able to assist the Company's personnel in carrying out their review and assessment.

Note C
(see p.245)

5.2 DE shall ensure that the Prototype/Equipment is at all times maintained in a safe condition and secure and agrees to make good any damage or loss caused by accident, omission, default, theft or negligence however arising and if unable to make good at its own cost any such damage or loss it shall indemnify the Company in respect of the cost incurred in arranging for the necessary repairs to be carried out or a replacement made.

6. The company's obligations

The Company shall:

6.1 Provide suitably experienced and qualified members of its staff to attend meetings with members of the staff of DE and to assist DE as may reasonably be required from time to time.

6.2 Notify DE of any information which comes into the possession of the

Company and which is relevant to DE in carrying out its obligations under this Agreement.

6.3 Make payment to DE within [twenty-eight] days of the receipt of each invoice rendered by it [in respect of each calendar month], specifying in sufficient detail the nature of the work for which payment is claimed, the time taken and the number and grade of personnel employed in carrying out the work.

6.4 Respond to DE within [four] weeks of receipt of the initial evaluation report stating either that it does not require any further work to be carried out and that this Agreement shall be terminated or that it wishes to discuss with DE the formulation of a further programme of development and evaluation work and to assess with DE the costs which will be involved, and if following such discussions the Company requires DE to carry out a further programme of work, it will authorise DE to do so in writing, specifying the payments to be made, but if not this Agreement shall be terminated by the Company on giving written notice to that effect.

7. Design and intellectual property rights Note D (see p.245)

If in the process of carrying out its obligations under this Agreement DE makes any improvement in the design of the Prototype/Equipment or in its technology which is capable of registration under the Registered Designs Act 1949, the Copyright, Designs and Patents Act 1988, or the Patents Act of 1949 and 1977 DE acknowledges that all such rights belong to the Company and DE shall assist the Company [without charge] in making application for registration of any such rights either under the current legislation or any modification or re-enactment of it for the time being in force.

8. Confidentiality Note E (see p.245)

DE shall not during the period of this Agreement, nor after its termination, however caused disclose or divulge or allow to be disclosed or divulged to any other person, firm or company information which it receives or obtains and which is confidential and relates to the Company's business generally or the Prototype/Equipment in particular, except as may be necessary to fulfil its obligations under this Agreement and provided that the consent of the Company is first obtained and that any such other party or person enters into an appropriate confidentiality agreement with the Company in terms similar to those contained in this clause.

9. Termination

The Company may at its sole discretion terminate this Agreement in writing immediately or on giving such period of notice in writing as the Company considers appropriate if DE:

9.1 Is in breach of the terms of this Agreement where although such breach is capable of remedy it has not been so remedied within twenty-one days of receipt of the notice from the Company specifying the breach and requiring its remedy.

9.2 Fails or refuses to carry out its obligations in such a manner or method as may reasonably and properly be required of it by [named individual or title of Company's nominee].

9.3 Fails to act upon or incorporate relevant information supplied by the Company.

9.4 Goes into liquidation or if a receiver of its assets is appointed.

10. Change of control of DE

If DE is acquired by any third party which does not have control of DE at the commencement of this Agreement, this Agreement shall terminate with effect from the date the acquisition of control occurred unless the Company elects in writing that this Agreement should continue.

11. Rights and obligations prior to termination

On the termination of this Agreement all pre-existing rights and obligations which have accrued to or by either of the parties under this Agreement shall continue in full force and effect.

Note F (see p.245)

12. Delivery and return of documents and materials on termination

In the event of the expiration or the termination of this Agreement however caused DE shall immediately deliver or return to the Company:

12.1 All documents and any copies, including memoranda, notes, manuals, reports, design drawings, specifications and papers and any other items or property belonging to the Company which relate in any way to the Company's business and/or the Prototype/Equipment and which DE may have in its possession or be under its control.

12.2 All materials (used and unused) and other equipment [specify in detail] devised either by the Company or DE for use in carrying out the testing and evaluation of the Prototype/Equipment.

13. Counter claim or set off following termination

The Company shall pay to DE any amounts due to it which are not in dispute unless the Company has a right of counter claim or set off against DE in which case no such payments shall be made.

14. Arbitration

All differences or disputes which may arise in connection with this Agreement, or its construction or effect shall be referred to a single arbitrator to be agreed upon by the parties, but in default of their agreement the President for the time being of the Chartered Institute of Arbitrators shall nominate an arbitrator in accordance with the Arbitration Acts 1950–1979 or any statutory modification or re-enactment for the time being in force.

15. Notices

Any notice, instruction or communication shall be sent by ordinary first class post, telex, facsimile transmission or by such other means as may be appropriate in the circumstances, and in the case of a notice served by first class post it shall be deemed to have been received by the party to whom it was sent forty-eight hours after posting, and in the case of any other form of transmission twenty-four hours after sending.

16. Entire agreement

This Agreement constitutes the entire agreement between the parties with respect to the matters dealt with and supersedes any previous agreement between the parties in relation to such matters.

17. Force majeure

In the event that either of the parties are unable to carry out all or any of their obligations under this Agreement as a result of matters arising beyond their reasonable control neither party shall have a claim against the other provided that notice of the event or events is given to the party not affected within forty-eight hours.

18. Restriction on assignment

This Agreement is not capable of being assigned by DE.

19. Sub-contracting by DE

DE may delegate in part to specialist sub-contractors with the consent of the Company provided that a written confidentiality agreement with the Company is entered into by any such specialist sub-contractor in terms similar to those contained in clause 8.

20. Law

This Agreement shall be governed by English law.

SIGNED by on behalf of the Company

SIGNED by on behalf of DE

Explanatory notes on agreement for the development and evaluation of a prototype or pre-production item of equipment

A. Duration (see p.239)

The period fixed for the duration of the arrangement will depend on a number of factors, one of which will be how often the parties have dealt with each other in the past and to what extent they have built up a degree of trust. If DE has to incur significant expense in setting up and designing equipment for the purpose of carrying out the work it may want the security of an agreement for a realistic term, although if a specific period is incorporated this would conflict with the flexibility that the company would require to enable it to decide whether or not to continue following receipt of the initial evaluation report. Alternatively, the agreement can continue until DE has fulfilled its obligations to the satisfaction of the company but this would be to the benefit of the company and may not be acceptable to DE. A further option is that the agreement simply continues until either party gives to the other a specified written period of notice.

B. DE's duties and obligations (see p.240)

DE is to prepare the initial evaluation report in consultation with the company's own engineers or technical personnel. The company's personnel are to be allowed access to attend at DE's premises for the duration of the agreement (which would include any not only the period which it takes to carry out the initial evaluation but during the course of any further programme which may be agreed) and to be provided with information. If such a provision was not incorporated DE would be entitled to refuse access to the Company's personnel other than by specific invitation, at its discretion.

Any subsequent programme for further work is to be carried out only if the company decides after discussion with DE as provided in clause 6.4.

If there is not to be a two stage arrangement and DE is to carry out a full programme from the outset, clauses 5.1.1., 5.1.2 and 5.1.3 should be deleted and a new clause 5.1.1 inserted as follows:

> Carry out in accordance with the appropriate standards of current practice and such regulations as may be applicable such engineering, mechanical, electrical and other tests as may be necessary to evaluate the design and capacity of the prototype/equipment and make recommendations as to how the design and capacity can be improved or modifications made so that the prototype/equipment can be manufactured or brought into production in a viable form, and shall take into account any request or proposal which may be made by [the Company's nominated engineer[s]] [specify person or persons by name] to the extent which it is reasonably practicable to do but where the

proposals or requests are rejected or not acted upon DE shall state the reasons in an interim report.

Clauses 5.1.4 and 5.1.5 should be renumbered 5.1.2 and 5.1.3 respectively. It also follows that clause 6.4 will be deleted.

C. Safe and secure maintenance of the prototype or equipment (see p.240)

Although the company's own insurance cover may be sufficient it would be prudent to include in the agreement an obligation on the part of DE, not only to keep the prototype/equipment safe and secure at all times but also to indemnify the company in respect of any loss or damage.

D. Design and intellectual property rights (see p.241)

Although the probability is that any invention or design rights capable of being patented or registered would vest in the company automatically, it is advisable to include in the agreement a specific acknowledgment by DE that this is so and that it will assist the company in making any appropriate applications for registration without further charge if the company requires it to do so. This may meet with resistance from DE in which case the necessary modification to the wording can be made.

E. Confidentiality (see p.241)

It is recognised that DE may from time to time need to employ specialist sub-contractors or involve the assistance of a third party but its ability to do so should be controlled.

F. Delivery and return of documents and materials on termination (see p.242)

This clause will need to be amplified or expanded to take account of the particular nature of the prototype or equipment which is being evaluated or developed.

Introduction to agreement for the cleaning of office/factory/ work place

This precedent is on the face of it fairly prosaic but the importance of such an agreement should not be minimised or overlooked. An agreement brings some order into the arrangement which otherwise would be missing. It deals with the questions of what the contractor is to do, when it is to do it, what the rate of payment will be for the various kinds of work and when payment will be made; and, importantly, specifies the insurance arrangements which should be made to cover not only the contractor's liability to its own employees but the company's liability under the Occupier's Liability Act 1957. Company secretaries are particularly concerned with the occupation and use of their company's property and to ensure that any legal responsibilities or obligations are complied with or observed.

Although in many situations the work to be carried out by the contractor will be of a relatively unskilled nature, important contractual and other relationships arise as a consequence of the company allowing a third party and its employees access to its premises at times when the premises may be otherwise unattended.

The principal statute which governs the company's duty to a visitor to its premises is the Occupier's Liability Act 1957. There is no doubt that a factory owned by a company would come within the description of premises covered by the Act. A company's duty under the Act relates to a visitor who is on the premises as a result of the invitation or permission of the company.

The 1957 Act imposes a duty of care which is defined as a duty to take such care as in all the circumstances of the case is reasonable to see that the visitor will be reasonably safe in using the premises for the purposes for which he is invited or permitted by the occupier to be there. There is, however, a specific proviso which applies to an independent contractor whose work is of an inherently hazardous nature and this would include a cleaning contractor where the work to be performed involves working at a height or in a precarious position. It is reasonable for the occupier to expect that such a person will be aware of the risks which are normally associated with the type of work to be carried out and will take the necessary precautions.

The 1957 Act entitles an occupier to modify or exclude its duty either by notice, warning or by contract. The scope for doing so, however, has been cut down by the Unfair Contract Terms Act 1977 and section 2 provides that an occupier cannot by contract or notice exclude or restrict its liability for death or personal injury resulting from negligence. Further, section 3 of the 1957 Act provides that where an occupier has by contract to permit people who are not parties to the contract to enter the premises it cannot exclude or restrict its duty of care to such people by the contract.

The duty of care extends not only to ensuring that the areas within which the invitees or visitors will be working are reasonably safe but those areas in which they would have to be in order to get to and from those parts of the premises where they were working.

It would nevertheless be advisable for a prudent company secretary to draw the attention of the contractor or its employees to any potentially hazardous parts of the company's premises or machinery.

The company's insurance cover should be carefully reviewed and any deficiencies in the extent of the cover or amounts payable made good and any uncertainties clarified. The agreement imposes on the contractor an obligation not only to insure its employees against personal injury and accident but to insure against any damage which it causes to the company's property. Although this requirement may introduce an element of duplication in the insurance cover, that would be preferable from the company's point of view as there will be the two options to consider in the event of an accident to persons or damage to property. The contractor is also required to produce copies of the relative insurance policy or a summary of its terms on request by the company.

If the contractor does not have its own form of agreement or terms and conditions, or they are not to be used, then the definition in clause 1.1 should be deleted, as should clause 2, and the remaining clauses renumbered accordingly.

If the contractor is an individual the appropriate minor adjustments to the wording should be made.

Agreement for the cleaning of office/factory/work place

Dated 19 .

The Parties:

LTD/PLC whose registered office is at ('the Company') (1)

LTD/PLC whose [principal place of business] [registered office] is at ('the Contractor') (2)

IT IS AGREED as follows:

1. Definitions and interpretation

1.1 These terms and expressions shall have the following meanings in this Agreement:

'CLEANING SERVICES' means the services referred to in clause 6 of this Agreement.

'THE CONTRACTOR'S TERMS AND CONDITIONS' means the Contractor's terms and conditions attached to this Agreement.

'THE COMPANY'S PREMISES' [set out fully by description or by address].

1.2 The headings to the clauses are for convenience and reference only and do not affect their interpretation.

2. The contractor's terms and conditions
Only conditions [refer to specifically by numbering or other means] of the Contractor's Terms and Conditions shall apply to this Agreement and be incorporated.

3. Appointment of contractor
The Company appoints the Contractor to provide the Cleaning Services in accordance with the provisions of this Agreement.

Note A (see p.251)

4. Variations
It is acknowledged by the Contractor that the Company may from time to time wish to review the scope, range and extent of the Cleaning Services to be provided under this Agreement and if the Company decides to increase or reduce the scope, range and extent of the Cleaning Services it may do so and notify the Contractor accordingly on giving [fourteen] days' notice in writing stating the date or dates on which the variation or variations are to take effect [and where the variation involves an increase in the Cleaning Services the Contractor shall within a period of [twenty-eight] days from the receipt of the company's notice confirm whether or not it will carry out the additional work].

5. Duration
This Agreement shall commence [with immediate effect] [on] and shall continue [for a period of [months] [years]] [until terminated by either party giving written notice to the other of not less than [ ] complete calendar month[s]].

Note B (see p.251)

6. The Cleaning Services
The Contractor shall:

6.1 Between the hours of and on each day [Sundays excepted] thoroughly [sweep] [clean] [wash] all the floor surfaces on each of the [ ] floors at the Company's Premises and remove [manufacturing waste deposit and] all items of rubbish and the like and empty all the waste paper receptacles at the Company's Premises, the rate of payment to be £ per [hour] [day] [week] [month].

6.2 On [specify days] in each week between the hours of and thoroughly clean the lavatories and the wash room[s] [specify any other areas to be cleaned] at the Company's Premises and vacuum all carpets in the reception area[s] and the stairs and corridors and where carpets are not laid, thoroughly to [sweep] [clean] [wash] all the floor surfaces of such areas not otherwise cleaned each day, the rate of payment to be £ per [hour] [day] [week] [month].

6.3 On [specify day] in each month between the hours of and thoroughly clean all the windows [inside and outside] of the Company's Premises, the rate of payment to be £ per month.

6.4 At least once in every [six] months [at a time or times to be agreed between the parties] carry out the following additional cleaning work [at a price to be agreed] [the rate of payment to be £ per] [specify in detail the work to be done and if appropriate the time or times when it is to be done].

7. Other duties and obligations of the contractor Note C (see p.251)

The Contractor shall ensure:

7.1 So far as is practicable that all persons employed by it are of good character, efficient and capable of carrying out the work.

7.2 That all personnel employed by it in carrying out the work are properly supervised by a suitably experienced manager.

7.3 That in carrying out the work all relevant statutory provisions and requirements are fully observed.

8. Insurance arrangements and indemnity Note D (see p.251)

The Contractor shall:

8.1 Maintain insurance in the minimum sum of £ in respect of all personnel employed by it in carrying out its obligations under this Agreement and also in respect of the Company's own employees or visitors to the Company's Premises against accident, personal injury or death, and shall indemnify the Company against all such liability.

8.2 Maintain insurance in the minimum sum of £ in respect of any loss or damage which may occur or be caused to the Company's property (including the personal property of any of its employees or visitors) as a result of the negligence, wilful action, default or omission of the Contractor or any person employed by it and shall indemnify the Company against all such loss or damage.

8.3 Produce a summary of all insurance cover taken out in accordance with clauses 8.1 and 8.2 or a copy of the respective policies [within seven days of the date of this Agreement] [when requested to do so in writing by the Company] and produce satisfactory evidence of the renewal of each policy on request by the Company.

9. The company's obligations

The Company shall pay the Contractor within [twenty-eight] days of the receipt of each invoice rendered by it [in respect of each calendar month], specifying in sufficient detail the nature of the work for which payment is claimed and the time taken in carrying out the work.

10. Termination

The Company may at its sole discretion terminate this Agreement in writing immediately or on giving such period of notice in writing as the Company considers appropriate if the Contractor:

10.1 Is in breach of the terms of this Agreement and although such breach is capable of remedy it has not been so remedied within twenty-one days of receipt of the notice from the Company specifying the breach and requiring its remedy.

10.2 Is incompetent or guilty of gross or serious misconduct or negligence in carrying out its obligations.

10.3 Fails or refuses to carry out its obligations in such a manner or method as may reasonably and properly be required of it by [named individual or title of Company's nominee] [the Company].

10.4 Goes into liquidation or if a receiver of its assets is appointed.

11. Rights and obligations prior to termination

On the termination of this Agreement all pre-existing rights and obligations which have accrued to or by either of the parties under this Agreement shall continue in effect.

12. Notices

Any notice, instruction or communication shall be sent by ordinary first class post, telex, facsimile transmission or by such other means as may be appropriate in the circumstances, and in the case of a notice served by first class post it shall be deemed to have been received by the party to whom it was sent forty-eight hours after posting, and in the case of any other form of transmission twenty-four hours after sending.

13. Entire agreement

This Agreement constitutes the entire agreement between the parties with respect to the matters dealt with and supersedes any previous agreement between the parties in relation to such matters.

14. Force majeure

In the event that either of the parties are unable to carry out all or any of their obligations under this Agreement as a result of matters arising beyond their reasonable control neither party shall have a claim against the other provided that notice of the event or events is given to the party not affected within forty-eight hours.

Note E (see p.252)

15. Restriction on assignment

This Agreement is not capable of being assigned by the Contractor.

16. Law

This Agreement shall be governed by English law.

SIGNED by on behalf of the Company

SIGNED by on behalf of the Contractor

Explanatory notes on agreement for the cleaning of office/factory/work place

A. Variations (see p.248)

Any variations should be in writing. The contractor may be given the option of deciding whether or not it wishes to carry out any additional work required by the company. The contractor does not have the corresponding right to determine the contract if the company wishes to reduce the scope, range or extent of the cleaning services to be carried out, and this may be unacceptable to the contractor. It should be left to the contractor to raise the point in the negotiations.

B. The cleaning services (see p.248)

The detail will depend on the particular requirements of the company. It is probably of benefit to the Company if the times and days on which the cleaning work is to be carried out are stipulated but it is up to the parties to decide if this is necessary.

C. Other duties and obligations of the contractor (see p.249)

Whether it is possible or even desirable to impose on the contractor an obligation to ensure that anyone employed by it is of good character is debatable. The point of including this provision is to encourage the contractor to be perhaps a little more careful in the way in which he selects his personnel for the work than he might otherwise have been.

D. Insurance arrangements and indemnity (see p.249)

As mentioned in the introduction there will be an element of duplication in the insurance arrangements between those which the contractor is obliged to arrange and those which the company would already have. The contractor will almost certainly have its own insurance arrangements in place anyway, but it is preferable to specify the basis upon which the question of any liability is to be apportioned or resolved in the event of an accident or damage to property. As the contractor is obliged to produce copies of the relative insurance policies a comparison can then be made with the cover that the contractor has and the cover that the company has. It will be noted that the obligation on the contractor to insure property is extended to the personal property of the company's employees and any of its visitors which would include persons who attend the premises in the course of the company's business. A situation can be envisaged where perhaps a floor surface is left in a dangerous condition which results in not only the injury to a company's employee or visitor but also to their personal property, for example spectacles.

E. Restriction on assignment (see p.250)

This clause prevents the contractor from assigning the contract at all and would also prevent an assignment to an associated company. This would enable the company to terminate the contract if such a situation arose and it wanted to review the position generally. The inclusion, therefore, of such a clause may meet with some resistance from the contractor.

Introduction to agreement for the maintenance of equipment or machinery

A number of the points which arise in connection with this precedent are similar to those in respect of the cleaning contract precedent. There are the same implications for the company arising out of its duty of care and its liability under the Occupier's Liability Act 1957, which is discussed on pages 246 and 247.

The type and nature of equipment and machinery will vary greatly from one company to another and it may be located in several different places. Consequently, the agreement provides for each item to be set out in a separate schedule which should also specify the location and the particular work to be carried out. In some cases the work must be sufficient in scope to ensure that the company complies with any statutory provisions to which the item of equipment or machinery is subject.

The payment for the services to be provided is based on a normal and emergency rate per hour for various grades of personnel. The contractor may require, in addition to such hourly payments, an annual service charge but this is something for the contractor to raise in the negotiations. The insurance arrangements are similar to those set out in the cleaning contract precedent but the contractor is also required, if it is feasible, to maintain a professional negligence insurance policy and to supply a copy of the policy to the company on request.

If the contractor does not have its own form of agreement or terms and conditions, or they are not to be used, then the definition in clause 1.1 should be deleted as should clause 2 and the remaining clauses renumbered accordingly.

Agreement for the inspection and maintenance of equipment or machinery

Dated 19 .

The Parties:

LTD/PLC whose registered office is at ('the Company') (1)

LTD/PLC whose [principal place of business] [registered office] is at ('the Maintenance Contractor') (2)

IT IS AGREED as follows:

1. Definitions and interpretation

1.1 These terms and expressions shall have the following meanings in this Agreement:

'MAINTENANCE SERVICES' means the services referred to in clause 6 of this Agreement.

'EQUIPMENT' means the equipment referred to in the separate Schedule annexed to this Agreement and marked 'Equipment'. Note A (see p.258)

'MACHINERY' means the machinery referred to in the separate Schedule annexed to this Agreement and marked 'Machinery'.

'THE MAINTENANCE CONTRACTOR'S TERMS AND CONDITIONS' means the Maintenance Contractor's terms and conditions attached to this Agreement.

1.2 The headings to the clauses are for convenience and reference only and do not affect their interpretation.

2. The maintenance contractor's terms and conditions

2.1 Only conditions [refer to specifically by numbering or other means] of the Maintenance Contractor's Terms and Conditions shall apply to this Agreement and be incorporated.

Note B (see p.258)

2.2 The rates per hour to be charged by the Maintenance Contractor in respect of each grade of employee shall be as follows until varied by agreement in writing by both parties:

Grade	[Normal] Rate per hour	[Emergency Rate per hour]
Manager		....
Senior Engineer/Mechanic	....	....
Mechanic	....	....
Other Personnel	....	....

3. Appointment of maintenance contractor

The Company appoints the Maintenance Contractor to provide the Maintenance Services in accordance with the provisions of this Agreement.

4. Variations

The Company is entitled to add to or subtract from the list[s] of items of [Equipment] [Machinery] set out in the annexed Schedule[s] and will notify the Maintenance Contractor accordingly in writing who shall, where items have been added, incorporate the additional [Equipment] [Machinery] into its programme of work as soon as practicable but no later than [twenty-eight] days from the receipt of such notice.

5. Duration

This Agreement shall commence [with immediate effect] [on] and shall continue [for a period of [months] [years]] [until terminated by either party giving written notice to the other of not less than [ ] complete calendar month[s]].

Note C (see p.258)

6. The maintenance services

6.1 The Maintenance Contractor shall:

6.1.1 ensure that the work will be carried out by suitably qualified and experienced personnel and that any materials, replacement parts or components used are of the necessary standard and quality;

6.1.2 inspect and carry out the routine maintenance of those items of [Equipment] [Machinery] at the location[s] and as far as practicable at the times and frequency indicated in the annexed Schedule[s] in accordance with the specification shown against each item;

[6.1.3 ensure that the Company complies with any statutory requirements which apply to the [Equipment] [Machinery];]

6.1.4 provide at its own cost all the requisite materials used in the course of carrying out the routine maintenance service;

6.1.5 keep the site where each item of [Equipment] [Machinery] is situated and the immediate vicinity in a clean and tidy condition [so far as practicable];

6.1.6 provide an emergency service and maintain such communication system as is necessary to ensure that any notification by the Company of the need for emergency work to be carried out is received by the Maintenance Contractor during a minimum of [sixteen] hours in any one day, including weekends and bank holidays, and carry out the emergency repair work as soon as possible but no later than [twenty-four] hours after notification that such work was required. Note D (see p.259)

6.2 If in the course of carrying out the inspection of an item of [Equipment] [Machinery] it becomes apparent that repairs should be made or components replaced other than would normally be done as part of the routine maintenance service, the Maintenance Contractor shall:

6.2.1 report orally to [specify individual or title] immediately if the repairs should be carried out or the components replaced in order to avoid breakdown of or damage to the [Equipment] [Machinery] or prevent personal injury;

6.2.2 in any other situation notify the Company in writing within [three] days giving details of the repair work which it is recommended should be carried out and specifying the components, if any, which should be replaced, identifying the relevant [Equipment] [Machinery] and indicating the likely cost involved.

6.3 On each occasion that work is being carried out to any item of [Equipment] [Machinery], the Maintenance Contractor shall ensure that there is in proximity to the item of [Equipment] [Machinery] a notice sufficient to warn any other person in the vicinity that the work is in progress.

7. Annual reports Note E (see p.259)

7.1 The Maintenance Contractor shall:

7.1.1 prepare an annual report dealing with the condition of each item of [Equipment] [Machinery] listed in the annexed Schedule[s] and will submit such report to the Company not later than [two] months after the expiration of each anniversary of this Agreement and shall include in the report an estimate of the length of the expected useful life of each item of [Equipment] [Machinery] and specify what additional work may be required, the components which it will be necessary to replace and the estimated cost of doing so;

[7.1.2 include in the report confirmation that where an item of [Equipment] [Machinery] is required to comply with certain statutory provisions that it does or does not so comply and where necessary include a full statement of the nature and extent of the work which has been carried out to the item of [Equipment] [Machinery] during the preceding twelve months and, where appropriate, recommend what additional work should be done or repairs made or components replaced to ensure that the statutory requirements will continue to be met.]

Note F (see p.259)

8. Insurance arrangements and indemnity

The Maintenance Contractor shall:

8.1 Maintain insurance in the minimum sum of £ in respect of all personnel employed by it in carrying out its obligations under this Agreement and also in respect of the Company's own employees or visitors to the Company's Premises against accident, personal injury or death, and shall indemnify the Company against all such liability.

8.2 Maintain insurance in the minimum sum of £ in respect of any loss or damage which may occur or be caused to the Company's property (including the personal property of any of its employees or visitors) as a result of the negligence, wilful action, default or omission of the Maintenance Contractor or any person employed by it and shall indemnify the Company against all such loss or damage.

[8.3 Maintain appropriate professional negligence insurance cover or similar insurance in the minimum sum of £ .]

8.4 Produce a summary of all insurance cover taken out in accordance with clauses 8.1 [and] 8.2 [and 8.3] or a copy of the respective policies [within seven days of the date of this Agreement] [when requested to do so in writing by the Company] and produce satisfactory evidence of the renewal of each policy on request by the Company.

9. The company's obligations

The Company shall:

9.1 Pay the Maintenance Contractor within [twenty-eight] days of the receipt of each invoice rendered by it [in respect of each calendar month], specifying in sufficient detail the nature of the work for which payment is claimed, the time taken and the number and grade of personnel employed in carrying out the work.

9.2 Provide the Maintenance Contractor with such information in relation to the [Equipment] [Machinery] that it may reasonably require.

10. Termination

The Company may at its sole discretion terminate this Agreement in writing immediately or on giving such period of notice in writing as the Company considers appropriate if the Maintenance Contractor:

10.1 Is in breach of the terms of this Agreement and although such breach is capable of remedy it has not been so remedied within twenty-one days of receipt of the notice from the Company specifying the breach and requiring its remedy.

10.2 Is incompetent or guilty of gross or serious misconduct or negligence in carrying out its obligations.

10.3 Fails or refuses to carry out its obligations in such a manner or method as may reasonably and properly be required of it by [named individual or title of Company's nominee].

10.4 Goes into liquidation or if a receiver of its assets is appointed.

11. Rights and obligations prior to termination

On the termination of this Agreement all pre-existing rights and obligations which have accrued to or by either of the parties under this Agreement shall continue in effect.

12. Delivery and return of documents and other property on termination

The Maintenance Contractor shall at the expiration or termination of this Agreement however caused immediately deliver to the Company or return to it all documents, and any copies, including memoranda, records, specifications and papers and any other items of property relating to or belonging to the Company which the Maintenance Contractor may have in its possession or be under its control.

13. Arbitration

All differences or disputes which may arise in connection with this Agreement, or its construction or effect shall be referred to a single arbitrator to be agreed upon by the parties but in default of their agreement the President for the time being of the Chartered Institute of Arbitrators shall nominate an arbitrator in accordance with the Arbitration Acts 1950–1979 or any statutory modification or re-enactment for the time being in force.

14. Notices

Any notice, instruction or communication shall be sent by ordinary first class post, telex, facsimile transmission or by such other means as may be appropriate in the circumstances, and in the case of a notice served by first class post it shall be deemed to have been received by the party to whom it was sent forty-eight hours after posting, and in the case of any other form of transmission twenty-four hours after sending.

15. Entire agreement

This Agreement constitutes the entire agreement between the parties with respect to the matters dealt with and supersedes any previous agreement between the parties in relation to such matters.

16. Force majeure
In the event that either of the parties are unable to carry out all or any of their obligations under this Agreement as a result of matters arising beyond their reasonable control neither party shall have a claim against the other provided that notice of the event or events is given to the party not affected within forty-eight hours.

17. Restriction on assignment
This Agreement is not capable of being assigned by the Maintenance Contractor.

18. Law
This Agreement shall be governed by English law.

SIGNED by on behalf of the Company

SIGNED by on behalf of the Maintenance Contractor

Explanatory notes on agreement for the inspection and maintenance of equipment or machinery

A. Definitions and interpretation (see p.253)

The precedent distinguishes between equipment and machinery. Where the Company only requires equipment or machinery to be maintained the one not required can be deleted.

B. The maintenance contractor's terms and conditions (see p.254)

Whether it is appropriate for the payment to be calculated on the basis of an hourly rate distinguishing between normal and emergency payments for each grade of personnel will depend on the particular requirements of each individual case and the nature of the work to be performed. As mentioned in the introduction there is no provision in the agreement for an annual service charge in addition to the hourly rate but this can be included if agreed.

C. The maintenance services (see p.254)

The schedule or schedules will need to be reasonably detailed specifying the particular items of equipment or machinery (including serial numbers so that it is quite clear which items are covered by the agreement) and where they are located. The contractor is to provide all the materials used in carrying out the routine maintenance service. If any components are to be included as part of the service without charge to the company, their type and nature should be specified so there is less room for dispute.

D. Emergency work (see p.255)

If it is important that the company should be able to call upon the contractor to carry out emergency work the contractor should be required to provide such a service and the communication system necessary to implement it.

E. Annual reports (see p.255)

It would be useful to the company for the contractor to provide a report annually and to include in the report reference to those items of equipment, if any, which have to meet statutory requirements. If the obligation to supply annual reports is not included in the agreement the contractor would be able to negotiate additional payments for doing so. It is also advisable to stipulate when the reports are to be available and to which period they are to relate.

F. Insurance arrangements and indemnity (see p.256)

These are similar to those included in the cleaning contract precedent and the general observations relating to insurance agreements in explanatory note D to that precedent should be referred to which appears on page 251. As mentioned in the introduction, it may be advisable that the contractor should be required to maintain (if it is feasible to do so) professional negligence insurance or similar cover for a specific amount so that if it carries out the work negligently and damage to the equipment or machinery is caused, compensation for some of the loss may be claimed against the contractor.

CHAPTER 13

SHAREHOLDERS' AGREEMENTS

Introduction to shareholders' agreement where two shareholders form a company for a new enterprise

Two individuals may decide to commence a new enterprise or business. They may perhaps have been made redundant or have left their previous employment specifically for the purpose of setting up the new venture.

Anyone contemplating a new business venture should take professional advice to determine whether or not the new enterprise or business should be operated in the form of a partnership or limited company both of which have advantages and disadvantages.

A partnership agreement has the benefit that there is no public record of its financial performance in the way that there is with a limited company which has to file accounts and annual returns. A limited company has the benefit, albeit a reducing one, of limited liability but there may be tax considerations which favour a partnership. A partnership can be dissolved at the instance of a partner whereas a limited company cannot be put into liquidation by one shareholder alone who has less than a 75 per cent shareholding because he would not be able to pass the necessary extraordinary resolution. There are some of the fundamental points to be considered in resolving the question of whether or not a limited company or partnership structure should be adopted.

After considering the various factors the likelihood is that (and it would depend on the nature of the business) the two individuals will come to the conclusion that limited liability is the preferred route for the new enterprise. Another advantage that a company has compared with a partnership is that a company can create a floating charge over its assets which may be useful in enabling finance to be arranged more readily.

The new company to be formed will have articles of association which will almost certainly be based on the Companies (Tables A to F) Regulations 1985. Table A, coupled with the provisions of the Companies Acts, contains a variety of remedies open to shareholders in the event that the affairs of the company are being conducted irregularly or illegally or are not being carried out properly, but there are very few remedies available to an aggrieved director/shareholder where the other director/shareholder is behaving unreasonably towards him. On the whole the way in which a quasi-partnership company is run on a day to day basis is dependent on how the directors relate to each other, and company law does not regulate their behaviour in minute detail.

Section 459 of the Companies Act 1985, however, does provide that a member of a company may apply to the Court by petition for an order that the company's affairs are being or have been conducted in a manner which is unfairly prejudicial to the interests of some part of the members or that a proposed act or omission is or would be so prejudicial. An application under section 459 would be available to one of two shareholders in a quasi-partnership company but its main purpose is to provide some protection for a minority shareholder.

Although the Court in response to an application under section 459 can make an order regulating the conduct of the company's affairs in the future and requiring the company to refrain from continuing to act in the way complained of by the aggrieved shareholder, these remedies may not be of much benefit to the aggrieved shareholder of a quasi-partnership company comprising two shareholders. The other remedy which the Court could order is that the shares of the aggrieved shareholder be purchased by the other shareholder but this poses the question of what value should be attached to those shares and at what date the valuation should relate to. The way in which the valuer appointed by the Court makes his valuation will depend on how the valuer exercises his discretion and what criteria he chooses to adopt. Far better, therefore, that the shareholders should at the outset of their relationship conclude a shareholders' agreement which will specify what is to happen in the event that one wishes to leave (in other words to dissolve the quasi-partnership) or is in default of his obligations under the agreement.

The problem, however, is that it is difficult to anticipate at the outset what circumstances may occur or problems arise which will lead to a breakdown in the relationship between the shareholders. Where deadlock between the shareholders occurs it will generally be difficult to resolve satisfactorily. An aggrieved shareholder cannot of his own volition institute the voluntary winding-up of the company in the event of deadlock, although it would be quite feasible to include in the shareholders' agreement an obligation on the part of the shareholders where there is deadlock to institute the voluntary winding-up procedure by requiring them to make the necessary statutory declaration and pass the extraordinary resolution placing the company in a members' voluntary winding-up. The precedent does not include this procedure because it could be used by one of the shareholders unreasonably who may for reasons of his own decide that the company should be wound-up and which if carried through could cause great difficulty to, and perhaps financial loss for, the other shareholder.

How to reconcile the requirements of the two shareholders while the business continues normally but at the same time provide a framework giving some degree of certainty in the event that relationships sour or one of the shareholders wishes to leave for genuine reasons or retire, is the fundamental problem which has to be addressed.

The formula incorporated in the precedent that attempts to resolve the problem is one which gives the remaining shareholder the option to acquire the outgoing shareholder's shares subject to a valuation to be made by the company's auditors. There is also a provision included enabling the remaining shareholder to acquire the shares and pay the purchase price over a period of time, not by specified instalments but on such basis as the remaining shareholder considers he can comply with. It may be that the remaining shareholder will have to raise the finance by borrowing and to make the necessary arrangements which will take time.

If the remaining shareholder does not or cannot exercise the option the outgoing shareholder can try and dispose of his shares to an outside party but the remaining shareholder will have the right of veto to any proposed share transfer because regulation 24 of Table A will have been amended.

There are a great number of matters that need to be resolved between the two shareholders which is difficult enough but where possible it is desirable to avoid complication so that the parties can understand the basis on which they operate and the consequences that will follow if they behave in a certain way or make certain decisions. The precedent is drafted on the assumption that Table A is adopted but with some amendments as follows:

1. Regulation 24 which deals with the transfer of shares should be amended so that the directors have an absolute right to refuse to register the transfer of any share without giving a reason. The wording might be as follows:

   The directors may in their absolute discretion and without assigning any reason therefor decline to register the transfer of a share whether or not it is a fully paid share and the first sentence of regulation 24 in Table A shall not apply to the company.
2. Regulation 50 and the fifth sentence of Regulation 88 should be deleted so as to deprive the chairman (if any) of a casting vote where there is equality of votes.

Circumstances which lead to a dissolution of the quasi-partnership may arise in one of three ways. The first is where one of the shareholders wishes to retire and leave the remaining shareholder to run the business. The retirement of the shareholder can be arranged on a mutually amicable basis and the retiring shareholder's shares would be purchased by the remaining shareholder in accordance with the formula contained in the agreement. It would be open to the two shareholders to agree, for example, that a longer period of time be given within which the purchase price should be paid if that suited them both, even though the agreement may provide for a shorter time. The remaining shareholder may also try and find a replacement for the retiring shareholder who could acquire the shares over a period of time or contemporaneously with the retiring shareholder's departure.

Secondly, the outgoing shareholder may wish to retire but to establish a new venture, either on his own or in conjunction with others. This dissolution may again be amicable and the arrangements for dealing with the shares of the outgoing shareholder are catered for in the precedent. Additionally, there may be included provisions preventing the outgoing shareholder from soliciting or dealing with the customers or clients of the company, and whether or not such provisions which are for the protection of both shareholders should be included must be carefully considered. Consequently, the precedent incorporates such clauses. In this situation it is assumed that the viability of the company will not be adversely affected and that if the remaining shareholder has to raise the necessary finance to acquire the shares of the outgoing shareholder he would be able and prepared to do so.

Thirdly, a situation may develop where either the relationship of the two shareholders has become acrimonious or one of the shareholders is in breach of his obligations under the agreement and is not prepared to remedy the breach, or the breach is so fundamental or material that it is not capable of being remedied. Where there has been default or breach by one shareholder, the remaining shareholder is in difficulty from a practical point of view in that he has to continue to be able to run the company properly and yet at the same time cope with the effects of the default or breach as the case may be. The remaining shareholder may consider it unfair if he is also obliged to pay the outgoing shareholder a significant amount for his shares, in a situation that has been forced on him through no fault of his own. However, as the outgoing shareholder's shares have to be valued and the value of the underlying business of the company will be one of the factors which the auditors would take into account in determining what the price for the outgoing shareholder's shares should be, this should discourage the outgoing shareholder from behaving in a way that is detrimental to the company. This is an example of where it would be particularly unfair to the remaining shareholder if the agreement provided that in such circumstances the shareholders were obliged to pass the necessary extraordinary resolution to wind-up the company and set in motion the winding-up procedure. The inclusion of the restraint clauses in this situation will have proved to be necessary from the remaining shareholder's point of view.

As the remaining shareholder has the right of veto in connection with any transfer of the shares to an outsider introduced by the outgoing shareholder, the remaining shareholder can as a condition of agreeing to the transfer require the incoming shareholder to agree to be bound by the terms of the agreement or a new agreement if that were considered more appropriate.

The precedent is drafted on the assumption that the company would comprise only two shareholders. Where there are more than two shareholders the general principles would also apply, although perhaps not for more than four shareholders, otherwise the arrangement could become unmanageable or unwieldy. If there are more than two shareholders the articles of association should include a *Bushell* v. *Faith* clause which would provide that where a resolution was proposed to remove a director, that director would have on that occasion only sufficient votes to match the votes on those shareholders who were in favour of the resolution. Otherwise the other shareholders could together remove the director as a director of the company with the consequence that his rights would be adversely affected and he would be unable to exercise any day to day control over the company's affairs. He may be able to claim that the behaviour of the other shareholders is unfairly prejudicial under section 459 but going to Court should be regarded as a last resort, particularly in cases of this kind for the reasons already mentioned.

Although in the precedent the company is joined in as a party this may not always be necessary. Generally it is preferable that the company should be a party and obligatory where it takes on specific obligations in its own right.

The agreement need not be executed as a deed but it may be considered better practice for it to be sealed by the company unless the seal has been dispensed with.

Shareholders' agreement where two shareholders form a company for a new enterprise

Dated 19 .

The Parties:

of ('Mr ') (1)

of ('Mr ') (2)

LTD whose registered office is at ('the Company') (3)

Recitals:

The Company is a private company limited by shares incorporated on the of 19 [having by Special Resolution changed its name with effect from the of 19].

The Company has at the date of this Agreement an authorised share capital of £ divided into shares of £ each of which have been issued and are beneficially owned and registered in the names of Messrs and as to share[s] each.

[The Company commenced to trade on the 19 .]

The Shareholders have agreed to co-operate in the management of the business of the Company whose principal object is that of .

The Company has agreed with the Shareholders that it will comply with the terms and conditions of this Agreement in so far as they relate to the Company.

The Shareholders are the only directors of the Company at the time of execution of this Agreement.

IT IS AGREED as follows:

1. Definitions and interpretation

1.1 These terms and expressions shall have the following meanings in this Agreement:

'THE ARTICLES' means the Articles of Association of the Company.
'THE AUDITORS' means the Auditors for the time being of the Company.
'THE SHARES' means the Shares of £ each in the share capital of the Company.
'LOAN' means, in relation to a Shareholder, any loan to the Company made by that Shareholder.
'THE SHAREHOLDERS' means Messrs and .

1.2 The headings to the clauses are for convenience and reference only and do not affect their interpretation.

1.3 Words importing the singular number shall include the plural and vice versa, words importing the masculine shall include the feminine and neuter and vice versa, and words importing persons shall include bodies corporate, unincorporated associations and partnerships.

2. Formal matters

At the date of this Agreement:

2.1 The auditors of the Company are
2.2 The bankers to the Company are
2.3 The accounting reference date is the
2.4 The secretary of the Company is

3. Additional financing Note A (see p.273)

3.1 Further capital which is required by the Company from time to time shall be provided in such manner and in such amounts as the Shareholders shall agree.

[3.2 Each Shareholder has at the date of this Agreement contributed by way of Loan to the Company the sum of £ .]

3.3 Any Loan made by either Shareholder shall only be repaid if both Shareholders agree.

3.4 Interest at the rate of [1] per cent above the Bank PLC base rate for the time being shall be payable on the balance of any Loan made by either Shareholder, such interest to be calculated on the accounting reference date in each year and to be payable in half yearly instalments on [ ] and [ ] in arrear.

4. Dividend policy and distribution Note B (see p.274)

Unless the Shareholders decide to the contrary, [per cent] of the amount of the Company's profits available for distribution as disclosed in the audited accounts in respect of each accounting reference period during the term of this Agreement shall be distributed by the Company to the Shareholders by way of dividend. If there is any disagreement between the Shareholders as to the amount of the profits of the Company which are available for distribution they shall request the Auditors to certify the amount available, if any. In giving their certificate the Auditors will act as experts and not as arbitrators and their decision shall be final and binding on the Shareholders.

Note C (see p.274)

5. Transfer arrangements relating to shares held by either shareholder who resigns as a director or is in default

In the event that either Shareholder resigns as a Director or commits a material breach or is in default of his obligations under this Agreement, or in the case of a breach capable of remedy fails to remedy the same within twenty-one days of being specifically required in writing to do so by the other Shareholder ['the remaining Shareholder'] the Shareholder who resigns or is in default ['the outgoing Shareholder'] shall be deemed to have offered to transfer his Shares to the remaining Shareholder on the following basis:

5.1 The remaining Shareholder shall implement the provisions of clause 6 within [fourteen] days of the occurrence of any of the events specified above.

5.2 Upon the price being certified by the Auditors the remaining Shareholder shall [within six months of the date of receipt of the Certificate of Value pay to the outgoing Shareholder the certified price in exchange for the executed stock transfer form and share certificate[s]] [have the option of paying the certified price for the Shares within a period of [three] years from the date of receipt of the Certificate of Value and if the remaining Shareholder exercises his option he shall do so in writing stating how the payment will be phased over the period of [three] years and stipulating how the transfer[s] of the Shares shall be effected].

5.3 If the remaining Shareholder does not exercise his option to acquire some or all of the Shares at the certified value within twenty-eight days of the receipt by him of the Certificate of Value the outgoing Shareholder may dispose of his Shares or the balance not acquired by the remaining Shareholder in any manner he may think fit but subject to the remaining Shareholder's right in accordance with Article [24] of the Articles to decline to register any such transfer.

Note D (see p.274)

6. Certification of price of shares by the auditors

6.1 Where the circumstances referred to in clauses 5 or 8 arise the Company shall request the Auditors [who shall act as experts and not as arbitrators so that any provision of law or statute relating to arbitration shall not apply] to certify by certificate in writing ['the Certificate of Value'] the price in their opinion of the Shares as between a willing seller and a willing buyer [on the basis of a sale of the Company as a going concern] [on a net assets basis] [on such basis as may be appropriate in the opinion of the Auditors] as at the date of the request for the valuation to be carried out.

6.2 The Company shall, as soon as it receives the Certificate of Value, send a copy to the outgoing Shareholder or the personal representatives of the deceased Shareholder as the case may be. The cost of obtaining the Certificate of Value shall be borne by the Company and the outgoing Shareholder or the estate of the deceased Shareholder jointly.

7. Life insurance arrangements in respect of both shareholders Note E (see p.274)

The Shareholders shall jointly effect with an insurance company insurance cover on the life of each other for so long as either own any Shares in the Company in the minimum sum of £ each (reviewable) for the benefit of and upon trust for the other at the date of the death of either Shareholder.

8. Transfer of shares by the personal representatives of deceased shareholder Note F (see p.274)

8.1 In the event of the death of either Shareholder the surviving Shareholder shall as soon as reasonably practicable implement the provisions of clause 6.

[8.2 The personal representatives shall within [twenty-eight] days of the receipt by them of the Certificate of Value transfer all of the Shares in the capital of the Company registered in the deceased Shareholder's name at the time of his death to the surviving Shareholder or his nominee upon payment by the surviving Shareholder to the personal representatives of the proceeds of the insurance policy maintained in accordance with Clause 7 together with such additional sum [to be payable by the surviving Shareholder over a period of [three] years from the date of receipt of the Certificate of Value] as may be certified by the Auditors in accordance with Clause 6.1. In default of the transfer of the said Shares by the personal representatives of the deceased Shareholder the surviving Shareholder may nominate himself to transfer the Shares and to do all that may be necessary to register such transfer.]

[8.2 Following receipt of the Certificate of Value the personal representatives may at their option offer to transfer all of the Shares in the capital of the Company registered in the deceased Shareholder's name at the time of his death to the surviving Shareholder or his nominee upon payment by the surviving Shareholder to the personal representatives of the proceeds of the insurance policy maintained in accordance with Clause 7 together with such additional sum [to be payable by the surviving Shareholder over a period of [three] years from the date of receipt of the Certificate of Value] as may be certified by the Auditors in accordance with Clause 6.1.

If the personal representatives do not offer to transfer the Shares the surviving Shareholder within [twelve] months of the date of the death of the deceased Shareholder may at his option offer to purchase the Shares on payment to the personal representatives the sum certified by the Auditors in accordance with Clause 6.1 on such basis as may be agreed.]

Note G (see p.275)

9. Insurance and administration

9.1 The Company shall maintain adequate insurance against all risks usually insured against for the full replacement or reinstatement value of all its assets and all other such insurance cover as may be appropriate for the Company's business.

9.2 Formal meetings of the directors shall be held as regularly as necessary and at least one board meeting held in every calendar month.

9.3 Cheques of a value in excess of £ shall be signed by both Shareholders.

Note H (see p.275)

10. Confidentiality

Neither Shareholder shall disclose or divulge or allow to be disclosed or divulged to any person, firm or company any information which he receives or obtains relating to the Company's business, finances, manufacturing methods and processes, trade secrets, or any other information relating to the Company including names and addresses of any parties who conduct business with the Company, and shall keep confidential all such information both during the period of this Agreement and after its termination whether such termination be by agreement or notice or as a result of default or material breach by either Shareholder.

Note I (see p.275)

11. Matters requiring consent of both shareholders

The Shareholders shall exercise their powers in relation to the Company to ensure that the Company does not except with their joint consent:

11.1 Make any material change in the nature of the Company's business.

11.2 Commence any legal or arbitration proceedings other than routine debt collection.

11.3 Make any claim, surrender, election or consent of a material nature for tax purposes.

11.4 Acquire shares or securities in any company.

11.5 Enter into any material contract other than in the ordinary course of the Company's business.

11.6 Permit or allow anything to be done which may lead to the winding-up of the Company.

11.7 Enter into any partnership or profit sharing agreement with any person.

11.8 Acquire or dispose of any subsidiary company.

[11.9 Issue any Shares or debentures in the Company.]

11.10 Acquire any leasehold interest in or other interest over land.

11.11 Enter into any contract or transaction or series of related transactions to a value of more than £

11.12 Sell, transfer, lease, assign or otherwise dispose of any part of the Company's undertaking or property.

11.13 Give any guarantee, indemnity or security in respect of the obligations of any other person.

11.14 Make any loan or give any credit in excess of £ other than in the normal course of business.

11.15 Make any changes in banking arrangements or facilities or arrange any overdraft or other borrowing facilities.

11.16 Create any fixed or floating charge or other security of any kind over the whole or any part of the Company's undertaking, property or assets.

12. Duration and termination

This Agreement shall continue until any one of the following events occur:

12.1 The Company cannot by reason of its liabilities continue its business and it is advisable to wind-up the Company.

12.2 The Company is wound-up compulsorily.

12.3 A receiver or administrative receiver is appointed of the whole or any part of the assets of the Company or the business of the Company shall be managed by an administrator appointed by the Court.

12.4 Either Shareholder commits a material breach of any of his obligations under this Agreement and fails to take all reasonable steps as may be necessary to remedy the same withih twenty-one days of being required in writing by the other Shareholder so to do or if the material breach is incapable of being remedied, then in any such case the other Shareholder shall give to the Shareholder in default written notice terminating this Agreement, stating the date of termination.

Provided that the terms of this Agreement shall continue to bind the Shareholders after its termination to such extent and for so long as may be necessary to give effect to the respective rights and obligations.

13. Non-solicitation Note J (see p.275)

The outgoing Shareholder shall not within [describe area or specific radius] and for a period of [ ] [months] [years] after the termination of this Agreement however caused, directly or indirectly, whether on his own account or on behalf of another business entity:

13.1 Solicit or procure business from any person, firm or company who or which during the course of this Agreement was a customer or client of the Company or generally or from time to time dealt with the Company.

13.2 Solicit the services of or endeavour to encourage any person who shall have been an officer, employee or consultant of the Company during the course of this Agreement to leave the Company's employment.

Note J
(see p.275)

14. Non-dealing

The outgoing Shareholder shall not within [describe area or specific radius] and for a period of [ ] [months] [years] after the termination of this Agreement however caused, directly or indirectly, carry on business or deal with any person, firm or company who or which was a customer, client, supplier, agent or distributor of the Company during the course of this Agreement.

Note J
(see p.275)

15. Non-competition

The outgoing Shareholder shall not within [describe area or specific radius] and for a period of [ ] [months] [years] after the termination of this Agreement however caused be engaged or assist in carrying on any business which competes with the business of the Company or otherwise be interested or concerned, either directly or indirectly, whether as a consultant, employee, director, partner, adviser, agent or in any other capacity in or with any person, firm or company whose business competes with the business of the Company.

Note K
(see p.276)

16. No partnership

Nothing in this Agreement shall constitute or be deemed to constitute a partnership between the Shareholders.

17. Restrictions affecting the shares of both shareholders

Neither Shareholder shall create any charge or encumbrance over all or any of his Shares nor grant any option or other rights, or dispose of any interest in all or any of his Shares.

Note L
(see p.276)

18. Conflict or ambiguity between the articles and this agreement

If, during the continuance of this Agreement, there is any conflict or ambiguity between its provisions and the provisions of the Articles then the provisions of this Agreement shall prevail.

19. Arbitration

All differences or disputes which may arise in connection with this Agreement, or its construction or effect shall be referred to a single arbitrator to be agreed upon by the Shareholders but in default of their agreement the President for the time being of [the Chartered Institute of Arbitrators] [the Institute of Chartered Accountants in England and Wales] shall nominate an arbitrator in accordance with the Arbitration Acts 1950–1979, or any statutory modification or re-enactment for the time being in force.

20. General

20.1 Notices. Any notices which are required to be given shall be in writing and shall be sent to the address of the recipient set out in this Agreement or such other address as may be designated subsequently. Any such notice may be delivered personally or by first class prepaid letter, facsimile or telex transmission and shall be deemed to have been served if by personal delivery when delivered by first class post forty-eight hours after posting and if by any other means on proof of receipt.

20.2 Assignment. Neither of the Shareholders may assign their interest in this Agreement without the prior written consent of the other Shareholder.

20.3 Entire agreement. This Agreement constitutes the entire agreement between the parties with respect to the matters dealt with and supersedes any previous agreement between them in relation to such matters.

20.4 Law. This Agreement shall be governed by and construed in accordance with English law.

SIGNED by the first Shareholder

SIGNED by the second Shareholder

THE COMMON SEAL of LTD was hereunto affixed in the presence of:

Director

Secretary

or

SIGNED for and on behalf of LTD by

Director

Explanatory notes on shareholders' agreement where two shareholders form a company for a new enterprise

A. Additional financing *(see p.267)*

The shareholdings must be kept in parity. It is unlikely that any further shares would be issued other than those which had been issued at the time the company was incorporated or shortly afterwards. Any further financing will probably be by way of bank borrowing or by shareholder loans. There is no reason why the shareholders cannot make loans in different proportions.

There is provision for interest to be payable on shareholder's loans which would provide some recompense in the event that one of the shareholders were to contribute a disproportionate amount by way of loan financing.

B. Dividend policy and distribution (see p.267)

Neither shareholder has an automatic right to receive a dividend. It would require the joint approval of both shareholders who would take account of the company's requirements for finance before declaring a dividend. However, one or both shareholders may want to ensure that a dividend of a certain percentage would be payable even if the other shareholder at the time would prefer it not to be. Even though profits are made it does not necessarily follow that to distribute them as dividends would be a sensible course of action to take. However, if there is a specific provision it will have to be implemented unless the shareholders both agree to a different arrangement at the time.

C. Transfer arrangements relating to shares held by either shareholder who resigns as a Director or is in default (see p.268)

The provisions are intended to strike a balance between the remaining shareholder's requirement to be able to keep the company running properly and the right of the outgoing shareholder to extract his share of his investment in the company. Other provisions could be included if the situation required it or the shareholders had their own particular reasons for wanting to do so.

D. Certification of price of shares by the auditors (see p.268)

The basis on which the auditors should make a valuation should be prescribed and the auditors should be consulted for their advice as to which formula should be specified.

E. Life insurance arrangements in respect of both shareholders (see p.269)

It is important that the shareholders themselves should take out the insurance policy on their joint lives. If the company undertakes to do so and to pay the premiums then the payments may fall foul of section 151 of the Companies Act 1985 as constituting the provision of financial assistance for the purchase of the shares in the company. If that were to be so then the transaction is void. The shareholders should therefore individually pay the premiums.

F. Transfer of shares by the personal representatives of deceased shareholder (see p.269)

There are two alternatives. The first constitutes an arrangement whereby the personal representatives of the deceased shareholder are obliged to sell his shares to the surviving shareholder and the surviving shareholder is obliged to purchase those shares.

This arrangement gives comfort to both shareholders because they know that their families will benefit from the guaranteed receipt of the payment for the shares which will be provided mainly from the proceeds of the insurance policy taken out for this purpose. However, the Inland Revenue will regard this kind of arrangement as being a binding contract for sale and as a result business property relief for Inheritance Tax purposes will not be available. Whether or not this will be a factor would depend upon the position of either shareholder and the extent to which their respective estates would be liable to Inheritance Tax at the time of their death.

The second alternative is a cross option arrangement. There is no binding contract for sale and, consequently, the potential to claim business property relief will not be prejudiced. However, there is no absolute guarantee that the surviving shareholder would acquire the shares of the deceased shareholder and pay the purchase price although the likelihood is that he would.

G. Insurance and administration (see p.270)

This clause should be expanded to include any other matters that are relevant to the requirements of the particular company or its business.

H. Confidentiality (see p.270)

In the event that one shareholder decides to determine the agreement and leave but the remaining shareholder wishes to continue the business of the company it is only reasonable that the outgoing shareholder should be prevented from disclosing information relating to the company to the detriment of its business and to the disadvantage of the remaining shareholder.

I. Matters requiring consent of both shareholders (see p.270)

A director by virtue of his appointment is in a position to commit the company in a wide range of different ways. The agreement should include some safeguards to prevent one director from acting unilaterally in certain respects or situations. Other matters which are directly relevant to the nature of the company's business should be incorporated if appropriate.

J. Non-solicitation, non-dealing and non-competition (see pp.271–272)

Reference should be made to the notes on these clauses on similar clauses on pages 202–203, although the clauses in this precedent do not specify a period preceding the termination of the agreement in which a customer or client dealt with the company or a person was employed, etc., by the company. The restrictions apply to all such customers or persons who dealt with or were involved with the company during the course of the agreement. As this is a shareholder's agreement, it is not considered necessary to include a clause similar to clause 22 on page 194.

K. No partnership (see p.272)

Although the arrangement may be described as a quasi-partnership it is to be conducted in the form of a company limited by shares. Nevertheless, it would be prudent to include a disclaimer that the arrangement does not constitute a partnership.

L. Conflict or ambiguity between the articles and agreement (see p.272)

The articles and the agreement run in parallel but at the same time should be complementary to each other. The agreement will not require registration at the Companies Registry provided that it does not include anything which it would be necessary to include in the articles of association and which would require to be filed at the Companies Registry.

Section 380 (4)(c) of the Companies Act 1985 requires registration of an agreement which has been agreed to by all the members of a company but which if not so agreed to would not have been effective for their purpose unless (as the case may be) they had been passed as special resolutions or as extraordinary resolutions.

Introduction to shareholders' agreement where a prospective director/shareholder acquires a minority holding in a wholly owned subsidiary of a parent company

The acquisition of a minority holding in a wholly owned subsidiary is not something to be undertaken lightly. On the whole the disadvantages outweigh any advantages. However, situations do arise where there is a requirement for a shareholders' agreement which caters for such an arrangement.

The kind of situation which is envisaged is where a private company with perhaps two or three directors commenced trading and became successful. Such a company may as time goes on wish to diversify or decide to manufacture components which it had previously bought in from other manufacturers or suppliers. The directors/shareholders incorporate a subsidiary company for the purpose of conducting the new element of its business and in the process employ a manager who may or may not be a director of the subsidiary. The subsidiary develops the new business and becomes successful in its own right and expands accordingly, and for a number of reasons the manager recruited to run the business may want to acquire a personal stake in it, partly because to do so would give him a degree of security and some sense of direct involvement and partly, should the decision ever be taken to dispose of the subsidiary, he could acquire a capital gain on the disposal.

It may happen that a manager inherits a reasonable sum of money and he may decide that he should invest in the subsidiary which employs him. Alternatively, the manager may be prepared to borrow the money to make the investment.

The precedent attempts to strike a balance between the interests of the holding company and its directors/shareholders and the interest of the subsidiary company director/shareholder. From the parent company's point of view it is important that the group structure cannot be affected or altered and that the parent company is always in a position to pass a special resolution. The parent company would also want to be in a position to acquire the shares of the subsidiary company director/shareholder should he die or leave or in the event of a breakdown in working relationships.

Reference should be made to the introduction to the shareholders' agreement, where two shareholders form a company for a new enterprise, on page 262 and in particular the right of a minority shareholder to apply to the Court under section 459 of the Companies Act 1985. Most of the judgments, if not all, which have been given, and there are not very many, have been in respect of situations where there has not been a shareholders' agreement and this has meant that the Court has had to make a decision between the conflicting interests and requirements of the parties. It is, however, unlikely that the Court would upset the terms of a shareholders' agreement freely entered into should a minority shareholder make an application under section 459.

The decision to enter into the shareholders' agreement should be minuted in the directors' minute books both of the parent company and of the subsidiary.

On balance it is preferable for the agreement to be executed as a deed.

Shareholders' agreement where a prospective director/shareholder acquires a minority holding in a wholly owned subsidiary of a parent company

Dated 19 .

The Parties:

LTD whose registered office is at ('the Parent Company') (1)

whose address is ('the Director') (2)

LTD whose registered office is at ('the Subsidiary') (3)

Recitals:

The Subsidiary is a private company limited by Shares incorporated on the of 19 [having by Special Resolution changed its name to on the of 19].

The Subsidiary has at the date of this Agreement an authorised share capital of £ divided into Shares of £ each of which have been issued and are beneficially held by the Parent Company.

The Director will, immediately after this Agreement has come into effect, be appointed a director of the subsidiary and be the holder of Shares credited as fully paid.

The business of the Subsidiary is that of .

[Names of Directors] also hold office as directors of the Subsidiary at the date of this Agreement and will continue to do so as appointees of the Parent Company.

The Director and the Parent Company have agreed to co-operate in the management of the Subsidiary for the purpose of carrying on its business and in accordance with the terms and conditions set out in this Agreement.

The Subsidiary has agreed with the Director and the Parent Company that it will comply with the terms and conditions of this Agreement in so far as they relate to the Subsidiary.

IT IS AGREED as follows:

1. Definitions and interpretations

1.1 These terms and expressions shall have the following meanings in this Agreement:

'THE ARTICLES' means the Articles of Association of the Subsidiary.

'THE AUDITORS' means the Auditors for the time being of the Subsidiary.

'THE SHARES' means the Shares of £ each in the share capital of the Subsidiary.

'LOAN' means, in relation to a Shareholder, any Loan to the Subsidiary made by that Shareholder.

'THE SHAREHOLDERS' means the Parent Company and the Director.

1.2 The headings to the Clauses are for convenience and reference only and do not affect their interpretation.

1.3 Words importing the singular number shall include the plural and vice versa, words importing the masculine shall include the feminine and neuter and vice versa, and words importing persons shall include bodies corporate, unincorporated associations and partnerships.

2. Formal matters

At the date of this Agreement:

2.1 The auditors of the Subsidiary are

2.2 The bankers to the Company are

2.3 The accounting reference date is

2.4 The secretary of the Subsidiary is

3. Subscription by the director for shares Note A (see p.286)

The Director shall subscribe for Shares at a price per share of £ and shall, immediately this Agreement comes into effect, deliver to the Subsidiary a completed application form accompanied by a [banker's draft] [a cheque] for the amount due.

4. Additional financing Note B (see p.286)

4.1 Further capital which is required by the Subsidiary from time to time shall be provided in such manner and in such amounts as the Shareholders shall agree.

4.2 Where additional financing is made by way of Loan advanced by either Shareholder repayment in part or in whole shall only be made if both Shareholders agree.

5. Dividend policy and distribution Note C (see p.287)

Where in respect of any accounting reference period the Subsidiary has profits available for distribution as disclosed in the audited accounts, the Shareholders shall procure that in the absence of agreement to the contrary, [25] per cent of such profits are distributed by way of dividend by the Subsidiary and [the Shareholders will be entitled to dividend in the same proportion that their respective shareholdings in the Subsidiary bears to its issued share capital] [the Director shall be entitled to receive per cent and the Parent Company per cent of the dividend declared].

6. Acquisition by the director of further shares Note D (see p.287)

6.1 The Director may utilise any dividend to which he is entitled to acquire additional Shares in the Subsidiary. The price at which such additional Shares shall be acquired shall be determined in accordance with the provisions of clause 7.1.

[6.2 The Director may at any time apply for additional Shares in the Subsidiary at a price to be determined in accordance with the provisions of clause 7.1.]

6.3 The maximum number of Shares which the Director may hold in the Subsidiary at any one time shall not exceed [25 per cent] of the issued share capital.

Note E (see p.287)

7. Certification of price of shares by the auditors

7.1 Where the circumstances referred to in clauses 6 and 8 arise, the Parent Company shall request the Auditors [who shall act as experts and not as arbitrators so that any provision of law or statute relating to arbitration shall not apply] to certify by certificate in writing ['the Certificate of Value'] the price in their opinion of the Shares as between a willing seller and a willing buyer [on the basis of a sale of the Subsidiary as a going concern] [on a net assets basis] [on such basis as the Auditors shall consider appropriate] as at the date of the request for the valuation to be carried out but with no account being taken of the fact that the Shares constitute a minority holding.

7.2 The Parent Company shall, as soon as it receives the Certificate of Value, send a copy to the Director or the personal representatives of the deceased Director as the case may be. The cost of obtaining the Certificate of Value shall be borne by the Subsidiary [and the Director or his estate jointly].

Note F (see p.288)

8. Transfer arrangements relating to shares held by the director during his lifetime

In the event that the Director resigns as a Director or is removed from office, the Director shall be deemed to have offered to transfer all of his Shares in the Subsidiary to the Parent Company or its nominee on the following basis:

8.1 The Parent Company shall implement the provisions of clause 7 within [fourteen] days of the resignation or removal of the Director.

8.2 Upon the price being certified by the Auditors the Parent Company shall [within six months of the date of receipt of the Certificate of Value pay to the Director the certified price in exchange for the executed stock transfer form and share certificate[s]] [have the option of paying the certified price for the Shares within a period of [three] years from the date of receipt of the Certificate of Value, and if the Parent Company exercises its option it shall do so in writing stating how the payment will be phased over the period of [three] years and stipulating how the transfer[s] of the Shares shall be effected].

[8.3 If the Parent Company does not within [twenty-eight] days of the date of receipt of the Certificate of Value exercise its option to acquire the Director's Shares at the certified price the Director may dispose of his Shares in any manner he may think fit but the Directors appointed by the Parent Company may decline to register any such transfer in accordance with the provisions in the Articles.]

9. Life insurance arrangements in respect of the director Note G (see p.288)

The Director shall effect with an insurance company insurance cover on his life [of not less than £] [as may be appropriate] (reviewable each year) and pay the premiums for so long as he owns any Shares in the Subsidiary upon trust and for the benefit of the Parent Company at the date of the Director's death provided that the Director shall complete all documentation that may be necessary from time to time to give effect to such arrangement and will deposit the policy with the Parent Company together with all endorsements and premium receipts.

10. Transfer of shares by the personal representatives of the director Note H (see p.288)

The personal representatives of the Director shall transfer all of the Shares registered in the name of the Director to the Parent Company or its nominee upon payment by the Parent Company which it shall be bound to make to the personal representatives of the proceeds of the insurance policy maintained in accordance with clause 9 for this purpose. In default of the transfer of the Shares by the personal representatives the directors appointed by the Parent Company may nominate one of their number to transfer the Shares and to execute such documentation as may be necessary.

11. The director's service agreement Note I (see p.289)

[11.1 The Director shall be appointed Managing Director of the Subsidiary.]

[11.2] The Subsidiary and the Director shall enter into a service agreement in the form of the draft already approved which shall supersede any terms and conditions of employment to which the Director was subject before the date of this Agreement.

12. The subsidiary's accounting and insurance obligations

12.1 During the continuance of this Agreement the Subsidiary shall prepare annual revenue and capital budgets which shall be submitted to the Shareholders within [two] [weeks] [months] of the commencement of each accounting reference period of the Subsidiary.

12.2 The Subsidiary shall keep true and accurate books of account and records in accordance with usual accounting practice and such books and records shall be audited by the Auditors.

12.3 The Subsidiary shall maintain adequate insurance against all risks usually insured against for the full replacement or reinstatement value of all of its assets and all such other insurance as may be appropriate for the Subsidiary's business.

12.4 Formal meetings of the directors of the Subsidiary shall be held as regularly as necessary and at least one board meeting held in every calendar month.

Note J
(see p.289)

13. Confidentiality

The Director shall not disclose or divulge or allow to be disclosed or divulged to any person, firm or company any information which he receives or obtains relating to the Subsidiary's business, finances, manufacturing methods and processes, trade secrets, or any other information relating to the Subsidiary including names and addresses of any parties who conduct business with the Subsidiary, and shall keep confidential all such information both during the period of this Agreement and after its termination whether such termination be by agreement or notice or as a result of the resignation or the removal of the Director from office.

Note K
(see p.289)

14. Matters requiring agreement of directors appointed by parent company

Unless the directors appointed by the Parent Company have first agreed the Director shall not exercise his powers in relation to the Subsidiary to:

14.1 Make any material change in the nature of the Subsidiary's business.

14.2 Commence any legal or arbitration proceedings other than routine debt collection.

14.3 Make any claim, surrender, election or consent for tax purposes.

14.4 Acquire shares or securities in any company.

14.5 Enter into any material contract other than in the ordinary course of the Subsidiary's business.

14.6 Permit or allow anything to be done which may lead to the winding-up of the Subsidiary.

14.7 Enter into any partnership or profit sharing agreement with any person.

14.8 Sell, transfer, lease, assign or otherwise dispose of any part of the Subsidiary's undertaking or property.

14.9 Give any guarantee, indemnity or security in respect of the obligations of any other person.

14.10 Make any loan or give any credit other than in the normal course of business.

14.11 Make any changes in banking arrangements or facilities or arrange any overdraft or other borrowing facilities.

14.12 Create any fixed or floating charge or other security of any kind over the whole or any part of the Subsidiary's undertaking, property or assets.

14.13 Enter into any contract or transaction or series of related transactions to a value of more than £ .

15. Duration and termination

Note L (see p.289)

This Agreement shall continue until any one of the following events occur:

15.1 The Subsidiary cannot by reason of its liabilities continue its business and it is advisable to wind-up the Subsidiary.

15.2 The Subsidiary is wound-up compulsorily.

15.3 A receiver or administrative receiver is appointed of the whole or any part of the assets of the Subsidiary or the business of the Subsidiary shall be managed by an administrator appointed by the Court.

15.4 The Director ceases to be a Shareholder,

Provided that the terms of this Agreement shall continue to bind the parties after its termination to such extent and for so long as may be necessary to give effect to their respective rights and obligations.

16. Non-solicitation

Note M (see p.289)

The Director shall not within [describe area or specific radius] and for a period of [ ] [months] [years] after the termination of this Agreement however caused, directly or indirectly, whether on his own account or on behalf of another business entity:

16.1 Solicit or procure business from any person, firm or company who or which within the period of [ ] year[s] preceding the termination of this Agreement was a customer or client of the Subsidiary or generally or from time to time dealt with the Subsidiary.

16.2 Solicit the services of or endeavour to encourage any person who shall have been an officer, employee or consultant of the Subsidiary within the period of [ ] year[s] preceding the termination of this Agreement, to leave the Subsidiary's employment.

17. Non-dealing

Note M (see p.289)

The Director shall not within [describe area or specific radius] and for a period of [ ] [months] [years] after the termination of this Agreement however caused, directly or indirectly, carry on business or deal with any person, firm or company who or which was a customer, client, supplier, agent or distributor of the Subsidiary within the period of [ ] years preceding the termination of this Agreement.

18. Non-competition

Note M (see p.289)

The Director shall not within [describe area or specific radius] and for a period of [ ] [months] [years] after the termination of this Agreement however caused be engaged or assist in carrying on any business which competes with the business of the Subsidiary or otherwise be interested or concerned, either directly or indirectly, whether as a consultant, employee, director, partner, adviser, agent or in any other capacity in or with any person, firm or company whose business competes with the business of the Subsidiary.

Note N (see p.290)

19. Restrictions affecting the shares of the director

The Director shall not create any charge or encumbrance over all or any of his Shares nor grant any option or other rights or dispose of any interest in all or any such Shares except as the Parent Company in its sole discretion may permit in writing.

20. Return of documents and other property on termination

The Director shall immediately on termination of this Agreement deliver to a director nominated by the Parent Company all documents (together with any copies), including notes, records, accounts, memoranda or papers and any other items or property relating to or concerning the business of the Subsidiary or any of its suppliers, agents, distributors or customers.

21. No partnership

Nothing in this Agreement shall constitute or be deemed to constitute a partnership between the Shareholders and neither of them may bind the other in any way.

22. Conflict or ambiguity between the articles and this agreement

If, during the continuance of this Agreement, there is any conflict or ambiguity between its provisions and the provisions of the Articles then the provisions of this Agreement shall prevail.

23. Undertaking by the Subsidiary

The Subsidiary undertakes with each of the Shareholders to comply with the terms and conditions of this Agreement.

24. Arbitration

All differences or disputes which may arise in connection with this Agreement, or its construction or effect shall be referred to a single arbitrator to be agreed upon by the Shareholders but in default of their agreement the President for the time being of [the Chartered Institute of Arbitrators] [the Institute of Chartered Accountants in England and Wales] shall nominate an arbitrator in accordance with the Arbitration Acts 1950–1979, or any statutory modification or re-enactment for the time being in force.

25. General

25.1 Notices. Any notices which are required to be given shall be in writing and shall be sent to the address of the recipient set out in this Agreement or such other address as may be designated subsequently. Any such notice may be delivered personally or by first class prepaid letter, facsimile or telex transmission and shall be deemed to have been served if by personal delivery when delivered by first class post forty-eight hours after posting and if by any other means on proof of receipt.

25.2 Assignment. Neither of the Shareholders may assign his interest in this Agreement without the prior written consent of the other Shareholder.

25.3 Entire agreement. This Agreement constitutes the entire agreement between the parties with respect to the matters dealt with and supersedes any previous agreement between the parties in relation to such matters.

25.4 Law. This Agreement shall be governed by and construed in accordance with English law.

THE COMMON SEAL of Parent Company Ltd was hereunto affixed in the presence of:

Director

Secretary

or

EXECUTED AS A DEED by and on behalf of Parent Company Ltd by

Director

Secretary

or

SIGNED for and on behalf of Parent Company Ltd by

Director

EXECUTED AS A DEED by the Director in the presence of:

SIGNED by the Director

THE COMMON SEAL of Subsidiary Company Ltd was hereunto affixed in the presence of:

Director

Secretary

or

EXECUTED AS A DEED by and on behalf of Subsidiary Company Ltd

Director

Secretary

or

SIGNED for and on behalf of Subsidiary Company Ltd

Director

Explanatory notes on shareholders' agreement where a prospective director/shareholder acquires a minority holding in a wholly owned subsidiary of a parent company

A. Subscription by the director for shares (see p.279)

The clause is drafted on the assumption that the director will pay in full for the shares contemporaneously with the completion of the agreement or shortly afterwards. If the director is to pay for the shares in instalments or the shares are to be allotted in instalments the clause should be amended accordingly as should the recital.

B. Additional financing (see p.279)

Additional financing may be required because the financial position of the subsidiary deteriorates or further capital is required for the expansion of its business.

If the need for additional capital arises as a result of financial difficulty, it may be raised by either a further issue of shares or loan finance. An imbalance will arise if only the director or the parent company has the resources to subscribe for his or its allocation of shares. If the director only is able to take up his allocation this would dilute the parent company's holding below 75 per cent which would preclude it from passing a special resolution. Conversely, if the parent company is the only party able to take up its allocation the director's interest would be diluted. Either of these possibilities should be considered at the outset so that the parties are aware of the implications.

If the additional capital is required for the purpose of expansion, then both parent company and the director would probably have a more optimistic attitude at the time the additional capital was required, although again there may be a problem if either is unable to raise their respective share of the finance, whether it be by share subscription or loans. The parties' room for manoeuvre may be restricted anyway if the company has already charged its property and undertaking as security for its current borrowings. If shareholder loans are contemplated then a clause similar to clause 3.4 in the other precedent should be included.

C. Divident policy and distribution (see p.279)

The entitlement to dividend is expressed either as a proportion related to the respective shareholdings or for the director and the parent company to receive a fixed percentage not necessarily in the same proportion as their shareholdings. A disproportionately higher rate of dividend may be agreed with the director as an incentive to him. There may, however, be taxation implications which should be discussed with the company's auditors. Consideration should be given as to whether the final two sentences of clause 4 of the previous precedent on page 267 should be included, although on balance from the Parent Company's point of view it would be better for the clause to remain as it is.

D. Acquisition by the director of further shares (see p.279)

The director has the option of either applying for further shares in return for the payment of the price by him if clause 6.2 is incorporated or he may utilise his entitlement to dividend to subscribe for additional shares, subject in both cases to the ceiling of 25 per cent which must be imposed to ensure that the parent company can pass special resolutions. The director may decide to take the dividend in cash and not subscribe for any additional shares. It may be tax efficient to take shares in lieu of dividend payments but that is something which should be considered as a matter of course.

E. Certification of price of shares by the auditors (see p.280)

This clause requires a great deal of consideration and care because the basis upon which the auditors value the shares of the company will be critical. The company's auditors should be consulted and their views taken into account in drafting this clause.

F. Transfer arrangements relating to shares held by the director during his lifetime (see p.280)

The periods of time stipulated within which the parent company can acquire the shares of the director are arbitrary and can be varied according to circumstances. Clause 8.2 incorporates two alternatives, one being an obligation on the part of the parent company to buy the director's shares at the certified price and the other being an option to acquire the shares but over a period of time. If the second alternative is the one incorporated in the agreement and the parent company does not exercise the option, the director would have great difficulty in trying to dispose of his shares, not only because they are unmarketable but because the directors nominated by the parent company would be able to decline to register any proposed transfer of shares in accordance with the provision in the articles. Where the second alternative in clause 8.2 is incorporated, clause 8.3 should also be incorporated, so that the period within which the parent company has to exercise its option can be specified. It would be quite inappropriate in most cases for an outsider to become a shareholder of the subsidiary, and a director entering into an agreement of this kind will have to accept that the value of his shareholding lies in the ability to sell the shares if the subsidiary is sold to a third party in its entirety.

G. Life insurance arrangements in respect of the director (see p.281)

This is a problem area in that it is very difficult to say at any one time what the value of the director's shareholding is. The only way that a reasonable assessment can be made is for the auditors to value the director's shareholding at the end of each accounting reference period and for the insurance cover to be varied accordingly, although if the shares were to increase in value to a great extent during the course of the succeeding accounting reference period, that increase would not be reflected in the insurance cover set at the beginning of the period. Reference should be made to explanatory note E of the previous precedent where the possibility of contravening section 151 of the Companies Act 1985 is discussed.

H. Transfer of shares by the personal representatives of the director (see p.281)

The second sentence of this clause is inserted primarily for the convenience of the parent company in that if the personal representatives of the director fail to make the transfer of the shares the subsidiary company's directors may nominate one of their number to do what is necessary to effect the transfer. The director receiving the payment from the Parent Company will hold the money as bare trustee on behalf of the deceased director's estate.

I. Director's service agreement (see p.281)

Whether or not it is appropriate for such a service agreement to be entered into will depend on the attitudes of the parties and the circumstances. The service agreement would be the matter of separate negotiation. It should be borne in mind that if the director is removed by the parent company as a director the director would still be entitled to payment in lieu of notice in accordance with the terms of the service agreement and may also be able to claim compensation for loss of office.

J. Confidentiality (see p.282)

Reference should be made to explanatory note H on the previous precedent as the general points made in that note apply equally in this case although the circumstances are somewhat different.

K. Matters requiring agreement of directors appointed by parent company (see p.282)

On a day to day basis the director will be left to get on with the job of running the subsidiary, and the persons with whom the subsidiary does business will probably regard the director as having considerable authority to bind the subsidiary, especially if the director is appointed managing director. Consequently, it would be prudent to include a number of matters which the director cannot deal with on his own and which require the approval of the parent company directors beforehand. The list is not exhaustive and other matters should be incorporated if the nature of the subsidiary's business requires their inclusion.

L. Duration and termination (see p.283)

If any of the specified events occur then the agreement is terminated. Other events could be included if appropriate and the clause as drafted should not be regarded as exhaustive.

M. Non-solicitation, non-dealing and non-competition (see p.283–284)

Reference should be made to the explanatory notes on these clauses on pages 202–203. As this is a shareholder's agreement, it is not considered necessary to include a clause similar to clause 22 on page 194.

N. Restrictions affecting the shares of the director (see p.284)

Although a minority shareholding in a private company is unlikely to have great value for security purposes it would be contrary to the underlying purpose and intention of the parties to this agreement for the director to be able to part with any interest in his shares in favour of a third party.

CHAPTER 14

JOINT VENTURE AGREEMENT

Introduction to joint venture agreement between the subsidiaries of a manufacturing company and a design and marketing company relating to the design, manufacture, marketing and sale of a new product

Joint ventures take many forms but generally a joint venture can be defined as a business arrangement entered into by two or more parties for the purpose of a common commercial objective.

As often as not the parties will form a new company specifically for the purpose of their joint venture business because of the inherent advantages of the company structure. Liability is limited and the rules relating to company administration are well defined. A company can enter into secured financing arrangements because it can create a debenture over its assets. None of these advantages is available where two or more parties form an unincorporated arrangement which technically constitutes a partnership. A partnership arrangement also has a number of advantages and disadvantages, a main disadvantage being that the liability of the participators is not limited and each is jointly and severally liable for the debts of the partnership. A partnership is not necessarily the appropriate arrangement where a long term venture is contemplated.

As a partnership is not treated as a separate entity for tax purposes, this may well discourage the use of an unincorporated joint venture arrangement. It does not always follow that a joint venture would be regarded as a partnership because it would be judged on the basis of whether or not the elements which comprise a partnership were present. It will be the substance of the arrangement and not the form or the label which the parties attach to it which will be the determining factor.

Two companies may, for example, wish to work together because they want to embark upon a single project and it makes more economic or commercial sense for them to be able to share the capital investment and employment of resources which the new project requires. The risks can be shared and this may be an attractive proposition where perhaps a new product is involved. A joint venture arrangement can also help to reduce manufacturing costs or other operational expenses where each company has complementary know-how or expertise which, combined, would result in benefits for them both.

A joint venture company may be formed where the project is likely to continue for a considerable period of time and a number of participators are involved with varying degrees of financial commitment and responsibility. One of the parties, for example, may be responsible for providing or procuring the funding, and another may be responsible for the management of the project in its initial stages, and another in operating the business once it has been established. If a joint venture company is formed for an undertaking of this kind the documentation which is generated will be substantial comprising a tailor made set of Memorandum and

Articles of Association, the joint venture agreement itself, a management agreement, shareholders' agreement, service agreements with the directors of the joint venture company who will have day to day responsibility for the conduct of the business; especially the managing director, mortgage and financing documentation and in some situations a technology licensing agreement if third parties are required to license the company to carry out its purpose. There will be an element of inter dependency between all the agreements involved.

A joint venture requiring this amount of documentation, and which comprises a number of participators with differing interests, will require a considerable degree of negotiation by and between the parties. Inevitably, solicitors would be involved in acting for each of the parties in finalising the structure of the joint venture.

A joint venture agreement of this kind just described will usually have provisions within it to deal with the problem of deadlock which may arise if some or all of the parties are unable to agree, in particular on how to arrive at a commercial decision. There will be a formula whereby one or some of the parties will be able to buy out the share of one or other of the parties and the basis on which the shares in the joint venture are to be valued will be specified.

These kinds of situations and agreements are beyond the scope of what a company secretary would need or require where, for example, his company wanted to enter into a collaboration agreement with another company for the purpose of a specific project or business venture. The two companies will probably have worked together in the past or have done business with each other and have found that in practice this has proved to be for their mutual advantage. They may then decide that it would be preferable for there to be a formal agreement governing their future business dealings in one specific area of mutually beneficial activity.

A typical example is where one company has design and marketing expertise with perhaps a distribution capacity, and the other company has the expertise and facilities to manufacture the product. The two companies see their abilities and capacity as being complementary but at the same time do not expect there to be any overlap in their respective functions which could give rise to potential conflict.

If a company secretary has a basic form of agreement available, he and his counterpart between them should be able to negotiate a perfectly acceptable working agreement where a detailed knowledge of their respective businesses is as much an important element in the arrangement as are the contractual and legal aspects.

Consequently, the precedent which follows does not involve the setting up of a joint venture company with all the ramifications which that would involve, but constitutes a straightforward working arrangement where one company designs, markets and sells the product and the other party manufactures it. The marketing is done in the name of the selling company with the manufacturing company receiving payment for the products which it manufactures plus a commission or royalty based on a percentage of the ultimate selling price.

There is always the possibility that a partnership arrangement will be deemed to have come into existence and it is therefore important that each company forms a wholly owned subsidiary as the vehicle through which its interest in the joint venture is to be held. Both subsidiary companies must not undertake any other business than that of the joint venture and their objects clauses should be restricted accordingly. As both newly formed companies will not have trading records and their purpose will only be the joint venture, if a partnership arrangement is held to have come into being the consequences will not be significant so far as each parent company is concerned.

Joint venture agreement between the subsidiaries of a manufacturing company and a design and marketing company relating to the design, manufacture, marketing and sale of a new product

Dated 19 .

The Parties:

LTD whose registered office is at
('the Manufacturer') (1)

LTD whose registered office is at
('the Seller') (2)

Recitals:

The business of the Manufacturer is the manufacture of Sprockets.

The business of the Seller is the design, marketing, distribution and sale of Sprockets [to the retail market].

The Seller has devised and designed a new and more advanced type of Sprocket and has carried out a programme of market research from which it has concluded that there is a demand for this type of Sprocket.

The Seller wishes to involve the Manufacturer in producing such Sprockets and to that end the parties have agreed to co-operate in the development, manufacture, marketing and sale of the Sprockets.

IT IS AGREED as follows:

1. **Definitions and interpretation**

1.1 These terms and expressions shall have the following meanings in this Agreement:

'SPROCKET' means [define or if more appropriate include by reference to separate document to be annexed].

'MANUFACTURING EQUIPMENT' means the equipment and machinery devised by the Manufacturer to produce the Sprockets and includes [if practicable define in detail the various items of equipment and machinery].

'INTELLECTUAL PROPERTY RIGHTS' means any patent, design, copyright, trademark or other industrial or intellectual property rights or invention capable of being registered under the patents, design, and copyright legislation in force from time to time.

1.2 The headings to the clauses are for convenience and reference only and shall not affect their interpretation.

2. Duration Note A (see p.300)

This Agreement shall commence with [immediate effect] [on] and shall continue [for a period of [months] [years] and subsequently] until terminated by either party giving written notice to the other of not less than [ ] complete calendar month[s].

3. The initial obligations of the parties Note B (see p.301)

3.1 The parties shall consider together the design of the Sprocket prepared by the Seller and carry out an initial evaluation to examine possible improvements which could be made to the Sprocket as it is presently designed.

3.2 Following the completion of the initial evaluation and review the Seller shall, if necessary, produce amended design drawings and specification within [ ] weeks of the completion of the initial evaluation and shall provide the Manufacturer with copies of the amended design drawings and specification in sufficient detail to enable the manufacturer to decide what Manufacturing Equipment will be required and how the manufacturing process will be carried out.

3.3 As soon as practicable following receipt of the final design drawings and specification from the Seller the Manufacturer shall prepare an analysis detailing the way in which the cost of producing and installing the Manufacturing Equipment is computed and shall send a statement of such costing to the Seller for the Seller's review and approval.

3.4 Once the parties have agreed on the level of expenditure to be incurred by the Manufacturer in producing and installing the Manufacturing Equipment the Manufacturer shall, as soon as practicable, proceed to install the Manufacturing Equipment.

3.5 When the Manufacturing Equipment has been installed the Manufacturer shall produce [ ] prototype Sprockets and send these to the

Seller for the Seller to evaluate and approve and the Seller shall notify the Manufacturer of its findings and suggestions for improvement, if any, in writing within [twenty-eight] days of receipt of the prototype Sprockets.

3.6 The Manufacturer shall prepare an analysis of the additional costs involved in developing the Manufacturing Equipment to enable it to produce Sprockets in sufficient volume to satisfy projected sales targets to be agreed by the parties as soon as practicable following their joint approval of the final design and specification of the Sprocket. The Seller shall pay [specify proportion] of all the costs incurred by the Manufacturer in producing and setting up the Manufacturing Equipment for the purpose of the joint venture and shall make such payment to the Manufacturer within [ ] [days] of receipt of the Manufacturer's invoice.

3.7 The parties shall as soon as practicable agree a production schedule for the period of [ ] months from the date on which commercial production of the Sprockets is expected to commence and after the expiration of such period the provisions of clause 6.2 shall apply.

Note C (see p.301)

4. Manufacturer's entitlement to payment

4.1 The parties shall at the commencement of each successive period of [twelve] months agree a price or range of prices depending on the quantities of Sprockets to be supplied by the Manufacturer in any one consignment, and the prices which are agreed shall apply for each period of [twelve] months, the first such period to commence on the date commercial production begins.

4.2 The Seller shall pay the Manufacturer for the Sprockets within [ ] days of receipt of the Manufacturer's invoice in respect of each consignment of Sprockets.

4.3 In addition to the payments to be made in accordance with clause 4.2 the Seller shall pay to the Manufacturer a royalty of [ ] per cent of the selling price of each Sprocket and shall account to the Manufacturer on [30 April] and [31 October] with its share of royalties in respect of the six monthly period expiring on the preceding [31 March] and [30 September] in each year.

Note D (see p.301)

5. Warranty and liability

1.1 The Manufacturer warrants to the Seller that the Sprockets manufactured by it shall be free from material defects for a period of [ ] [months] [years] after delivery to the Seller provided that the Sprockets are correctly handled, installed or maintained in accordance with the appropriate standard practice.

6. Other obligations of the manufacturer

6.1 The Manufacturer shall use the Manufacturing Equipment for the production of Sprockets exclusively to supply to the Seller and shall not produce such Sprockets for sale to any other party.

6.2 The Manufacturer shall accept all orders for Sprockets received from the Seller provided that the period between the date of receipt of the order by the Manufacturer and the date requested for delivery of each consignment of Sprockets shall be at least [ ] and each order is for a minimum of [ ] and a maximum of [ ] Sprockets.

7. Other obligations of the seller

Note E (see p.301)

7.1 The Seller shall not purchase Sprockets from any other third party and shall retain the Manufacturer as its sole source of supply of Sprockets.

7.2 The Seller shall consult with the Manufacturer and take into account the opinions of the Manufacturer in designing the marketing and publicity material to be issued by the Seller to promote the sale of the Sprockets, and shall ensure that on all such marketing and publicity material there appears an acknowledgment in sufficient prominence that the Manufacturer has manufactured the Sprockets.

8. Meetings between the parties

Meetings between representatives of both the Manufacturer and the Seller to discuss the business and progress of the joint venture shall be held at least once every [ ] month[s] at the offices of the Manufacturer and Seller alternately, or such other venue as shall be agreed from time to time. Minutes of the meetings shall be prepared and circulated.

9. Design and intellectual property rights

Note F (see p.302)

9.1 Where either of the parties is at the date of this Agreement the owner of existing Intellectual Property Rights, that party shall retain solely the benefit of such rights.

9.2 Where any Intellectual Property Rights are created as a result of or for the purpose of this joint venture by either party such rights shall belong to the originating party.

9.3 Where any Intellectual Property Rights have been created as a result of the joint efforts of the parties they shall hold such rights jointly, and where such rights are capable of registration they shall jointly apply to do so and the cost shall be treated as a joint venture expense.

9.4 Each party grants to the other licence to use its Intellectual Property Rights [if any] for the purposes of this Agreement.

9.5 Neither party shall use any of the Intellectual Property Rights belonging to the other party except for the purpose of this Agreement.

9.6 If it comes to the notice of either party that any third party is infringing or appears to be infringing any Intellectual Property Rights of the other it shall notify the other party and give such information or evidence as it has in support of its belief.

10. Confidentiality

The parties shall not during the period of this Agreement nor after its termination disclose or divulge or allow to be disclosed or divulged to any third party information which it receives or obtains and which is confidential and relates to either party's business generally or the Sprockets in particular except as may be necessary to fulfil their respective obligations under this Agreement.

Note G (see p.302)

11. Termination

Either party may terminate this Agreement in writing in the following circumstances:

11.1 If either party is in breach of the terms of this Agreement where although such breach is capable of remedy it has not been so remedied within twenty-one days of receipt of the notice from the party specifying the breach and requiring its remedy.

11.2 If in the reasonable opinion of either party the design of the Sprockets or the method of manufacture has become outmoded so that the joint venture business is no longer capable of being economically carried on.

11.3 If either party is acquired by any person or group of connected persons who do not have control of either party at the commencement of this Agreement in which event termination shall be with effect from the date the change of control occurred unless the party which has not been acquired elects in writing to continue this Agreement.

11.4 If either party goes into liquidation or if a receiver of its assets is appointed.

12. Rights and obligations prior to termination

On the termination of this Agreement all pre-existing rights and obligations which have accrued to or by either of the parties under this Agreement shall continue in effect.

13. Consequences of termination

In the event of termination however caused each party shall as soon as practicable but within [fourteen] days in any event deliver or return to the other party:

13.1 All documents and information whether supplied by that party or not but which relates to that party's business.

13.2 All engineering materials, memoranda, calculations, specifications, reports, design drawings, and any copies, specifically devised by the other party for use in carrying out the purposes of this Agreement.

14. The manufacturing equipment following termination
The parties shall jointly decide whether or not the Manufacturing Equipment should be destroyed following the termination of this Agreement or to sell it to a third party. Any proceeds resulting from any such sale shall be shared between the parties [equally].

15. Counter claim or set off following termination
The Seller agrees that it shall pay to the Manufacturer any amounts due to it which are not in dispute unless the Seller has a right of counter claim or set off against the Manufacturer in which case no such payments shall be made.

16. No partnership
The parties agree that this Agreement relates only to the single joint venture for the production and sale of the Sprockets and does not constitute a partnership.

17. Taxation Note H (see p.302)
The parties shall account separately to the Inland Revenue for the taxation due on their respective share of income from the joint venture and neither party shall bear any liability whatsoever for the taxation in respect of the income of the joint venture attributable to the other party. The parties mutually covenant with each other that they shall immediately, upon receipt of a demand from the Inland Revenue, each pay direct such taxes as shall from time to time be due on their own share of income from the joint venture [if any] and each shall fully and effectively indemnify the other against any costs, liability or expense that the other may at any time or times incur or expend as a result of the other failing to pay direct to the Inland Revenue such taxes as shall from time to time be due on their share of income from the joint venture.

18. Arbitration
All differences or disputes which may arise in connection with this Agreement, or its construction or effect, shall be referred to a single arbitrator to be agreed upon by the parties, but in default of their agreement the President for the time being of the Chartered Institute of Arbitrators shall nominate an arbitrator in accordance with the Arbitration Acts 1950–1979 or any statutory modification or re-enactment for the time being in force.

19. Notices
Any notice, instruction or communication shall be sent by ordinary first class post, telex, facsimile transmission or by such other means as may be

appropriate in the circumstances, and in the case of a notice served by first class post it shall be deemed to have been received by the party to whom it was sent forty-eight hours after posting, and in the case of any other form of transmission twenty-four hours after sending.

20. Entire agreement

This Agreement constitutes the entire agreement between the parties with respect to the matters dealt with and supersedes any previous agreement between the parties in relation to such matters.

21. Force majeure

In the event that either of the parties are unable to carry out all or any of their obligations under this Agreement as a result of matters arising beyond their reasonable control neither party shall have a claim against the other provided that notice of the event or events is given to the party not affected within forty-eight hours.

Note I
(see p.302)

22. Restriction on assignment

This Agreement is not capable of being assigned by either party.

23. Law

This Agreement shall be governed by English law.

SIGNED by on behalf of the Manufacturer

SIGNED by on behalf of the Seller

Explanatory notes on joint venture agreement between the subsidiaries of a manufacturing company and a design and marketing company relating to the design, manufacture, marketing and sale of a new product

A. Duration (see p.295)

Almost certainly it will be a requirement that the Agreement should continue for a minimum period and after the expiration of that period to continue until terminated by either party on giving a suitable period of written notice. The length of the period of notice will depend on a number of factors but is likely to be longer rather than shorter.

B. *The initial obligations of the parties (see p.295)*

It is envisaged that the design prepared by the seller may require some modification before the manufacturer is in a position to devise the manufacturing equipment and there should be some time scale laid down governing the process by which the final version of the product is to be approved by both parties. In a number of situations the cost of producing and installing the manufacturing equipment will be substantial, and as the arrangement is a joint venture it is not unreasonable to expect the seller to contribute to the cost at an early stage. If, however, the seller has already incurred significant expense in designing the product and carrying out a market research programme then it would not be unreasonable for the seller to be given some credit for that expense and, consequently, it may be appropriate for the seller only to pay a proportion of the cost of producing and installing the manufacturing equipment and not a full half share.

C. *Manufacturer's entitlement to payment (see p.296)*

It would be impracticable for a price or range of prices to be set for too long a period when the joint venture is still in its formative stages and the level of demand for the new product has yet to be tested. Some arrangement will need to be agreed and the formula in the precedent is an attempt to strike a balance between the respective interests of both parties. It is assumed that the manufacturer will pitch its prices at a rate which covers overheads and a modest profit element and that the normal rate of commercial profit will be obtained by way of a royalty payment expressed as a percentage of the ultimate selling price although the manufacturer would have little control over what this should be. Where royalty or commission payments are to be made by the seller in this way, the dates on which the payments are to be made and the periods to which the payments relate must be specified.

D. *Warranty and liability (see p.296)*

Although both parties will probably have their own respective sets of standard terms and conditions, the precedent is intended to stand on its own and represent the complete arrangement between the parties. Consequently, a warranty provision should be incorporated.

E. *Other obligations of the seller (see p.297)*

Whether or not it is appropriate for the manufacturer to be consulted by the seller with regard to publicity material and the like is a matter to be considered in each case.

F. Design and intellectual property rights (see p.297)

In many situations the question of such rights will not arise because although the product may be new it is an improved version of an existing product or range of products. This clause is included as a reminder to consider whether or not the matters referred to are likely to or could arise.

G. Termination (see p.298)

This clause provides, among other things, for the agreement to be terminated in the event that there is a change of control of either party. Whether or not this particular provision needs to be included should be carefully considered.

H. Taxation (see p.299)

It is important that there be included a categoric statement to the effect that each party will be responsible for its own tax liability arising out of the joint venture arrangement.

I. Restriction on assignment (see p.300)

It is important that this clause be included for the reasons mentioned in the introduction in that the two subsidiary companies will have been specifically formed for the purpose of the joint venture and consequently the benefit and obligations of the agreement must be retained.

INDEX